THE WELSH
KINGS

THE WELSH KINGS

Kari Maund

TEMPUS

First published 2000
Paperback edition published 2002, reprinted 2004

Tempus Publishing Ltd
The Mill, Brimscombe Port
Stroud, Gloucestershire GL5 2QG
www.tempus-publishing.com

British Library Cataloguing in Publication Data.
A catalogue record for this book is available from the British Library.

ISBN 0 7524 2321 5

Typesetting and origination by Tempus Publishing
Printed in Great Britain

Contents

Acknowledgements

In writing this book I have received valuable advice, assistance and feedback from colleagues and friends. I should like to thank the National Library of Wales for permission to reproduce the picture of Mascen Wledig from N.L.W. MS 17520A, fo.3; the British Library, for permission to reproduce the picture of Gruffudd ap Llywelyn ap Iorwerth from London, British Library MS Royal 14.C.VII, f.13v; and the British Museum, for permission to reproduce the photograph of the Hywel Dda penny. Thanks are due, too, to my colleague Bill Zajac who generously allowed me to make use of photographs from his collection; to James Cooke, who took photographs for me of Cricieth Castle, and to Christine Linton. My mother, Irene Maund, provided me with the line drawings and watercolours, for which I am very grateful. Thanks are also due to my colleagues, friends, and students in the School of History and Archaeology, Cardiff University, for their support. I am indebted to Professor David Dumville and Professor Simon Keynes, of the Department of Anglo-Saxon, Norse and Celtic, University of Cambridge, for many years of patient advice, assistance and guidance. I also wish to thank Jonathan Reeve of Tempus books, and Nicola Watson for preparing the index. My partner, Phil Nanson, has not only put up with the writing of this book in all its gory details, but accompanied me on many trips to historical sites and assisted patiently in the process of producing maps and genealogical charts: this book is for him.

List of abbreviations

List of figures

List of illustrations

List of colour plates

Introduction

Wales in the middle ages is hard to define. At different times its borders varied, sometimes including areas now part of England, sometimes losing areas now considered Welsh, to rulers from Anglo-Saxon or Anglo-Norman England. The shape of the land was to a large extent the product of a long process of invasion, representing the territories retained by the native Britons after the invasion of Britain by the Angles, Saxons, Jutes, and other Germanic peoples in the late Roman and sub-Roman period. Even the words Wales and Welsh are not the products of native speech. They are terms coined by these Germanic neighbours: Anglo-Saxon *Wealas* and *Wealisc*, meaning foreigners. In earlier centuries, the Welsh wrote of themselves as *Britones*, Britons, remembering their origins as the dominant native people of the island of Britain, speaking a common tongue and possessing a common history and cultural heritage. From the seventh century another word, *Cymry*, from Old Welsh *Combrogi*, compatriots, came into use, and, from the twelfth century, would become the dominant native term.[1] For all this, however, Wales was not a single, unified political entity, and even in periods when much of the country was ruled by a common overking, local and regional identities were strong. Throughout nearly all of the period covered by this book, Wales was made up of a number of separate kingdoms, each with their own royal dynasty, their own administration, and their own identity. The numbers of these kingdoms varied over time, with a tendency for smaller kingdoms to be absorbed into larger, more powerful units as the centuries passed, but unlike England or Scotland, Wales was never to achieve permanent political unity under a single native ruling house.

One result of this was that Wales had a very large number of native kings, princes and rulers: there are something of the order of ninety-seven in the eleventh century alone. Many of these rulers, especially those who lived in earlier centuries, are little more to us now than names, their histories either cloaked in layers of legend and myth, or lost entirely. There are few surviving written historical sources from medieval Wales, and much of what does survive is thin, particularly for the earlier period. These sources are not unbiased or objective, and have been subject to reworking and recasting in the interests of politically dominant families and institutions. As a result, our knowledge of some leaders is filtered through lenses of positive or negative propaganda. Some Welsh leaders impinged noticeably on affairs in England or Ireland, and as a result were recorded in English and Irish chronicles. These sources are valuable, but they are not always favourable to the Welsh, and one cannot now hope to recover details which they may have omitted or misrepresented. There are many questions still open about the characters, actions, and motivations of the men who ruled the kingdoms of Wales

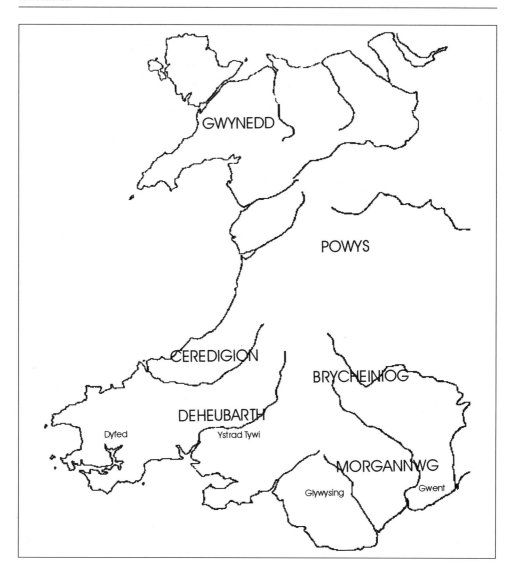

Map 1: Kingdoms of early medieval Wales.

between the fall of the Roman Empire and the loss of Welsh independence to Edward I in 1283.

The purpose of this book is to provide an introduction to the kings and princes of the independent Welsh kingdoms. As said above, many of these rulers are now little more than names to us: the book will therefore focus in the main upon those figures whose careers are more fully documented, or who in some way played key roles in the evolution of Wales. It has drawn upon historical, archaeological and literary sources not only from native Wales but also from its neighbours. The period of Welsh independence – roughly from the early fifth

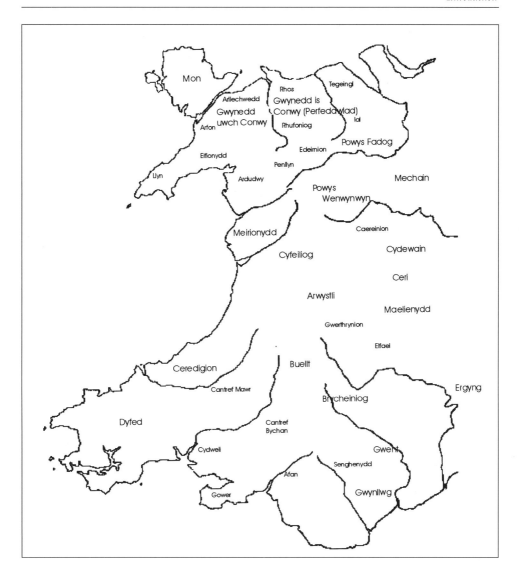

Map 2: Districts of Wales.

century down to the end of the thirteenth century – was to be one of the most dynamic periods in the history of the British Isles. At its beginning, Britain was part of the wide empire of Rome, subject to a centralized administrative and military structure, and linked by trade, governance, religion and scholarship to much of Western Europe and the Mediterranean. Wales, as such, did not exist as a separate territory: it would come into being as a result of the invasions and colonization in Britain by the Anglo-Saxons, who drove the Britons out of most of eastern, southern and central Britain into the west (modern Wales and Cornwall) and also the north (into what is now Cumbria and parts of southern

13

Scotland). The development of the Anglo-Saxon kingdoms, and, later on, of a unified kingdom of England, presented new challenges and threats to the kings in Wales, who faced not simply enemies and invaders but also potential allies and opportunities to expand their influence out of Wales back into the wider British arena. The expansion throughout Europe from the later eighth down to the eleventh centuries of the Vikings also was to have its effects in Wales, particularly in south Wales, and was to play a role in reshaping Welsh political life: indeed, at least one king of Gwynedd had Viking blood. In 1066, the Anglo-Saxon kingdom of England was conquered by Duke William of Normandy, and with the arrival of the Normans came a new set of influences on and threats to Wales. The Normans were aggressive and expansionist towards their new neighbours, and would have a dramatic impact upon Welsh political geography. Yet at the same time Norman administrative and governmental practices were adopted and transformed by the native Welsh to their own advantage, allowing some Welsh leaders to strengthen considerably their range of powers and resources, and others to protect and retain their hereditary lands in the face of new legal concepts and officers. The rule over Gwynedd of Llywelyn ap Gruffudd (1246-1282) was very different in its nature, scope and form than the kingships enjoyed by the leaders who flourished in the fifth and sixth centuries.

1 From Vortigern to Merfyn Frych:

the fifth century to *c.*825

Roman Wales is an artificial definition. The area now known as Wales did not exist in that form under Roman rule: it was simply part of Britain. The Romans first invaded western Britain in around AD 47 when the general Ostorius fought there against the *Deceangli*. Shortly afterwards, he fought another western people, the *Silures*, who were the allies of the powerful British leader, Caractacus. This war spread into the hill territory of north-east Wales, inhabited by the *Ordovices*, only ending with the defeat of Caractacus in AD 51. There were to be further conflicts in this area, especially against the *Silures*, until they were finally subdued in the 70s. By this time, the peoples of the south-west, the *Deceangli* and the *Demetae,* had submitted to Rome: the *Ordovices* rebelled in AD 79, but were soon brought into submission, and from this point all of modern Wales seems to have been under Roman rule.

The area fell into two zones, upland and lowland. The upland was controlled through a system of roads and forts at strategic locations. The lowland, and in particular south-east Wales, was governed from a local capital at *Uenta Silurum*, Caerwent, from whence taxes were collected, laws enforced, and public works undertaken. Roman villa-type sites have been found in south-east Wales, and the area may have been more extensively and lastingly influenced by the Romans than the rest of Wales.[1] Although other parts of Wales were less thoroughly integrated into the Roman way of life, Rome was nevertheless to have a lasting legacy for Wales. In later centuries, late- and sub-Roman leaders were remembered in Welsh tales, histories and genealogies. Welsh royal houses claimed descent from the Emperor Constantine III (and, through confusion of names, from his predecessor, Constantine the Great, who made Christianity the official religion of the Roman Empire) and from the usurping emperor of the west, Magnus Maximus, known in Welsh as Macsen Wledig. Latin words were borrowed into Welsh.[2] Perhaps the most significant long-term effect was the introduction of Christianity. No details survive as to the conversion of Wales, but by the fifth and sixth centuries, it seems to have been a largely – perhaps completely – Christian society, and thus it would remain.

Roman rule in Wales declined from the fourth or even the later third century. Written sources depict a growing threat from Irish raiders, and in certain places, like Cardiff and Holyhead Island, coastal forts were built or strengthened. Around the same time, there is evidence of an increase of activity at Welsh hill-forts – the centres of native tribal culture and politics.[3] This might indicate that Roman dominance was weakening, and native power-structures were beginning to re-assert themselves. The Latin historian Ammianus Marcellinus recorded raids by

Irish and by Picts (from what is now Scotland) in Britain in AD 360. By the later fourth century, the Roman Empire was under increasing pressure politically and militarily, and had decreasing resources to spend on its more remote provinces. Magnus Maximus, a Roman soldier of Spanish origin stationed in Britain, took advantage of the growing chaos, and, with the backing of much of the army in Britain, made himself emperor over Britain, Gaul and Spain between AD 383-388.[4] To support his campaigns in Gaul and Spain, Magnus withdrew the soldiery from Britain. Britain remained in contact with the rest of the western Empire after the defeat and death of Magnus, but it seems likely that despite continued communication, many parts of Britain were by the end of the fourth century effectively self-governing. In some places, a Roman-style way of life centred on villas and towns may have continued; in others, the old structures of tribal chiefdoms centred on hill-forts and dependent on military prowess may have reasserted itself.

The traditional date for the end of Roman rule in Britain is AD 410. For much of the next two centuries, the history of Britain as a whole, let alone Wales, is uncertain, and based on later, mainly foreign, sources. It is possible to outline a chronology of events, although this outline is incomplete and uncertain. Writing in the sixth century, the Byzantine historian, Procopius, believed Britain to be inhabited by three peoples: Angles, Frisians and Britons, each subject to their own rulers and independent from each other. He wrote of ongoing migrations from Britain of native Britons into neighbouring Gaul, and particularly into Armorica (modern Brittany). Other writers also recorded barbarian invasions of Britain in this time, and political disruption.[5] The first decade of the fifth century saw considerable upheavals, with a succession of emperors elected in Britain and subsequently overthrown. The most successful and famous of these was Constantine, who was elected in 407, and gathered together most of the army which remained in Britain, taking it with him into Gaul, where he enjoyed considerable success until 409. Zosimus, writing during the sixth century, using earlier records, recorded that *c.*408 Constantine's general, Gerontius, allied with barbarian invaders and rebelled against the usurping emperor. At around the same time, Britain and part of Gaul rose against the surviving Roman officials and expelled them, subsequently establishing their own authorities.[6] The sources are difficult to interpret, but it seems likely that in the early part of the fifth century, facing pressure from foreign invaders, the Britons increasingly took their own government and defence into their own hands. Constantine died in 411, and no subsequent Roman emperor made any attempt to regain Britain. The British writer, Gildas, writing during the sixth century, paints a very bleak picture of this period. He did not set out to write history: his work, *On the Ruin of Britain,* is a sermon designed to educate and remonstrate with his contemporaries. He included no dates, and his few references to historical figures are difficult to interpret. We do not know exactly when he wrote, nor where, and it seems likely that he was selective in his use and interpretation of material.[7] However, he is the sole native writer whose account survives from this early period, and his book had a lasting influence. Later Welsh writers, such as the author of the early ninth-century *Historia Britonnum (HB)* and the compilers of the Welsh Chronicles, as well as English writers such as Bede and the compilers of the Anglo-Saxon Chronicle, drew on Gildas to construct a history of Britain in the fifth and sixth centuries.

Vortigern, Ambrosius and Arthur

Gildas described how, faced with increasingly dangerous raids from Picts and Scots, a certain proud tyrant and his council invited three ship-loads of Saxons to Britain, to become protectors of the Britons against the raiders. These mercenaries were given land in eastern Britain. After some time, complaining of ill-treatment and inadequate resources, the mercenaries turned on their employers and began to plunder and ravage on their own behalf.[8] The major settlements were destroyed, and the invaders rapidly overran most of the island. Many Britons were killed, others fled overseas. Finally, some of the remainder united under the leadership of Ambrosius Aurelianus and inflicted a series of defeats upon the Saxons, culminating in a decisive siege at Badon Hill. After that victory, peace was restored for around half a century, enduring into Gildas's own time, although, he cautions, already the Britons have returned to their old sinful ways, and are courting punishment.[9] His account is couched in Biblical terms, so that the Saxons become the agents of a wrathful God, sent as a punishment upon the sinful Britons: it cannot be taken as accurate history.[10] Yet his narrative would form the basis for the orthodox historiography of the Anglo-Saxon settlement eras in both early Wales and Anglo-Saxon England, and has continued to exercise an influence on perceptions of the settlement era down to this day.

   Gildas did not name the proud tyrant, but by the time that the Anglo-Saxon monk, Bede, wrote his *History of the English Church and People* in the early part of the eighth century, the tyrant was said to have been Vortigern.[11] It is not clear how Bede came by this name. It has been suggested that Gildas's Latin phrase *superbus tyrannus*, proud tyrant, may reflect a translation of a British name or title, *mor tigern*, great king.[12] Gildas's story is unlikely to reflect an accurate historical tradition, but Vortigern has come to occupy a considerable role in the legendary history of early Britain. It cannot be stated with any certainty whether he existed or not: if he did exist, it certainly cannot be discovered whether there is any amount of truth in any of the stories which accrued to his name. The leaders of the Saxon mercenaries whom he supposedly invited into Britain acquired names, Hengist and Horsa.[13] According to *HB*, Hengist tricked Vortigern into marrying Hengist's daughter, and then used this tie to persuade Vortigern to make substantial grants of land to the Saxons, and permit greater numbers of them to enter Britain. Vortigern's son Vortimer resisted this policy, and fought valiantly against the Saxons. But he died before he was able to achieve his goal, and his father's pro-Saxon policy held sway. Hengist then persuaded Vortigern to summon a peace conference, and, once the British leaders were assembled, Hengist and his men fell on them and slew all of them apart from Vortigern himself, who was imprisoned, and only released after ceding large tracts of land.[14] The weak judgement and sinful ways of Vortigern were not restricted to his dealings with the Saxons, according to *HB*. He conducted an incestuous relationship with his own daughter, incurring the wrath of St Germanus, a reforming bishop from Gaul.[15] He listened to the advice of wizards and contemplated human sacrifice when planning a new fortress.[16] After the treachery of Hengist, Vortigern fled first to Gwrtheyrnion and then to a fort on the River Teifi, whence he was followed by St Germanus, who sought to reform him. Vortigern did not listen, and was destroyed in a divine fire along with all his wives.[17] This tale is not the sole account of the death of Vortigern: *HB* gives two more. According to one, he became a landless outcast, despised by all, and died alone. According to the other, he was swallowed up by the earth in punishment for his sins.[18]

The surviving tales about Vortigern are little more than legend, but he remains an important figure in early Welsh history.[19] In later centuries, native Welsh royal dynasties – and in particular one major ruling house, the First Dynasty of Powys – claimed him as an ancestor, and one early kingdom, Gwrtheyrnion, has him as its eponym. At some point in the mid-ninth century, Cyngen, king of Powys, erected a monument in honour of his ancestors, and in particular of his grandfather Elise. It was inscribed with a description of Elise's activities along with a genealogy of his line.[20] At the time that the monument was erected, the ruling family of Powys faced aggression not only from the Anglo-Saxons on their eastern borders, but from their northern and western neighbours, the kings of Gwynedd. Cyngen would die an exile in Rome. The monument thus represents a statement of the ancestry and antiquity of this ruling house in its last years of dominance: Vortigern occupies a key position in the doctrine of their legitimacy which the pillar embodies, presented as the father and friend of saints, the honourable descendant of the Romans, and the successful master of a wide territory. This picture is at odds with the stories recounted in the *HB*. The latter text was written in Gwynedd, under the influence of the aggressive royal dynasty of that kingdom. Its negative portrayal of Vortigern reflects the ambitions and desires of the royal house of Gwynedd in the ninth century.[21] Alongside its negative portrait of Vortigern, *HB* gives an unflattering account of another figure who featured as the ancestor of a ruling house of Powys, Cadell Ddrynllug (Cadell of the gleaming hilt).[22] Cadell is depicted as a good and honest man, but of servile, rather than noble birth, and owing his promotion to the ranks of kingship to piety, and to the intercession of St Germanus, rather than to inheritance or military prowess (the approved routes to legitimate kingship in early Wales). This image of Cadell is less negative than that of Vortigern, but it too raises questions over the status of his descendants – they belong, by implication, to the servile class, and their claims to high lineage are problematized. The testimony of *HB* tells us more about the political agenda of Gwynedd in the early ninth century than about the realities of the fifth and sixth centuries. It is uncertain whether Vortigern and Cadell existed and ruled in central mid Wales (or some part thereof); it is certain that by the eighth and ninth centuries, they were claimed as ancestor figures – conveyors of legitimacy – by the kings who ruled the kingdom of Powys in that later age.[23]

Both Gildas and *HB* mention another sub-Roman British leader, Ambrosius. Even more than Vortigern, he is obscure. Gildas describes him as a Roman and a gentleman.[24] To Gildas, the Romans represented the forces of civilization and order, in contrast to the sinful and weak Britons, and the barbarian invaders. His description of Ambrosius may imply that Ambrosius came of a line which in the sixth century still had some pretence of Roman-style authority, but this cannot be proved. Gildas neither claims nor denies that Ambrosius was a contemporary of Vortigern and it should be remembered that we do not know the extent of the power and influence of any leaders in post-Roman Britain. By the time of the writing of *HB*, however, a connexion between Vortigern and Ambrosius was assumed. *HB* presents Ambrosius as the rival of Vortigern, and attributes Vortigern's invitation to the Saxons as in part a response to fear of Ambrosius.[25] Its account of Ambrosius is less elaborate and more confused than its account of Vortigern. It relates a tale of Ambrosius's unusual birth and prophetic powers, and it seems that by the early ninth century, the leader of late Roman-British resistance had become inextricably confused with another legendary figure, perhaps an antecedent of the Merlin Ambrosius of Arthurian myth. Alongside this, *HB* attributes to Ambrosius a kind of overlordship over the Britons after the death of Vortigern.[26] This has lead to speculation about the existence in the sixth century of a concept of a British overkingship, perhaps based on the approval of a council, perhaps based on political ability, perhaps based on military prowess, and modelled on Roman administrative and governmental practice.[27] Yet this theory rests on no more secure basis than *HB,* which possessed only barely more evidence than survives to us today – the idea of British overkings resisting the Saxons thus becomes simply early medieval Welsh legend. Traditionally, the name associated with resistance to Saxon invasion is Arthur. The earliest reference in an historical text to him is in *HB,* where he is described not as a king, but simply as the battle leader, *dux bellorum,* of the Britons.[28] The bulk of the material relating to Arthur dates to the twelfth century and later, and is literary, rather than historical. Unlike Vortigern, who from an early period occupied a key role in the pedigree of the royal line of Powys, Arthur was not claimed as an ancestor figure (the same is true of Ambrosius). Genealogy in early Wales was used as much to justify claims to legitimate power and to reinforce lordship as it was to define kinship and descent. In early medieval Wales, Arthur was not drawn upon as a legitimating figure (although he occurs occasionally in poetry as a type of a fine warrior, and in late eleventh/early twelfth century Saints' Lives as a pattern of tribal leadership to be questioned and improved by the behaviour of the Saints).[29] Arthur was a legendary hero, and not a forebear or a great king of antiquity, and the upsurge of interest in him during the twelfth century owed more to Anglo-Norman and French pressure upon the native Welsh polity, and to European literary initiatives than to any genuine remembrance of the sixth-century past.

The archaeological record suggests a rather more realistic picture of a network of kingdoms based on local power. In the area that would become Wales, these were probably centred on elite defended sites (sometimes Iron Age hill forts which had been reoccupied in the fourth or fifth centuries, sometimes in former Roman towns). At Coygan Camp, Dyfed, south Wales, high status occupation of a native (as opposed to Roman) site is attested from the fourth century through to the sixth, showing a continuity of native political and social activity at elite level from the last century of Roman dominance through into the post-Roman age.[30] With the end of Roman domination and the increase in pressure from overseas raiders, it seems likely that overlapping small kingdoms and chiefdoms grew up among the native Britons to provide centres of government and defence.

Gildas's Five Kings

Gildas's account supports the idea of the development of small local kingdoms. The proud tyrant belonged to the past; Ambrosius to the period of Gildas's birth. In his own day, Gildas wrote of kings whom he considered little better than tyrants. He accused them of wide-ranging sins: extortion, adultery, incest, robbery, ill-governance, false justice, and impiety. He singled out five in particular: Constantine of Damnonia; Aurelius Caninus; Vortepor, tyrant of the Demetae; Cuneglasus; and Maglocunus.[31] It cannot be proved that Gildas's account was accurate or truthful; we cannot now know what he may have omitted or recast to serve his polemic purpose. We cannot establish with any certainty the nature of the powers possessed by these men or the extent of the territories they ruled.[32] He gave territorial details for only two of them: Damnonia, (probably Dumnonia, now Devon and Cornwall), and the Demetae. The latter refers to one of the future kingdoms of Wales, Dyfed, whose name is derived from this old tribal name. Few details survive concerning Vortepor, but his name is recorded in the genealogy of the early kings of that kingdom.[33] More importantly, the name Vortepor occurs in the inscriptions on a monumental stone from Castelldwyran near Carmarthen. One inscription, in Latin, reads *memoria Voteporigis protictoris*, to the memory of Vortepor the protector. A second inscription on the same stone, in Irish, reads simply *Votecorigas*, an Irish form of Vortepor. The stone has been dated to the mid-sixth century, and while the dating partly rests on the evidence in Gildas, the monument provides substantial supporting evidence for the existence of Vortepor and his kingship over the people of Dyfed. The nature of the inscription may also suggest that, despite Gildas's negative portrait, Vortepor was better thought of in his own kingdom –

The Vortepor stone.

or wished to leave such an impression to posterity. The use of the word *protector* is interesting, as it suggests a claim to an affiliation of some kind with Roman practice. It may be that Vortepor's kingship sought to emulate Roman models of governance, as well as native ones.

The remaining three of Gildas's kings are not given any specific geographic location. Nevertheless, it may be possible to make tentative identifications. Maglocunus is probably Maelgwn Gwynedd, to whose name a certain amount of tradition had accrued by the early ninth century. *HB* referred to him as *Mailcunus magnus*, Maelgwn the great.[34] He is said to be the descendent of Cunedda, the founding figure of the first royal line of Gwynedd. Gildas's depiction of him suggests a man of practical action and ruthless disposition, who made himself king by overthrowing his uncle, and showed himself as liberal to his followers as he was callous to his enemies. He was an educated man – Gildas writes of his monastic training and background – but he turned away from monastic life in order to pursue his kingship.[35] The tone in which Gildas wrote is one of regret: his picture of Maelgwn suggests a man of great ability but few scruples. Maelgwn was claimed as an ancestor by almost all later kings and princes of Gwynedd, and, with Vortigern, stands as one of the dominant figures in the landscape of early Wales, although his career is now lost to us.

The identity and location of Aurelius Caninus and Cuneglasus are much harder to establish. Caninus may be a word-play on the Welsh name 'Cynin'.[36] This name occurs in the pedigree of the first dynasty of Powys.[37] However, this can only be speculation – Cynin is not an uncommon name, and the name in the Powys pedigree could refer to another individual. Moreover, the pedigree, in its earliest surviving form, dates to the mid-tenth century, and has been subject to manipulation in favour of a different (and alien) ruling line. It is defective in its early sections, where there is evidence for several generations having been lost. Lloyd suggested that Aurelius Caninus may have been a descendent of Ambrosius Aurelianus, an argument which is no more provable than the thesis based on the pedigrees.[38] We cannot say who Aurelius may have been, nor identify where he ruled. Cuneglasus is equally problematic. He has generally been accepted as Cynlas who appears in later pedigrees as a king of Rhos in north Wales,[39] but this cannot be certain.[40] Like the argument associating Aurelius Caninus with Powys, it depends on the witness of a pedigree which survives from a much later period and has been manipulated in the interests of a politically dominant royal line of a much later period. As with Aurelius Caninus, Cuneglasus is a mystery.

The early history of the Welsh kingdoms

Early medieval Wales was a land of many kingdoms. We lack detailed knowledge of many of these: most of the earliest kings remain no more than names in pedigrees. Nevertheless, it is possible to draw in outline something of the history of the early kingdoms, and in particular, of the kingdoms of Dyfed, Gwynedd and Powys.

Dyfed

The medieval kingdom of Dyfed in south-west Wales had its origin in the Roman tribal area of the Demetae, and was an apparently independent political entity by the middle of the sixth century. Gildas wrote of raids and incursions by the Irish in the late Roman and sub-Roman periods,[41] and a variety of evidence – written, archaeological, monumental and linguistic – indicates a settled Irish presence in early Dyfed. A medieval Irish prose tale, *The Expulsion of the Déisi*, reads as follows[42]:

> Eochaid, son of Artchorp, with his descendants, went over the sea
> into the land of Dyfed, and his sons and his grandsons died there.
> And from them is [descended] the race of Crimthann over there.

The text goes on to give the pedigree of the descendants of Eochaid, son of Artchorp, in Wales, including *Gartbuir*, an Irish spelling of Vortepor, who appears as the great-great-great grandson of Eochaid. The Déisi were a people from Mide in Ireland, who had been expelled from their lands. The tale relates how they migrated to Wales, where they imposed themselves as the ruling dynasty in the old tribal area of the Demetae. The final name in the pedigree is *Tualador*, representing Welsh Tewdwr or Tewdos.

The tale gives one reason for the Irish presence in Dyfed – the Déisi were fleeing from enemies in Ireland and seeking a new place to settle. However, a variety of other reasons also suggest themselves. *HB* refers to the Irish settled in west Wales,[43] and surviving Welsh genealogies of the royal line of Dyfed also record a layer of Irish names. The Welsh records preserve the memory of Irish ancestry but show an adaptation to later political needs and desires – certain Irish names are omitted in favour of a territorial eponym, *Dimet*, and a number of Roman names. The earliest Welsh pedigrees were written down by the middle of the tenth century at the latest, and composed rather earlier: by this time, there was unlikely to be any vested interest in inventing an Irish connexion for the kings of Dyfed. Their author seems unaware of *The Expulsion of the Déisi*. What we possess, therefore, is two separate and independent traditions of the Irish origins of the early kings of Dyfed. The Welsh genealogies add an extra dimension to the ancestry of these kings, continuing it back beyond the Irish layer to give a Roman dimension. This latter element owes far more to the needs of tenth century Welsh politics than to reality. A claim to Roman descent legitimized and reinforced the authority of kings, making it appear they had an ancient right to rule. Pedigrees are not the easiest or most reliable of sources: they are subject to rewriting to reflect the changing political needs of later generations, to errors caused by scribal carelessness, and to deliberate omission where a former link has lost its value, meaning or interest. They contain no dates, nor can it be certain that everyone named within a pedigree was a king or a ruler – in later centuries, when we possess fuller chronicle evidence, it is clear that many kings were outside the main line of the dominant ruling houses, or did not belong to any known ruling house.

They are the records of the successful leaders of the age in which they were composed, and for earlier ages they must be used with care. However, the weight of evidence in the pedigrees makes it likely that the first dynasty of Dyfed had an Irish origin. Other categories of evidence back this up. There is a corpus of inscribed stones found across south-west Wales and dateable to the fifth century onwards. These commemorate individuals of high status – the Vortepor stone referred to earlier is one such example. They are inscribed in Latin, using the Latin alphabet, but a number of them also have inscriptions in Irish, using a form of script native to early Ireland, ogom. The majority of ogom-inscribed stones lie in the Dyfed area, strongly suggesting an Irish presence there at an early date, perhaps concentrated among the elite classes of society.[44] The practice of erecting memorial stones was not an Irish one, but seems rather to have been adopted in imitation of Rome. The use of Irish names and script on such memorials is further testimony of an assimilation between local Welsh and Irish cultures, with the incoming settlers following the practice of the more Romanized natives.

The incidence of ogom on inscribed stones and the occurrence of Irish names over several generations in the pedigrees of Dyfed, suggests that the Irish royal dynasty retained a sense of its Irishness at least until the end of the sixth century. By the mid-tenth century at the latest, however, the Dyfed royal line had largely forgotten or elided its Irish origins. The pedigree of the royal line was recast to derive its ancestry – and its claim to legitimacy – from Magnus Maximus, the usurping emperor of Britain and Gaul. But the true origins of the family lay in Ireland.

Gwynedd

Under the Romans, the area that would become the kingdom of Gwynedd was the homeland of the *Ordovices*. It was a military zone, and the native population was relatively un-Romanized. As in Dyfed, Gwynedd was partially settled by Irish colonists in the late Roman period. The early Irish *Cormac's Glossary* refers to a fort in Britain owned by the sons of Liatháin.[45] This is probably a reference to the Irish tribe, Uí Liatháin, whose name may be preserved in the name Llŷn.[46] Moreover, there is a scattering of memorial stones in north-west Wales whose inscriptions include names of Irish origin, such as *Cunogusos*, on a stone from Llanfaelog,[47] and *Maccvdecceti* on a stone from Penrhos Llugwy,[48] both considered to date from the sixth century. There is also a small number of stones with ogom inscriptions, including the *Iaconus* stone from Treflys in the Llŷn peninsula,[49] and the *Icori* stone from Bryncir, Eifionydd,[50] both also dated to the sixth century. Further ogom inscriptions exist from eastern Gwynedd, one on the stone of Prince Similius, from Clocaenog, Dyffryn Clwyd, dated to the late fifth century;[51] and perhaps the stone reading *Brohomagli Iatti* from Pentrefoelas, Rhufoniog, dated to the mid-sixth century.[52] This is a small corpus of evidence by comparison with the material for Dyfed, and it is necessary to conclude that the Irish formed only a minority element in Gwynedd.

The Maccvdecceti stone.

The Iaconus stone.

Embedded in the *HB* is the foundation legend of Gwynedd, and of the ancestors of Maelgwn Gwynedd. It reads:

> Cunedda, with his sons, who numbered eight, had come formerly from northern parts, that is the region called Manau of Gododdin, one hundred and forty six years before Maelgwn ruled, and they expelled the Irish, with very great destruction, from these regions, so that they never came back again to live there.[53]

Manau of Gododdin was a British kingdom in north Britain, in the region of the Anglo-Scottish border. This kingdom, and neighbouring north British kingdoms like Strathclyde and Elmet, formed the background to a considerable amount of later Welsh tradition surrounding the struggle of the Britons against the Saxons. North British ancestry would, like descent from Roman figures, become a badge of legitimacy and antiquity in Welsh pedigrees. As it stands, the foundation legend of Gwynedd shows the influence of ninth century aspirations and beliefs. It states

25

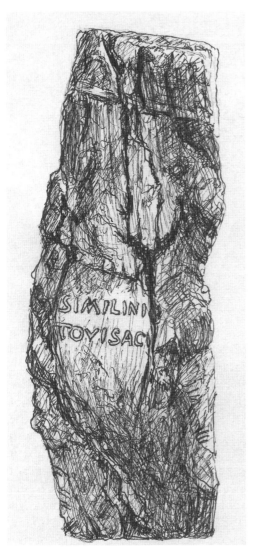

The Similius stone.

that Cunedda and his sons drove the Irish not simply out of Gwynedd but out of all Wales, a statement at odds with the evidence in southern pedigrees for a continuous Irish presence in Dyfed. It may reflect on the ninth-century context of *HB*, compiled at a time when the rulers of Gwynedd advanced claims to primacy over all of Wales. It would have been in their interest to represent Cunedda as a pan-Welsh figure. Pedigrees add further detail to the Cunedda legend:

> These are the names of the sons of Cunedda, who numbered nine. Tybion was the first-born, who died in the land called Manau of Gododdin and thus did not come with his father and aforesaid brothers. Meirion his son divided the possessions amongst his [Tybion's] brothers: Oswael the second born, the third Rhufen, the

The Brohomagli Iatti stone.

fourth Dunod, the fifth Ceredig, the sixth Afloeg, the seventh Einion Yrth, the eighth Dogfael, the ninth Edern.[54]

The names of the sons of Cunedda became attached to territories within Gwynedd, although we cannot now discover whether the names were derived from the territories, or whether the territories were named from the tradition of the sons. By the tenth century, when the earliest extant pedigrees were recorded, the divisions of Gwynedd were held to originate in the holdings of the sons of Cunedda, giving an impression of antiquity to the unity of the kingdom in the hands of a single family.[55] Either the legend had developed in the period since the composition of *HB*, or the pedigree recorded a variant version, as its account gave Cunedda nine – rather than eight – sons. We cannot determine which, if any, of the sons should be considered as the extra one. Tybion at first appears the logical candidate, as he is said to have died before his father moved south, but *HB* gives no names to the sons, and Ceredig is as least as likely as Tybion to be a later accretion. Ceredig is the eponym of the kingdom of Ceredigion, and the reputed ancestor of its royal line. There is no reliable evidence that Ceredigion was dominated from an early date by the royal line of Gwynedd. Rather, it was an independent kingdom, which by the ninth century had become a bone of contention between the kings of Gwynedd and of Dyfed. The affiliation of Ceredig to the line of Cunedda in the pedigree may be an attempt by a pro-Gwynedd writer in the ninth or tenth centuries to prove that Ceredigion belonged by right to the heirs and descendants of Cunedda. This raises another issue: we cannot be sure that Gwynedd itself had always been a unity. The fact that its sub-divisions bear the names of Cunedda's sons makes it possible that at some point, perhaps the fifth or sixth centuries, these sub-divisions were themselves separate states, whose eponyms and ancestor figures became absorbed by the tradition of the dynasty of Gwynedd. In the case of Meirionydd, independence from the overkingship of Gwynedd may have persisted into the ninth century. Meirion is said in the pedigree to have been a grandson, and not a son, of Cunedda. The Cunedda legend might best be regarded as a manifesto as to how various petty kingdoms were absorbed into the control of a single royal line, that of Maelgwn Gwynedd,[56] as well as an explanation for the relatively slight layer of Irish influence in Gwynedd. Dark has argued that this line may have had its heartland in Anglesey.[57]

It remains to be asked if any faith may be placed in the Cunedda legend. Certainly, by the early ninth century, the royal line of Gwynedd saw itself as descended from a north British hero, and owing its position to right of conquest. Cunedda has attracted scholarly debate, and there is no consensus of opinion on his historicity.[58] The ancestry given to him in the pedigrees hints at a Roman background (or at a belief in such a background by the time the pedigrees were composed). He is said to have been a grandson of Padarn *Peisrud* (of the Red Robe), a name which may reflect Latin *Paternus*. On the basis of this, it has been suggested that he was the descendant of some Roman or sub-Roman official, perhaps in the vicinity of Hadrian's Wall.[59] More elaborately, it has been suggested that his migration to Gwynedd was part of a deliberate policy imposed by a pan-British overlord, perhaps Maximus, or Vortigern, or even Coel Hen the Old King Cole of the nursery rhyme.[60] More cautious historians have stressed the retrospective nature of the pedigrees and its susceptibility to manipulation by later dynastic need.[61] It would be unwise to place too much emphasis on Cunedda's putative Roman ancestry, or upon theories associating him with some sub-Roman British empire. However, archaeological evidence may throw some light upon the supposed connexion between Gwynedd and north Britain. Square-ditched graves found near Tandderwen, Clwyd, may have features in common with barrows, burials and forts found in north Britain,[62] and a number of nuclear fort type sites found in north Wales may be related to sites in the Fife peninsula.[63] This might support the idea of an elite migration into north Wales in the fifth century or a little earlier. The evidence is not without its problems, however: the Fife sites lie not in the old kingdom of Manau of Gododdin, but rather in territory which at that period would have been part of Pictland. This does not rule out a connexion between Gwynedd and north Britain, but it may cast doubt on the traditional association between Cunedda and Manau of Gododdin. Dark has pointed out that at least one of the ogom-inscribed stones, that of Prince Similius, lies quite close to Tandderwen, and argued that foreign elements in Gwynedd may represent the presence of foreigners settled there, drawn by the existence of an established and eminent kingdom.[64] None of these need to have been Cunedda, and he may be no more than a dynastic fiction.[65] What can be said is that the ninth century account of *HB*, of a north British migration at aristocratic level into Gwynedd in the fifth century, may be supported to a degree from archaeological evidence, and that from the early ninth century at least the name of Cunedda became attached to this migration.

By the mid-seventh century, the ruling family of Gwynedd had risen to considerable prominence. The Anglo-Saxon colonization of England was well-advanced, and their new kingdoms were in the process of expansion, at the expense both of the surviving British kingdoms, and of other Anglo-Saxon kingdoms. Much of this expansion was in the north, but the eastern borders of Wales also saw warfare and conflict. The Anglo-Saxon monk, Bede, recorded in his *History of the English Church and People* that in AD 615, Aethelfrith, king of a northern Anglo-Saxon kingdom, Northumbria, fought a battle against the Britons of north Wales near Chester.[66] This is the earliest certain reference to warfare between the Welsh and the Anglo-Saxons, although it is unlikely that it was the first such conflict. In north Britain, there was warfare between the north British kingdoms and the Anglo-Saxons, but there was also intermarriage and perhaps alliance.[67] In at least one Anglo-Saxon border kingdom, that of the *Magonsaete,* the ruling dynasty may have had Welsh blood.[68] Welsh traditions commemorate the heroic activities of north British heroes such as Urien of Rheged (whose name was later drawn into Arthurian legend), and hint at an element of north British involvement in the conversion to Christianity of some of the northern Anglo-Saxons.[69] These figures, some historical, some legendary, were to be remembered in Wales, especially north Wales, but the details of their struggle with the Anglo-Saxons are obscure. Bede, who was close both in time and geography to the conflict between the north Britons and the Anglo-Saxons, recorded almost nothing of it. He believed that the Britons had refused to evangelize the Anglo-Saxons, and had reservations about their doctrinal correctness, which may have led him to omit instances of non-confrontational relations between the Anglo-Saxons and the north Britons. His reservations coloured his attitude to the Welsh. In the year of the battle of Chester, the Welsh Chronicles note the death of Iago ab Beli, a member of the ruling house of Gwynedd. If Iago was involved in the battle, which is uncertain, this might suggest that Chester lay in the sphere of influence of the kings of Gwynedd at this time. The phrasing of the obituary notice for Iago hints that he may have been in religious orders,[70] and Bede recorded that monks from the Welsh monastery of Bangor-on-Dee were present at the battle, perhaps to pray for victory for their countrymen.[71] Iago may have been a member of the royal house of Gwynedd who had retired into a monastery, but had been driven by political necessity to return to the world; he may have taken monastic vows on his deathbed after receiving fatal wounds in the battle; or, as Lloyd argued, he may not have been involved at all[72] – in default of further evidence, we cannot know. But while Iago is obscure, his son Cadfan, and more particularly his grandson, Cadwallon, are better recorded, and Cadwallon can be located not only as ruler of Gwynedd, but also as a major political force in mid-seventh century Britain.

An inscribed stone from Llangadwaladr, Anglesey, reads: *Catamannus rex sapientissimus opinatisimus omnium regum*, King Cadfan, the wisest and most renowned of all kings.[73] The stone almost certainly records Cadfan ab Iago, and

The Catamannus stone.

its location increases the likelihood that his dynasty had its heartland in Anglesey. It is possible his son was responsible for raising it. Cadwallon ap Cadfan is the best documented of all the early rulers in Wales – his deeds are recorded by Bede and remembered in native Welsh tradition. On the death in 616 of Aethelfrith, his kingdom was seized by Edwin, a member of a rival dynasty. Edwin carved out for himself a position of supremacy amongst the Anglo-Saxons.[74] Bede also credited him with the conquest, at least temporarily, of Anglesey and the Isle of Man;[75] perhaps the first Anglo-Saxon king to secure power west of the Pennines. Welsh sources confirm this aggression towards Welsh territories: the Triads record resistance to Edwin in the Llŷn peninsula by a local king or prince, Belyn,[76] who died *c*.627. Cadwallon was besieged on Anglesey by Edwin in around 632, and the Triads add to this that he was forced to flee to Ireland.[77] The Triads also claim that Edwin had spent time in Gwynedd while his rival Aethelfrith was king.[78] Triads are difficult to interpret: their form is highly conventional, and they are often cryptic. But the combined witness of Bede, the Welsh Chronicles, and the Triads demonstrate that in the earlier part of the seventh century, the kings of Northumbria took an interest in Gwynedd. Cadwallon's period of exile was short, for by 633 or 634 he was again in Gwynedd, and on the offensive. He allied with one of Edwin's major rivals, Penda, the king of the midland Anglo-Saxon kingdom of Mercia. In 633 or 634, they invaded Edwin's lands, and met him in battle at Hatfield Chase, where Edwin was killed.[79] Cadwallon and Penda were not satisfied with this. They continued the war in Northumbria and by the end of 634, they encompassed the deaths in battle of not one but two putative successors to Edwin, Osric and Eanfrith.[80] The campaign lasted a full year, during which time Cadwallon imposed himself as ruler over all Northumbria, not as a victorious king but a savage tyrant.[81] Cadwallon's success proved short-lived: Eanfrith was succeeded by his brother, Oswald, who in 634 or 635 defeated and killed Cadwallon at *Hefnfelth*, Heavenfield, near Hexham.[82] The location of the battle, and the amount of time which had passed since the overthrow of Edwin, is testimony to the strength and determination of Cadwallon, who carried the war out of his native Gwynedd across the Pennines into the heart of Northumbria, and continued to pursue his aim of dominance far from his own power-base. He may have had some support in this from the local population (some of whom may have had British blood): Bede, however, gives us no clues as to how Cadwallon resourced his campaign.

Bede's account of Cadwallon is hostile. This is partly rooted in the purpose with which he wrote his *History*. The centre of his narrative was the conversion to Christianity of the Anglo-Saxons, and he was a native of Northumbria. Edwin, and even more Oswald, were key figures in the conversion in the north. Bede had a clear idea of the nature, duties and rewards of Christian kingship. Cadwallon violated his standards. He was a Christian king, who made war on his fellow Christians in alliance with the pagan Penda, and who pursued vengeance without mercy. Bede constructed the Welsh in negative terms, a model derived in part from the harsh depiction given of them by Gildas, and partly upon his own distaste for a people whom he perceived as failing in their Christian duty. Cadwallon, to Bede, was a reprehensible example of a weak and faithless people, whose sufferings at the hands of the Saxons was a divine punishment. The invasion of Gwynedd by Edwin thus became a manifestation of divine favour, and Cadwallon's response a example of apostasy. To modern eyes, Cadwallon's actions appear more understandable: he acted in defence of his sovereignty, seeking to regain what had been taken from him, and to inflict damaging reverses on his enemies, perhaps in the hope of discouraging further invasions of his lands, perhaps in the hope of putting an end altogether to the new and dangerous northern states. Penda, whose lands lay adjacent to the borders of Wales, and who had his own reasons to be opposed to the expanding power of the Northumbrians, may well have appeared a useful ally. We do not know the terms of the agreement between them, but until Cadwallon's death their actions appear coordinated and amicable, and, after Cadwallon's death, we have no certain record of Penda taking the offensive against Gwynedd. It may be that the alliance was founded on friendship and respect, as well as political need. It was to the advantage of both kingdoms to have a dependable ally on their borders. Cadwallon's death in Northumbria may have resulted in some disruption in Gwynedd. He left a son, Cadwaladr, who may not have succeeded him, or may have been restricted only to the western part of the kingdom. According to *HB*, Cadwallon was followed as king by one Cadfael ap Cynfedw, whose antecedents are completely obscure.[83] The same text hints that Cadfael, like Cadwallon, enjoyed amicable relations with Penda.[84] Penda had continued the war against Northumbria beyond Cadwallon's death, and in 642, he killed Oswald near Oswestry,[85] in a battle which may have involved the Welsh of Powys, if not also those of Gwynedd. In 655, Penda went to war against another Northumbrian king, Oswiu, and according to *HB*, was in the wake of battle able to restore to the Welsh treasures which had been stolen from them.[86] Later in the same year, Penda fell in battle against Oswiu at *Winweard*,[87] and *HB* implies that Cadfael was present at this battle, allied with Penda.[88] His subsequent career is obscure to us.

A continued alliance with Mercia had practical advantages for the kings of Gwynedd, and not solely for the defence of both kingdoms against Northumbria. Mercia largely bordered on the mid-Welsh kingdom of Powys, and relations between Powys and Gwynedd were often hostile. An alliance between Gwynedd and Mercia may have permitted both to expand at the expense of Powys. Place names in the territory of medieval Powys suggest an Anglo-Saxon colonial presence there in the age of Penda: both Llannerch Penna, near Ellesmere, and Pontesbury, in the Shropshire/Powys border, may contain the name Penda as an element, and might perhaps indicate settlements made under his aegis, or that of his close descendants.[89] In later centuries, alliance between Gwynedd and Mercia proved fruitful for both sides: the alliance of Cadwallon with Penda is thus the first recorded instance of a major theme in Anglo-Welsh relations.

Powys

Powys in the early period is difficult to define geographically. Its later shape probably reflects processes both of early absorption of smaller original units (such as Gwrtheyrnion) into a larger over-kingdom, plus gradual erosion of the larger unit by its neighbours, in particular Gwynedd and Mercia. Moreover, little material evidence survives for early Powys, and the written evidence is confused, sometimes contradictory, and shows later manipulation to the detriment of Powys by writers working in the interests of the later rulers of Gwynedd. Unlike Gwynedd and Dyfed, there is no evidence of any Irish settlement within Powys. Rather, the kingdom was of native origin, and it has been argued that in its earliest years, it may have included lands now in Shropshire and southern Cheshire. The name Powys may derive from Latin *pagenses*, people of the country.[90] This raises the question of whether the name was bestowed by the people of Powys, or by a neighbour. Dark has argued that the name may have resulted from a propaganda campaign on behalf of an urban-based elite at an early date, and intended to disparage yokel neighbours or rivals;[91] another suggestion is that the name reflects an area which had a high level of paganism.[92] The problem with both these suggestions is that we do not know when a discrete kingdom of Powys emerged, and both arguments assign the name to a late-Roman or sub-Roman context, whereas the kingdom proper may not have arrived at an established form until the late sixth or early seventh centuries. Extant genealogical traditions are little help, as none of them were recorded until considerably later. It is likely that Powys, like Gwynedd, was formed from a number of smaller units, whose traditions and pedigrees were later rationalized or combined to give an impression of a greater chronological depth for the kingdom. We know of named kings from the Powys area in the late sixth and early seventh centuries. However, the contexts in which these names occur are difficult to interpret.

Offa's dyke, near Knighton, Powys.

The earliest reference to a dynast from Powys is at the battle of Chester, *c.*616. Bede's account of this does not name the Welsh leaders (apart from a certain Brochfael, who had been assigned to guard the monks of Bangor on Dee, who were present to pray for Welsh success).[93] As was discussed above, this battle was against aggressors from Northumbria, and perhaps involved forces from Gwynedd, as well as Powys. The Welsh Chronicles, in their account of the battle (which was written after Bede's time, and probably by an author aware of Bede's work), state that one Selyf ap Cynan was killed there. Selyf is named in the extant Powys pedigrees as a member of its royal line. Apart from the circumstances of his death, and the possibility that he was in some way acting in conjunction with the forces of Gwynedd in this battle, we know nothing of him (and the bare entry in the Welsh Chronicles does not preclude that he was, in fact, fighting on the side of the Northumbrians – we have no way of knowing how advanced the rivalry of Gwynedd and Powys was at this period).

When Edwin of Northumbria overran Gwynedd in the 620s, he might have had to have gone through Powys. No details survive regarding this, and this is further evidence to the degree to which surviving Welsh sources are not only relatively late in date, but biased away from Powys. The Welsh Chronicles note intermittent conflict between the Anglo-Saxons and Powys along the eastern

33

boundary of the kingdom from the later seventh century onwards. This conflict continued into the eighth century, and it was in this time that Offa's dyke may have been at least partially constructed.[94] Offa, like Penda, was king of Mercia and enjoyed substantial status and influence throughout most of Anglo-Saxon England. The purpose of the dyke is debated: it is unlikely to have been a simple defence, but it may have marked a frontier, or a buffer zone, or a barrier to raiding parties, or a line to which Anglo-Saxon settlers within the Welsh border might retreat.[95] Offa made a number of raids into Powys, perhaps to subdue the population, perhaps to prepare the way for the construction of the dyke, and possible new Anglo-Saxon settlement. Aggression towards Powys did not end with the construction of the dyke: raids continued after the death of Offa, and in 822 it was overrun, probably by the Mercians, who reached as far west as Degannwy, and seized control of the kingdom.

Anglo-Saxon domination did not endure. In 855, the Welsh Chronicles record the death at Rome of Cyngen, king of Powys, and last of his line to rule. Cyngen had not fled from fear of the Anglo-Saxons, but as a result of the aggression of Gwynedd, which, by the ninth century, was under the control of a new, dynamic and expansionist dynasty. Cyngen's perception of the events of his reign were recorded by him on the Pillar of Elise.[96] In addition to recording the genealogical traditions of his family, it also served to commemorate the expulsion from Powys of the Anglo-Saxons. The inscription (which when it was recorded was already damaged) on it read:

> Concenn son of Cattell, Cattell son of Brohcmail, Brohcmail son of Eliseg, Eliseg son of Guoillauc. Concenn therefore being great-grandson of Eliseg erected this stone to his great-grandfather Eliseg. It is Eliseg who annexed the inheritance of Powys... throughout nine [years] from the power of the English, which he made into a sword-land by fire. Whosoever shall read this hand-inscribed stone, let him give a blessing on the soul of Eliseg. It is Concenn who... with his hand... to his own kingdom of Powys... and which... the mountain... the monarchy Maximus... of Britain... Concenn, Pascent... Maun, Annan. Britu, moreover [was] the son of Guorthigirn [Vortigern], whom Germanus blessed and whom Sevira bore to him, the daughter of Maximus the king, who slew the king of the Romans. Conmarch painted this writing at the command of his king, Concenn. The blessing of the Lord upon Concenn and all members of his family and upon all the land of Powys until the day of judgement, Amen.[97]

According to this, Cyngen's grandfather, Elise, had driven the English out. This may refer to an earlier period than the invasion of 823, but the latter probably did not endure for very long. The aggressor, Mercia, was itself under attack from a neighbour, the southern Anglo-Saxon kingdom of Wessex, and is unlikely to have men and resources to spare for Wales. The pedigree section of the pillar has been discussed above: the problem of the multiple origins claimed by the differing sources for the dynasty of Powys reflects ninth century propaganda from Gwynedd, but it also probably hides earlier traditions in which the descendants of Vortigern, Cyngen and his predecessors, may have ruled over a separate territory to that held by the descendants of Cadell Ddrynllug. The two may have become associated through absorption or conquest. The question of the origins of the Powys line – and the likelihood that Powys was formed out of several earlier kingdoms – is further evidenced in surviving poetry, about early Powysian dynasts, notably Cynan Garwyn, the father of that Selyf who died in the battle of Chester, and about his father Brochfael, and about one Cynddylan, said to be a descendant of Cadell Ddrynllug. Poetry is difficult to interpret, and none of the extant poems about early Powys predate the ninth century – and some of them may be as late as the eleventh century. Brochfael – who may or may not be the man of that name who unsuccessfully defended the monks at the battle of Chester – and Cynan Garwyn are little more than names, presented in the poetry as warrior heroes, and rulers of wide lands. Such imagery may well owe more to poetic convention, and later medieval claims to Powysian glory, than to any reality. The Cynddylan poetry poses further questions, hinting at the possible existence at some early stage of yet another dynasty in Powys (or at a cadet line of a known dynasty) who may have held land – perhaps as a discrete political unit – in an area that now lies in Shropshire, and fell under English dominance at an early date.[98] Like the question of the sons of Cunedda, the poetic traditions concerning Powys are witness above all to the complex origins of the kingdom, and are probably best considered in the light of tradition and legend grown up around origins which were fragmented, and perhaps by the ninth century no longer wholly understood.

The other kingdoms

The origins and early history of the other Welsh kingdoms are even less clear. Some, such as Buellt and Ceredigion, had their own royal lines, but their rulers are now no more than names. Similarly, the rulers of the kingdoms of the south-east, Gwent and Glywysing, are seldom referenced in historical sources, and material surviving in the twelfth-century *Book of Llandaff* is controversial, difficult to date, and, again, reveals little to us other than a handful of names.[99]

Brycheiniog, in the eastern part of Wales, had certain features in common with Dyfed. Pedigree evidence, surviving from the eleventh century, if not earlier, points to an Irish element in the royal line, and the evidence of inscribed stones supports this.[100] Like Dyfed, Brycheiniog shows a local concentration of inscriptions in ogom and with Irish names. This suggests that Brycheiniog also saw settlement, at least at elite level, by the Irish, in the fifth and sixth centuries. The pedigrees from Brycheiniog also have another odd feature, in that Brychan, dynastic founder of the royal line and eponym of the kingdom, is said to have fathered a large number of saints. This probably reflects more on later ecclesiastical claims than on reality. Brycheiniog may have come under the influence of Dyfed in the eighth century, but it retained its own royal family into the ninth century, when its last known king, Tewdwr ab Elise, entered into an alliance with the Anglo-Saxon king, Alfred the Great.[101] The dynasty survived into the tenth century, when the kingdom was finally absorbed by a neighbour.

Ceredigion in the west was long subject to claims of overlordship from its neighbours, and was to be a battleground between north, south, and mid Wales on into the twelfth century. It was ruled by its own native kings until the ninth century, when it was overrun by the kings of Gwynedd, and its founder, Ceredig, was attached to the Cunedda legend as a putative grandson.

The early centuries of Wales are largely shadowy. Many kings are little more than names: others are inextricably bound up in later legend, myth and propaganda. The fifth through to the eighth centuries found Wales a land of many kings and many kingdoms, but at the end of the eighth century, a new figure, Merfyn Frych, emerged. He, and the dynasty he founded, would change the political face of Wales forever.

2 From Rhodri Mawr to Hywel Dda:

c.844 - c.949

The ninth century was a turning point in the history of Wales. In England, it saw the rise of a new, centralizing political force, the royal house of Wessex, which would ultimately unify all of England under one king. It was also the peak of the first Viking Age: throughout the British Isles, raiders attacked settlements, killed or kidnapped their inhabitants, seized goods, and colonized. Wales escaped the worst of this, but was not untouched by the consequences of the raids and settlements in England. The century also saw the rise within Wales of a major new political power, the descendants of Merfyn Frych[1]. This dynasty would play a major role in Welsh political life down to the conquest of Wales in 1283.

Viking raids on the British Isles had begun in the late eighth century: the first recorded raid occurred in Lindisfarne, off the north-east coast of England, in 793. In the same year, Viking ships raided the churches of Inismurray and Inisboffin in Ireland, as well as the church on Lambay island. Raids continued on both England and Ireland on into the early part of the ninth century, and from the middle part of the century, the Viking raiders began to over-winter in England, the first stage in a process leading to settlement. By the 870s, the Vikings had overrun and colonized almost all the English kingdoms, with the sole exception of Wessex in the south-west. The date of the first Viking raid on Wales is not certainly known. The first recorded attack was in 850, when a Welsh leader named Cyngen (we do not know from which of the Welsh kingdoms he came) was killed by Viking raiders. Three years later, in 853, Anglesey was ravaged, and in 855, a Viking leader, Ormr, fought the king of Gwynedd, Rhodri Mawr. However, given the level of Viking activity in the Irish sea and along the north-west coast of England and Scotland from the early part of the century, it is unlikely that these raids of the 850s are the first which Wales suffered. There are traces of Viking settlement within Wales.[2] The bulk of the evidence lies in place-names, although there is an increasing amount of archaeological material also.[3] However, during the ninth century, the greatest threat faced by the kingdoms of Wales was not the Vikings but each other, and in particular the powerful new royal line of Gwynedd, descended from Merfyn Frych.

Merfyn Frych and Rhodri Mawr

In 816 the Welsh Chronicles record the death of Cynan ap Rhodri, king of Gwynedd. He was descended in the male line from Cadwaladr and Maelgwn Gwynedd, and had, for the three years before 816, been involved in a struggle for control of Gwynedd against his brother, Hywel. Around the same time, the king of Mercia, Cenwulf, was pursuing a determined campaign against Wales, ravaging Gwynedd and annexing Rhufoniog. Two years later he attacked Dyfed in the south-west, suggesting perhaps that he had been able to maintain an overlordship in Gwynedd itself, and by 823 the Anglo-Saxons had overrun Powys. They had doubtless benefited from the internal frictions within the Welsh kingdoms: Gwynedd was weakened by the conflict of the brothers Cynan and Hywel; while in Powys, the king, Elise ap Cyngen, found it necessary to kill his brother, Griffri, in 814, probably to secure his own power. Internal conflict was by no means uncommon within the Welsh kingdoms, but it led to a reduction in resources and to the development of factions, thus leaving kingdoms more vulnerable to outside aggression. Hywel ap Rhodri had survived his brother in Gwynedd (albeit perhaps under the overlordship of Cenwulf of Mercia), and died in 825. He was the last known member in the direct male line of the descendants of Maelgwn to hold Gwynedd. The *HB* records for us the name of his successor, one Merfyn Frych ap Gwriad.[4]

Although Merfyn's descendants would dominate the kingdoms of Wales for much of the centuries down to 1283, and although many of our surviving native sources were written or rewritten in their interests, Merfyn himself remains obscure. The pedigrees in London, British Library MS Harleian 3859 (HG), compiled in the mid-tenth century under the patronage of Merfyn's great-great-grandson, Owain ap Hywel Dda, claim that Merfyn was related to the old royal line of Maelgwn through his mother.[5] She is said to have been Essyllt, daughter of that King Cynan ap Rhodri who died in 816, and niece of Hywel ap Rhodri (died 825). However, several of the other genealogical manuscripts state that Essyllt was Merfyn's wife, not his mother,[6] and while HG probably represents the earlier tradition regarding Merfyn among his descendants, by the later twelfth century when the *History of Gruffudd ap Cynan (HGK)*, commemorating another of his descendants, was composed, the tradition seems to have been that Essyllt was Merfyn's wife.[7] The HG pedigrees were composed in Deheubarth; *HGK* was written in Gwynedd: they may represent variant traditions regarding Merfyn preserved in south and north Wales. By the mid-tenth century at the latest, the members of Merfyn's dynasty were engaged upon legitimating his control over Gwynedd. The fabrication of a link through the female line to the former ruling house was a convenient way to do this (and such links were to be claimed repeatedly by Merfyn's descendants). It must be said, however, that given the lapse of time between Merfyn's life and the composition of the pedigree in HG, that the connexion via Essyllt ferch Cynan, must at best be regarded as tradition, and may be simple fiction.

Merfyn is associated in the literary record with *Manaw*. Later tradition claims that he came from that land (*Meruin vrych o dir manaw*).[8] By the later twelfth century, he was provided with a patrilineage affiliating him to a legendary figure from north Britain, Llywarch Hen,[9] and as a result, it has been suggested that his family came from Manaw of Gododdin, the supposed homeland of Cunedda.[10] The descendants of Llywarch Hen had a traditional association with Powys.[11]

Perhaps Merfyn originated amongst the nobility of that kingdom, and turned his attention westward due to Anglo-Saxon pressure. As Lloyd pointed out, Manaw could equally refer to the Isle of Man.[12] An inscription found on Man, perhaps of the early ninth century, reads *crux guriat*, the cross of Gwriad. Gwriad was the name of Merfyn's father, and it is possible that the inscription refers to him, although again this cannot be proved. What is certain is that Merfyn was not a member in the male line (and inheritance to land and title in early Wales passed in the male line) of the original royal house of Gwynedd, and his rise to power there was the result of usurpation. No details survive as to this, although it is unlikely to have been achieved without warfare, even if he had married into the original royal house. We should regard him as a successful and determined warrior and politician, who was able to bring an alien kingdom under his control through a mixture of battle and diplomacy, persuading the local magnates to accept and support his leadership in place of their native dynasty. If the old house had died out with Hywel ap Rhodri in 825, then Merfyn may have been able to capitalize upon a power vacuum, and manipulate local rivalries or political confusion, as well as troubles caused by Anglo-Saxon invasions (and perhaps by Viking raids) to his own advantage. He remained king of Gwynedd until his death in 844, and, if he was not married to Essyllt, he may have formed an alliance by marrying into the royal line of neighbouring Powys.[13] This marriage is attested in two later pedigrees.[14] Such a marriage, if it is genuine, might represent the traces of an alliance between Gwynedd and Powys in the early ninth century, perhaps to resist the aggression of the English. Alternatively, it might reflect an attempt by Merfyn's descendants to justify their intrusion into Powys. Merfyn died in battle in 844, probably as king of all Gwynedd. The events of his reign and indeed the context of the battle in which he fell are not recorded for us. He left a son, who would be known to later generations as Rhodri Mawr, Rhodri the Great.

As with Merfyn, some confusion attaches over the identities of Rhodri's wife and mother in the pedigrees. According to the pedigree in Oxford, Jesus College MS 20 (JC 20), Rhodri's mother was Nest, the daughter of Cyngen, king of Powys.[15] However, the pedigrees in National Library of Wales Mostyn MS 117 (MG),[16] and in the *Achau Brenhinoedd y Thywysogion Cymru (ABT)*,[17] give his mother as Essyllt ferch Cynan. There are no very good grounds for accepting either as reliable. What the confusion tells us is that a claim connecting the Line of Merfyn by marriage to the old royal house of Powys was considered credible, and perhaps necessary by the time of the composition of the earliest of the pedigrees involved.[18] The pedigrees reflect a period in which the royal house of Gwynedd was promoting claims to overlordship and control over most of Wales: supposed blood-links to the ancient ruling lines of other kingdoms supplied later members of the Line of Merfyn with a superficial layer of legitimacy in their attempts to dominate and intrude into neighbouring kingdoms. This process of genealogical manipulation was employed to explain and legitimize the eventual expansion of this dynasty into Ceredigion and Dyfed, as well as Gwynedd and Powys. It cannot be proven that any of the claimed marriages ever occurred, although equally they cannot be disproved. It is unlikely that women could transmit rights to land or dominion to their husbands or their sons in early medieval Wales – the texts of the Welsh laws which survive to us were written down no earlier than the late twelfth century, and their provisions exclude women from inheriting land and titles.[19] It is unclear that these later law codes operated in identical form in earlier centuries – indeed it is probable that they did not. However, there is no indication in any surviving Welsh records that women were considered capable of transmitting legal title to kingship or lordship. Thus, even if the claimed marriages of early members of the Line of Merfyn are genuine, it is unlikely that the marriages conferred any meaningful legal rights to lordship. However, a marriage tie was a useful way of forming an alliance, and of opening up lines of communication and connexion with the leading men of a given kingdom. A man married to a member of a native royal line would probably be better positioned to gather around himself the necessary network of political and military support for making a bid for kingship.

Rhodri Mawr came to power in an auspicious time for Wales. The kings of Mercia had pursued an aggressive policy towards Wales in the first part of the ninth century, but during the later 820s and 830s, Mercia faced increasing external pressure, from its southern neighbour, Wessex. Under King Egbert, Wessex had annexed much of southern England, and in the 820s and 830s, extended its overlordship over Mercia and Northumbria. As a result, Mercian aggression towards Wales was reduced. Egbert made a raid into Wales in 830, but he did not show a sustained interest in Wales, in contrast to the persistent aggression of Cenwulf of Mercia. Furthermore, from the 830s onwards, the level of Viking activity in southern England increased. The Vikings began to spend winters in England from the 850s. This pressure contributed further to a reduction in Anglo-Saxon military interest in Wales. Wales too was being raided by Vikings, and there was a clump of raids in the 850s, but these were predominantly hit and run affairs, targeting vulnerable coastal settlements.

The lull in Anglo-Saxon aggression gave Rhodri Mawr time to consolidate his own position in Gwynedd after his father's death. These years also provided him with the opportunity to expand his power outside Gwynedd. Up until the ninth century, the question of relations between the various kingdoms of Wales is hard to establish, although it seems likely that, just as smaller units like Rhos and Rhufoniog slowly became annexed or incorporated into larger kingdoms, so the larger units were involved in border warfare and conflicts over debatable lands. From the ninth century, however, our source materials become fuller, and we can establish a clearer picture of Welsh political life. In 856, the king of Powys, Cyngen (the father of Nest), died in exile in Rome. This Cyngen had been responsible for the erection of the Pillar of Elise,[20] which laid out both the official pedigree of the kings of Powys, and their successes against the Anglo-Saxons. The exact context of the inscription is not known, but Dark has argued that it may have represented a deliberate and permanent public record of the history and status of the kings of Powys in the face of increasing pressure from Gwynedd, represented either by Merfyn or, after 844, by Rhodri Mawr.[21] *HB* contains a series of attacks

The Pillar of Elise.

upon the legitimacy and ancestry of the royal house of Powys. It was written in Gwynedd, in the reign of Merfyn Frych, and possibly under his influence. This suggests that the new royal house of Gwynedd adopted a hostile attitude towards Powys. If there had been a marriage between the new kings of Gwynedd and Cyngen's daughter, it did not secure a peaceful alliance between the two kingdoms. Cyngen died in exile, and he is not known to have left a successor of his own blood to rule in Powys. It is not certain that Rhodri Mawr took firm possession of Powys during the mid-ninth century: but the native Welsh Chronicles name no further independent kings of Powys until the last quarter of the eleventh century. The conquest of Powys by the kings of Gwynedd may have taken place over an extended period, and parts of the kingdom may have been controlled intermittently by local lords or forgotten descendants of the original ruling house. The details of the conquest are lost, and it may not have been completed in the lifetime of Rhodri. The West Saxon King Aethelwulf raided Wales, again perhaps Powys, in 853, and may have had interests in the border area. He may also have been anxious to check the advance of Rhodri, who presented a potential threat to the borders of the Anglo-Saxon lands.

In addition to the claims that Rhodri had a link by blood or marriage to Powys, the later pedigrees supply him with a link to Ceredigion. According to JC 20,[22] and to *ABT,*[23] he married Angharad ferch Meurig, the sister of Gwgan ap Meurig, king of Ceredigion. Gwgan drowned in 872, and, like Cyngen of Powys, was to be the last known member of his dynasty to rule over Ceredigion. Perhaps, on Gwgan's death, Rhodri annexed his kingdom and may even have been responsible for Gwgan's death, although, as with Powys, there is no direct evidence for this. However, from the later ninth century, Ceredigion was absorbed into the political sphere of the Line of Merfyn, and – unlike Powys – it would not recover its independence from that house. Ceredigion lay on the route between Gwynedd in the north and Dyfed in the south, and was a key area for any group seeking to dominate Wales. Possession of Ceredigion would have provided Rhodri and his successors with access into the agriculturally desirable lands of the south, particularly Pembrokeshire, and with dominance of much of the western seaboard of Wales. While Powys was to be something of an uneasy possession, which would eventually pass into the hands of a new family unrelated to the Line of Merfyn, Ceredigion became a property of Merfyn's descendants, and its native traditions were affiliated onto the foundation legend of Gwynedd, creating the impression that an attachment between Ceredigion and the north was legitimate and antique.

Rhodri Mawr was a forceful and effective military leader. There are records of a Viking raid on Gwynedd in 853, and in 856 Rhodri is known to have killed in battle Ormr, the leader of a Viking band operating in Wales. It is possible that the relatively low incidence of recorded Viking activity within Wales in the lifetimes of Merfyn, Rhodri, and Rhodri's sons reflects their prowess. They may have been capable of mounting an organized resistance to Viking harassment, and this, combined with the fact that much of Wales presents a difficult and intractable terrain for colonization, may have discouraged Viking interest. Rhodri's heartland was in the north-west, including the attractive and agriculturally valuable island of Anglesey. If he mounted a strong defence of the good lands within his kingdom, (and it seems very probable that he did), then potential Viking settlers may simply have decided to move on to easier targets in Ireland, England, and the Western Isles.

Towards the end of his reign, however, Rhodri's fortunes took a down-turn. Viking interest in England intensified from the 860s and Wales saw a renewal of Viking attacks in 871. In 877 Rhodri was briefly expelled from his kingdom by Viking raiders and fled to Ireland. In the same year, part of Mercia was settled by Vikings, leaving Wessex as the sole English kingdom free from Viking dominion. Rhodri was reinstated in Gwynedd by 878, but his enjoyment of his restoration was to be short-lived. He was killed in battle that year, fighting the Anglo-Saxons. The context of this battle is not known, but it may well be that the Anglo-Saxon enemies came from Mercia, either seeking refuge from Viking rule, or operating under Viking control to expand hegemony, and defend the border area against potential Welsh hostility.

The sons of Rhodri

Rhodri left sons. Traditionally, they numbered six,[24] but their identities (and indeed number) are unstable. JC 20 names eight: Cadell, Merfyn, Anarawd, Aeddan,

Meurig, Morgan, Tudwal and Elise.[25] *ABT* lists seven: Anarawd, Cadell, Meurig, Merfyn, Tudwal, Gwriad and Gwydelig.[26] These pedigrees are extant only in relatively late manuscripts, and their testimony is probably a reflection of later medieval claims to descent from Rhodri than an accurate statement of ninth-century fact. However, the earliest reference to six sons is in Asser's *Life of King Alfred*, written in the later ninth century.[27] This text does not name the sons, and thus we cannot be sure that the sons who have appeared in the later pedigrees are genuine – indeed, it is possible that the reference to six by Asser is an error in the transmission of his text.[28] The Welsh chronicles mention only four sons by name: Anarawd, Cadell, Merfyn, and Gwriad. These seem to be the politically active descendants of Rhodri, and amongst these four only Cadell and Anarawd made a major impact on Welsh history. The late twelfth-century writer, Gerald of Wales, recorded that after Rhodri's death, his surviving sons divided his lands between them. [29] However, in the Welsh Chronicles the brothers are usually recorded acting together, and it seems more likely that no strict division occurred, but rather the brothers shared control of their father's kingdom, although Anarawd may have been the senior and leader among them.[30] They adopted an aggressive, expansionist policy towards their neighbours, continuing the practice of their father and grandfather. In 878, the king of Wessex, Alfred, won a major victory over the Vikings and, as a result, imposed a peace treaty between the remaining independent Anglo-Saxons and the Scandinavian settlers. By this time, the Vikings had colonized East Anglia, Northumbria, and the east Midlands; the royal lines of most of the old Anglo-Saxon kingdoms had been destroyed or disrupted, and Alfred emerged as the single most important English leader. He brought part of Mercia under his own control, leaving the remainder to the Vikings, and consequently he came into contact with the Welsh. Before about 885, all the known kings of the southern Welsh kingdoms had submitted to Alfred as overlord and protector. Their reasons are recorded by Alfred's contemporary biographer, Asser, who was himself a Welshman – a cleric from the church of St Davids.[31] The king of Glywysing in south-east Wales, Hywel ap Rhys, and his neighbours, Brochfael and Ffernfael, sons of Meurig, kings of Gwent, turned to Alfred in search of help against the Mercians, who were at the time under the leadership of Alfred's son-in-law and subordinate, Aethelred. The king of Dyfed, Hyfaidd ap Bledri, and the king of Brycheiniog, Tewdwr ab Elise, sought Alfred's protection against another enemy: the sons of Rhodri Mawr, who were seeking to impose their power over central and south Wales. It seems that the power of the Line of Merfyn was such that outside assistance was the best solution for those members of older royal lines who still survived in control of their kingdoms, and who feared that their power would be eclipsed or stolen.

Anarawd and his brothers were initially unwilling to submit to Alfred. Rather, they had formed an alliance of their own, with the major rival power to Alfred within England. This was the Scandinavian kingdom of York, whose power extended across the Irish Sea to Dublin. As such, it was a neighbour to Gwynedd, and a valuable ally against English power. The alliance may explain the lack of Viking interest in Wales in the later ninth century: as a friend to York, Gwynedd may have been protected from harassment. Nevertheless, in the long term, the alliance proved unsatisfactory. Before 893, Anarawd and his brothers sought an alternative alliance with Alfred. Asser relates that Anarawd journeyed to meet Alfred in person, and was received with honour. He was accorded the same rank in his relations with Alfred – who was promoting himself as the leading political figure in southern Britain – as Aethelred, the Mercian leader.[32] We do not know the status in Alfred's eyes of the other Welsh kings, but the implication is that they occupied a lower rank, and later events seem to bear this out. The 880s saw a reduction in Viking activity, as the settlers concentrated on building their new settlements, but in 892, a new Viking force arrived in Britain from Scandinavia, and embarked on a series of campaigns. The Welsh allies joined with their West Saxon overlord to resist this army in the Severn-Wye area in 893, but this did not put an end to its activities. In 894, the army seized control of Chester and raided north Wales: perhaps Anarawd and his brothers put up stern resistance, for it shortly turned southwards, and instead entered into battle with the Anglo-Saxons. This Anglo-Saxon force apparently remained in the area for some time afterwards: in the next year, Anarawd attacked Ceredigion and Ystrad Tywi, with the help of an Anglo-Saxon force. No king of Ceredigion or Ystrad Tywi is listed among those who submitted to Alfred in the 880s, but the territories may have been in contention between the sons of Rhodri and the king of Dyfed. Hyfaidd of Dyfed, who had been Alfred's client, had died in 893, and his successor may not have renewed the relationship with Alfred, which may explain the Anglo-Saxon presence in Anarawd's force. Alternatively, Alfred may have decided that Anarawd and his brothers represented the most powerful – and hence most useful – bloc within Wales, and elected to lend them his support. This raid on the south demonstrates that the troubles caused by Viking activity had not been sufficient in their effect or scope to deflect Anarawd from his plans to expand. However, Viking interest in Wales was not finished. In 896, they raided Brycheiniog, Gwent and Gwynllŵg, all in the east. Anarawd's lands went unscathed, and he and his brothers were to have nearly a decade to consolidate their holdings in north and central Wales. In 903, a Viking band under one Ingimund came to Anglesey, having been expelled from their home in Dublin by the Irish. He established at least a brief settlement, but his actions did not escape reaction from the sons of Rhodri. In 904, Merfyn ap Rhodri fell in battle against Vikings, probably those of Ingimund, and Ingimund eventually moved on from Anglesey to the Wirral, where he was granted land to settle by the Mercian leader, Aethelflaed, daughter of Alfred and widow of Aethelred.[33] The renewed Viking threat may have led Rhodri and his surviving brother, Cadell, to decide that it was time to reinforce their power, perhaps in search of new resources, if they were temporarily without Anglesey, perhaps in response to changing circumstances in Wales.[34] They had established a southern bridgehead in the 890s, and their father Rhodri had probably put Ceredigion under pressure (and perhaps put an end to its native royal line, even if he was unable to establish Venedotian power there firmly). In 904, the king of Dyfed, Llywarch ap Hyfaidd, died. His heir was his brother

Rhydderch, but the latter survived him by only a year, being executed in 905. Rhydderch was the last member of the old line of Dyfed to rule there, and the manner of his death suggests that his power was not unquestioned or unchallenged. Anarawd and Cadell had taken advantage of Llywarch's death to launch an invasion (this suggests that by this time they were confident of their power over Ceredigion, through which lay their route into Dyfed). Rhydderch doubtless attempted to resist or repel them, but without success, and the southern lands fell into the hands of the sons of Rhodri, whose descendants would henceforth claim kingship over them down to the Edwardian conquest. Cadell ap Rhodri established himself as king in the south-west, probably holding Dyfed and Ystrad Tywi as one unit, and thereafter these two areas were considered one kingdom, known as Deheubarth, the southern half. Anarawd ap Rhodri continued to rule the north, holding Gwynedd and probably also Powys. On Cadell's death in 910, his lands passed to his son, Hywel, who was to become the founder of the new royal line of Deheubarth, known as the southern branch of the Line of Merfyn. Hywel coexisted peacefully with his uncle, Anarawd, who continued to rule Gwynedd until 916.

In their notice of his death in 916, the Welsh Chronicles commemorate Anarawd as king of the Britons, a title which they reserve for the most powerful and wide-ruling of Welsh kings. He and his brothers had succeeded in holding Gwynedd against Viking pressure and against the growing power of Wessex by battle and by alliance. They had expanded their power to control Ceredigion and the south-west, as well as Powys (whose conquest may have been due at least in part to the activity of Rhodri Mawr). On the testimony of Asser, they had also begun to threaten the eastern kingdom of Brycheiniog. Anarawd left sons, who took control of Gwynedd, and henceforth the Line of Merfyn split in two, with the descendants of Anarawd ruling in the north, and those of Cadell in the south-west. This division of interest – which became increasing marked over time – was perhaps an inevitable side effect of the expansion of the dynasty. As its sphere of influence grew, and as the number of politically active members of the dynasty increased, their interests and needs tended to diverge, and they were more likely to come into conflict with one another. Anarawd and his brothers, having grown up together, probably had more vested interest in common action – and more experience in cooperation. Their sons, however, may not have grown up together, and may not have perceived cooperation as desirable or advantageous. In early Wales, the principle of the succession to power of the eldest son in the senior male line was not established: rather, all male members of a royal line had, in theory at least, a right to attempt to gain a share in power and to try to impose themselves as king.[35] Cousins could thus appear as threats, and potential sources of division and conflict, rather than as natural allies. The split in the dynasty was geographic, but it was also political, and after the early tenth century, northern and southern dynasts had separate goals, interests and intentions. By the twelfth century, the northern branch was promoting itself as the senior line within the dynasty, with rights of overlordship over their kinsmen of the south. During the tenth century, however, propaganda emanating from one member of the dynasty put forward the opposite notion, of the pre-eminence of the southern branch. This had its roots in the career of one particular member of the southern branch: Hywel ap Cadell ap Rhodri, better known as Hywel Dda, Hywel the Good.

Hywel Dda and Idwal Foel

Hywel Dda occupies a special place in the history of Wales. This is partly because he is rather better documented than most other Welsh kings from this early period and this is in itself a by-product of the age in which he lived – and partly because his name was became attached in later centuries to the process of the codification of native Welsh law. Professor David Kirby has argued that the surviving medieval Welsh material relating to Hywel may be interpreted as an indication that after his death Hywel became at least temporarily the centre of a cult, focusing upon ideas of him as an ideal of kingship – just, pious and effective militarily.[36] This image seems to have emanated initially from the court circle of Hywel's son and successor, Owain, although we have no evidence to connect him to the production and revision of Welsh law codes earlier than the late twelfth century. The epithet *Dda*, the good, is unique in Wales. The epithets of other Welsh kings and lords refer to political or military prowess, such as *fawr*, the great; to physical features, such as *foel*, bald or *goch*, the red; or to seniority, such as *hen*, the old and *fychan*, the lesser or younger. Hywel's nickname is not recorded before the twelfth century, and is associated with the tradition connecting him to legislation. Thus we cannot say if he was regarded as good by his contemporaries, or whether this was an image of him fostered subsequently by his descendants, and in particularly by those who sought in the twelfth and thirteenth centuries to establish a long-lasting, legitimate and royal context for the Welsh law.

The first half of the tenth century was a relatively peaceful period for Wales. The frequency and seriousness of Viking raids decreased, in England as well as in Wales, and did not resume to any major degree until the 970s. In England, Alfred the Great's son, Edward the Elder, king of Wessex, and daughter Aethelflaed, Lady of the Mercians, who between them dominated those parts of Anglo-Saxon England still in English hands, turned their attention towards re-conquering the lands seized by the Vikings. They built a series of fortified strongholds, known as burhs, across southern and midland England, which formed both defences for English lands and centres from which military and administrative affairs might be coordinated. One of these burhs was at Rhuddlan, suggesting either that parts of north-eastern Wales were under Anglo-Saxon control, or that some collaboration for mutual defence between the ruler of Mercia and the king of Gwynedd existed.[37] Edward and Aethelflaed also began the process of pushing back the boundary of Danish rule in England, and of establishing the hegemony of the kings of Wessex over all the kingdoms within Britain, not only those in Scandinavian and Anglo-Saxon hands, but also the kingdoms in Wales and

Scotland. Edward continued Alfred's policy of drawing the Welsh kings into submission. In 916, Aethelflaed attacked the border kingdom of Brycheiniog, perhaps to discourage expansionism by the Line of Merfyn from north or south, perhaps as a warning to its ruler, Tewdwr ab Elise. In 916 or 917, a Viking force made a raid along much of the Welsh coast, particularly in the south and south-east, and inland into Gloucestershire and Herefordshire, and met with resistance from Edward's armies. The raiders had taken hostage a Welsh bishop from Ergyng in the south-east border of Wales, and Edward ransomed him back,[38] a move which probably brought him into contact with the shadowy kings of Gwent and Glywysing, if not with those further west. In *c*.921, according to the Anglo-Saxon Chronicle (ASC),[39] Hywel and Clydog of Deheubarth, and their northern cousin, Idwal Foel, made submission to Edward. The latter may have been taking advantage of the aftermath of the English resistance to the Vikings in order to enforce his overlordship on the kings of Wales. It was in Edward's interest to discourage any potential alliance between any of the Welsh and the Vikings, while Hywel Dda and his kinsmen may have viewed Edward as a more reliable ally than any Viking leader. The raiding army of 916/7 had come from Brittany: an alliance with the Vikings of, say, York, would be little protection against such opportunist raiding from different Scandinavian colonies. Edward, whose lands abutted most of the Welsh borders, was a more permanent presence with an established military reputation. It might have seemed preferable to have him as an ally, even on terms of accepting his overlordship, than to have him as an enemy. Moreover, any attempt by the kings in Wales to create an alliance with the Scandinavians settled in England might well have resulted in swift reprisals from Edward or Aethelflaed.

In 920, Clydog ap Cadell died, leaving Hywel as sole ruler in Deheubarth. His claim to the territory was further strengthened by his marriage to Elen, daughter of Llywarch and niece of Rhydderch, the last kings of Dyfed in the old royal line. Unlike the marriage alliances claimed in the pedigrees for Hywel's ancestors, this marriage is attested in contemporary tenth-century records. Although the marriage did not give Hywel a direct right to kingship, it probably made it easier for him to build vital relationships with the native aristocracy of Dyfed.[40] Elen's death is noted by the Welsh Chronicles, also, one of the very few women to be mentioned by them.[41] The marriage bolstered Hywel's status as king in Deheubarth: certainly no resistance to his power nor any rivals are recorded in Dyfed. In 924 Edward of Wessex died, to be succeeded by a son, Athelstan. Edward is not known to have had any direct dealing with Hywel after the submission in 918, but in the year of his death he faced a revolt against his power in the Chester area, in which the king of Gwynedd, Idwal Foel, may have been implicated.[42] Idwal was to prove uneasy in his alliances with the English, a fact which contrasts with the behaviour of his cousin Hywel. Athelstan became one of the most successful of all the kings of Wessex, forming alliances across Europe and imposing his dominion over much of Britain. In 927, he moved to establish his relations with Hywel and other Welsh rulers, just as Edward had done. ASC names the kings who submitted as Hywel, and Owain, king of Gwent: it may be that Idwal of Gwynedd was maintaining a position of hostility to English domination.[43] The twelfth-century writer, William of Malmesbury,[44] adds further details to the account, stating that, on this occasion, Athelstan fixed the southern border between England and Wales along the River Wye, and demanded a large tribute from his new Welsh subordinates. According to William also, Athelstan drove the unfriendly Idwal out of his kingdom of Gwynedd, but restored him subsequently upon terms favourable to Athelstan. William omits the names of Hywel and Owain, and calls Idwal king of the Britons, suggesting he may have been influenced by twelfth century north Welsh claims to overlordship over all Wales. The tale of tribute and of negotiations over the siting of the border also could well be reflections of practices current in twelfth-century Anglo-Welsh relations, rather than of tenth-century affairs. There is no evidence that any such tribute – if it was demanded – was ever paid, and the details of William's account probably cannot be relied upon. All this suggests that while the southern Welsh were willing to submit, albeit perhaps reluctantly, Idwal of Gwynedd was less tractable.

Documents – charters – surviving from Athelstan's reign recording grants of land and privileges made by him to churches and to followers provide further evidence for relations between Welsh and English in this period.[45] Welsh kings, and Hywel in particular, seem to have been regular visitors to Athelstan's court. The names of these Welsh kings appear as witnesses to a number of grants made by Athelstan, usually given the title *regulus*, little king, or *subregulus*, under-king. These are not autographs, but rather lists kept by clerks of those who were present to ratify the grant, and the ordering of names within the lists of witnesses is significant in terms of indicating the relative status of those present. The names of the Welsh kings were generally recorded after those of Athelstan and of the English archbishops (if the latter were present), but ahead of the bishops and nobility. This suggests that they were considered to be figures of very high status. On those occasions when more than one Welsh king was present, Hywel's name nearly always occurs first amongst the Welsh, and always before that of his cousin Idwal. This suggests that Hywel was accorded particular respect in English circles, and perhaps that he was held to be senior amongst the Welsh kings.[46]

Hywel made a number of trips to the English court over a number of years, and in 929 he was to make a pilgrimage to Rome, making him one of the earliest Welsh kings known to have made long journeys outside his kingdom for reasons other than exile. This, combined with the tradition associating him with legal reform, led Lloyd to propose that Hywel maintained a pro-English policy, and even that he may have modelled himself upon Alfred the Great.[47] Hywel's behaviour towards the English certainly contrasts with that of Idwal. During the mid-930s, as a move against Athelstan, the Vikings of York formed a coalition with the Scots, which was finally defeated at the battle of Brunanburh in 937. In records surviving from after Brunanburh, the Welsh kings seem no longer to have been present at the English court. No Welsh king attested any grant made by Athelstan's brother and successor Edmund. It may be that after the victory at Brunanburh, Athelstan loosened his hold over the Welsh, and that the weaker Edmund was unable to reassert it. As Kirby has argued, moreover, the compliance of Hywel in these years may have been more apparent than real: his attitude to Athelstan may have been tempered not with admiration, but with a pragmatic acceptance of Athelstan's superior power, leading him to avoid confrontation or provocation until such time as a less effective king was ruling in England.[48]

The Welsh reappeared at the English court in the reign of Edmund's successor, Eadred. They may have made their first visit for his coronation in 946, and they certainly were present in 949, at a point when Eadred needed to ensure the submission of the Welsh to his lordship. He was under political pressure, facing resistance from the Vikings of York, and would have wished to avoid the formation of any new anti-English coalition. By 949 circumstances in Wales had changed considerably. During the 940s, the English kings had been largely occupied fighting the Vikings of York and Dublin, and had paid relatively little attention to Wales. In 942, Idwal rebelled and launched an attack on the English. The ensuing battle resulted not only in his death, but in that of his brother Elise. Idwal left a number of sons, but before they could establish themselves in Gwynedd, Hywel invaded from the south, expelled the sons of Idwal, and seized Gwynedd for himself. This demonstrates that his power in the south was secure and that he possessed sufficient resources to be able to expand his power. It left him the pre-eminent king in Wales, and, indeed, the ruler of almost all of Wales. The south-eastern kingdoms of Gwent and Glywysing were still in the hands of their native royal lines, but the small kingdom of Brycheiniog fell to the Line of Merfyn by 944, probably due to the aggression of Hywel. There exists in the British Museum a single coin bearing the name of Hywel. This is the sole coin surviving of a Welsh king. It was minted not in Wales itself, but at Chester, where there was an English mint, and which was an English possession, hinting perhaps at a dimension of the relations of Hywel with the kings of England. The coin may be a medal, struck for commemorative purposes, rather than a coin intended for circulation in the economy, and its genuineness cannot be established. However, if it is genuine, then it is clear testimony of the status and aspirations of Hywel.

Hywel is the first king in Wales for whom we have clear evidence of such wide power and influence. This is not to say that his position was uniformly accepted or approved. The Welsh poem *Armes Prydein Fawr*, which dates from the tenth century, sets out to depict an imaginary but desirable alliance of all the non-English peoples of the British Isles – Welsh, north British, Scots, Picts, Scandinavians and Irish – together with the Bretons, against the English. Such an alliance, it is envisaged, might sweep the English from the islands entirely and restore old glory. The poem was composed in south Wales and quite possibly in the reign of Hywel.[49] It has been suggested that the poem was written around 930, after the submission of the Welsh to Athelstan, and in the early years of the coalition against him: in this interpretation, the poem might have been a reproach to Hywel for a pro-English, or anti-war stance.[50] Dumville has argued, however, that the poem might better be dated after the battle of Brunanburh, and even after

The Hywel Dda coin.

Hywel's death, and as thus is a reflection less on Hywel's policies than on the generic state of the relations of the non-English kingdoms in Britain with the English kings.[51]

Hywel died in 949, still ruling both Deheubarth and Gwynedd. The events of the later part of his reign are not known to us. It appears to have been a period of relative peace, largely free from Viking raids and problems in the borders. This attests to the strength of Hywel and his ability to maintain peace and order. It is to this period of his reign that his legislative activities have been assigned.[52] Traditionally, he summoned an assembly of the leading men of his lands to deliberate upon the nature and form of the laws in Wales. Welsh law had developed by custom, not through royal decree, and thus was not regarded as a possession or prerogative of any king. A council of twelve noblemen, aided by a representative of the church compiled a revised code, and it was then promulgated by Hywel.[53] However, there is no evidence at all from the tenth century to confirm this story, and thus no sound evidence that Hywel in fact instituted any revision of law.[54] The nature of Welsh law before the thirteenth century is much debated, and there is no certainty that any of the laws written down in the thirteenth century existed in an earlier period in their extant form. While it is not impossible that Hywel may have taken an interest in law (perhaps seeing control of law as a means to strengthen his own power), equally it is not impossible that the association of Hywel with the law reflects more on twelfth and thirteenth century south Welsh attempts to re-establish the importance and influence of their line in an age dominated by the princes of Gwynedd.

What can be said is that while Hywel achieved a position of great power in the lands conquered and held by the Line of Merfyn, he did not pass on to his sons more than the southern part in which his own career had begun, and in which, probably, his power was based. His death led not to the smooth succession of a new pan-Welsh king, but to warfare and conflict between the next generation of the Line of Merfyn.

3 From Owain ap Hywel to Gruffudd ap Llywelyn:

c.949 - 1063/4

The later tenth century

Hywel Dda had been an effective and wide-ranging ruler: his sons perhaps hoped to inherit his hegemony. It was not to be: Hywel had driven his cousins, the sons of Idwal Foel, out of Gwynedd in 942, and had ensured that they presented no further threat to him in his lifetime. But while they were defeated, they were not discouraged: almost immediately on Hywel's death, Idwal's sons – Iago, Idwal, Ieuaf, Rhodri and Meurig – returned to Gwynedd and reasserted their hereditary claim. Hywel's sons – Owain, Rhodri and Edwin – were not willing to accept such a reduction of their power, and the two sides met in battle at Carno, on the Venedotian-Demetian border. The location suggests that Idwal's sons already controlled Gwynedd and were able to draw upon the support of the local nobility. The battle was a victory for the sons of Idwal, who spent the next years consolidating their power in the north. In 952, two of them, Iago and Idwal, launched two raids into the heartland of Deheubarth, suggesting that they were sufficiently secure in Gwynedd to spare time and resources for expansion. Within three years of Hywel's death, the hegemony of Deheubarth had evaporated. The conclusive battle between north and south, for this generation, was fought in 954, at Llanrwst in Gwynedd. The Welsh Chronicles have not recorded the outcome of the battle, but it is likely that the sons of Idwal won.[1] Later the same year, they raided Ceredigion: it is unlikely that they would have been able to do this had they been defeated in their own lands only months beforehand. This marked the end of the conflict between the sons of Hywel and the sons of Idwal: for the remainder of their lifetimes, neither side is recorded as having troubled the other further. Instead, each concentrated their efforts upon other areas and other problems.

Edwin ab Hywel Dda died in 954,[2] perhaps as a consequence of the warfare of that year. His death left his brother Owain as the sole ruler of Deheubarth, a position he took seriously. Frustrated in his ambitions in the north, he turned attention to the one remaining direction, south-east.

The south-eastern Welsh kingdoms are among the least documented in Wales. Power in the south-east was vested in the hands of a series of often obscure kings. The Welsh Chronicles paid very little heed to this area, recording its rulers usually only when they impinged in some way upon the kings of Deheubarth or Gwynedd, or when their lands were subject to external

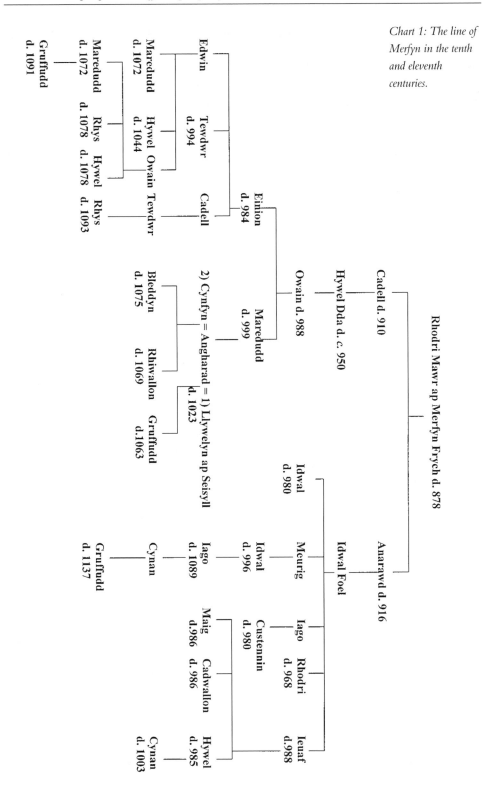

Chart 1: The line of Merfyn in the tenth and eleventh centuries.

aggression. A late source, the *Book of Llandaff*,[3] records a few fragments about rulers of Gwent and Glywysing, and in particular about their relations with the church. However, the reliability of the *Book* is far from certain, and much of the information – attacks on church lands, breaches of sanctuary and the like – may well reflect more on the rights and privileges Llandaff hoped to claim in the twelfth century than on historical fact from earlier centuries.[4] In the later ninth century, Hywel ap Rhys, king of Glywysing, and his neighbours, Brochfael and Ffernfael, sons of Meurig, kings of Gwent, had submitted to the overlordship of Alfred the Great, and Hywel may be further attested by an inscribed stone now in the church of Llantwit Major, Glamorgan. During the earlier part of the tenth century, Morgan ab Owain of Glywysing was one of the kings who attested the charters of Anglo-Saxon kings. He reigned until 974; his brothers, Gruffudd and Cadwgan, held lands in the south-east, perhaps under his overlordship. Gruffudd ruled Gower, until his death at the hands of the men of Ceredigion (perhaps at the instigation of Hywel Dda) in 933/4. Cadwgan died in battle against the Anglo-Saxons in 950, and seems to have had lands near Margam. Gwent in this period was subject to its own kings, drawn from a number of different families. This suggests that in the tenth century the region was relatively weak, subject to civil upheavals and with an independently-minded nobility whose ambitions might well overrule their loyalty. Gwent was particularly vulnerable to Anglo-Saxon incursions, and along its eastern border the territory of Ergyng (Archenfield) transferred between Welsh and English control several times. This vulnerability may have contributed further to the political instability of its kings.[5] Morgannwg may have appeared to Owain ap Hywel as an easy target. He raided it in 960, and during the 970s his son Einion made repeated attacks on Gower. By the end of the tenth century, Gower seems to have passed into the hands of the kings of Deheubarth: the campaigns initiated by Owain laid the foundations of this conquest.

Owain enjoyed a long reign, and it is to his circle that we owe our knowledge of many of the events of tenth-century Wales and earlier. He survived until 988, although in later life he was too ill or infirm to play a major role in politics or war. During the 970s and 980s, his son Einion took over as military leader of Deheubarth. Relations between Owain and Einion, and between these two and Owain's second son Maredudd, were amicable (a distinct contrast to the state of affairs in Gwynedd). The amity within the family probably contributed to the production, in Owain's lifetime, of one of our most important surviving records of early Wales, the A-text of the *Annales Cambriae (AC A)* and its associated genealogies, both now preserved in British Library MS Harleian 3859. It is clear from the contents of these works that they were produced in Deheubarth. The A-text was written at St Davids, using earlier records, and providing an account of events in Wales from the fifth century down to the death of Hywel Dda.[6] The text in its later section shows a clear interest in the activities of the Line of Merfyn, and in particular in its southern branch. Given that it ends with the death of Hywel, it is likely that it was composed not long after that event, and in a circle sympathetic to him: we cannot be certain Owain was involved in its composition, but St Davids was the chief church of his kingdom, and its monks and clergy may have been anxious to retain his favour. The collection provides the ancestry of the leading royal lines of the kingdoms of Wales, down to the mid-tenth century. It commences with pedigrees for the lines of Gwynedd and of Deheubarth, traced to Merfyn Frych and beyond. In both cases, they end with Owain ap Hywel Dda. This suggests that the compilation was in some way official, enshrining the political and ideological claims of Owain. He had been driven out of Gwynedd by 954 at the latest, but he clearly had not forgotten his father's domination there, and was not ready to surrender the claim it left him. The pedigree of the rulers of Gwynedd in Harleian MS 3859 is traced via Cadell ap Rhodri Mawr, and includes Hywel Dda. Anarawd ap Rhodri and his sons and grandsons (including Idwal Foel, and Idwal's sons, Owain's contemporaries) are omitted entirely. It seems that during the middle and later tenth century, a doctrine developed amongst court circles in Deheubarth whereby the southern branch of the Line of Merfyn was promoted as senior within the greater dynasty, and as the legitimate claimants to power not only in Deheubarth, but also over north Wales.

Einion ab Owain's position in Deheubarth is difficult to assess. His entire career took place during the lifetime of his father, and it is by no means certain that Owain ceased to be considered king, even in his later years. We have no evidence to suggest that he retired into a monastery or laid down any aspect of his kingship other than the leadership of armies: equally, we have little evidence as to how Einion was regarded by the Demetian nobility, whose support was crucial to the maintenance of a ruler's position. We can say that Einion seems to have been regarded as a perfectly acceptable and proper person to lead the warband of Deheubarth, and, perhaps, to coordinate the campaign of expansion south-east. He may have held the position of *penteulu*, head of the warband, a prestigious rank within the courts of Welsh kings which was often conferred on close family members. A *penteulu* wielded considerable influence, particularly amongst the free men of fighting age who formed the core of the warband. Such men could easily help to undermine or overthrow a weak or unpopular king. If Einion was *penteulu* then either it is testimony to a high level of trust between father and son or we must envisage Einion as *de facto* king, ruling in the name of an incapacitated or otherwise weak father. This latter view receives some support from the extant written records: in 983, the king of Gwynedd, Hywel ab Ieuaf, launched a raid south, striking at the more easterly territories of the southern branch. The areas attacked are described in the Welsh Latin Chronicles as all the lands of Einion ab Owain: the Welsh vernacular Chronicles, compiled slightly later than the Latin texts, read Brycheiniog and all the lands of Einion ab Owain.[7] This suggests that Einion was *de facto* leader of the southern branch. At this remove we cannot know with any certainty his exact rank: it should be reiterated, however, that the St Davids annalist whose work underlies all the surviving Welsh Chronicle accounts of this period shows nothing but approval of him (and, later on, of his brother, Maredudd). The link between Owain and St Davids has already been noted: the approval of Einion in the St Davids text may thus be some further evidence that his position in his father's lifetime was official.

The expansion south-east had begun under Owain, but Einion proved the more determined aggressor. He attacked Gower in 970 and again in 977. Lloyd considered Gower by this time to be mainly under the power of the kings of Deheubarth, and Einion's attacks as retribution for temporary incursions into the territory by the men of the south-east.[8] But while the written records demonstrate Owain's interest in the south-east, they do not prove any more than that. The Chronicles do not state that Owain or Einion seized control of Gower. It is more likely that the 960s and 970s saw a continued campaign by the royal family of Deheubarth to annex Gower, perhaps in an attempt to secure interests already held in the more northerly territories of Brycheiniog and Buellt. The campaign may have been partly driven by the exclusion of the southern branch from Gwynedd, but it may also have been fuelled by pressure on the south-west coast of Wales from Viking raids, which occurred sporadically during the later tenth century, and which placed pressure on the resources of Deheubarth. Expansion east was an effective means of acquiring goods to replace property and resources lost to foreign raiders. By the 980s, the eastern campaign may have been well-advanced, and may have put Einion in a position to begin to present a threat to the northern branch, for in the 980s conflict between north and south recommenced. By 983, Einion held Brycheiniog and other lands of interest to the king of Gwynedd, Hywel ab Ieuaf. Hywel, in alliance with an Anglo-Saxon nobleman, launched an attack upon Einion's lands. Einion responded with force, and inflicted serious casualties upon the invaders, repelling them. His victory had a heavy personal cost. The following year, he was killed by the noblemen of Gwent. These were the people whose lands and rights were threatened by his expansion, and who stood to gain the most by his removal. It may be that the warfare of 983 had weakened Einion's forces and left him more vulnerable. Equally, it is possible that there was a direct connexion of some kind between Hywel's raid, and the murder of Einion: the leading men of Gwent may have collaborated with the forces from Gwynedd. Owain was still alive, but the impetus to avenge Einion was left to another son, Maredudd, who succeeded his brother as the active force in Deheubarth after 984. Maredudd dominated Welsh political life for the rest of the century.

While the ruling house of Deheubarth was occupied with eastwards expansion, what of the north? The second half of the tenth century was marked in north Wales by a period of dynastic in-fighting. The sons of Idwal Foel had cooperated in their resistance to the sons of Hywel Dda in the 950s, and probably also against Viking and English raiders in the 960s, but their unity did not endure. The early deaths of his brothers had left Owain ap Hywel Dda in a strong position in the south, and his brothers left no sons who challenged his power. The circumstances were very different in Gwynedd, where Iago, Idwal, Rhodri and Meurig, sons of

Idwal Foel, all survived into the late 960s.[9] But by the end of the 960s, tensions developed amongst them. In 968, Rhodri ab Idwal was killed in Anglesey, and his death provoked a power-struggle between his surviving brothers. By the end of 969, Idwal had been captured and imprisoned and Iago had imposed himself as sole native authority in Gwynedd. He was not long to enjoy this new status: the 970s saw a new wave of Viking attacks on Wales, and particularly on north-west Wales (where it is possible that the Viking raiders were seeking to impose some kind of overlordship).[10] Iago's territories were harassed repeatedly in the earlier 970s. Moreover, English interest in Wales had re-awakened. Welsh kings had ceased to visit the English court after the reign of Eadred, and after 949 no Welsh king attested a charter of an Anglo-Saxon king. In 973, however, King Edgar came to Chester, and met with a number of kings with lands in and around the Irish Sea. The purpose of the meeting was probably to create a network of alliances against Vikings operating in the Irish Sea.[11] This was an issue of importance to most of the parties involved, whose lands were vulnerable to harassment and attempts at colonization. That Iago entered such an alliance is testimony to the seriousness of the raids he had experienced. Edgar may have imposed himself as the senior partner in this alliance, but unlike his predecessors in the early part of the tenth century, he seems not to have required his new allies to attend his court or serve in his army.

The alliance may have sought to reduce dangers from seaborn raiders, but it had no power to protect Iago from attack from within his own dynasty, and this was not slow to materialise. In 974, his nephew, Hywel ab Ieuaf, raised an army and drove him at least temporarily out of Gwynedd. Hywel may already have gained a measure of power in the north – he accompanied his uncle to the meeting with Edgar and would dominate the politics of Gwynedd for the next decade. Iago returned to the kingdom but could no longer remain as sole king: he was forced to cede both a share of power and land to Hywel.[12] The two coexisted uneasily down until 978, in which year Hywel attacked the monastery of Clynnog Fawr. Clynnog was a centre with strong links to the Line of Merfyn, and probably lay in Iago's sphere of influence: by attacking it, Hywel was directly challenging Iago's authority. The raid challenged Iago in another way, also, for in it Hywel was supported by troops from Anglo-Saxon England, possibly provided by Aelfhere, earl of Mercia. Whatever settlement had been negotiated between Iago and Edgar in 973 did not preclude English interference in his lands nor secure to him personally permanent English support. Hywel followed up this raid with a more direct attack in 979, and this time overran all of his uncle's possessions. Iago never regained them: in the same year he was captured by a Viking band, perhaps in the pay of Hywel, and vanishes from our records. Iago was the last of the sons of Idwal Foel to hold any kind of power in Gwynedd, but Hywel was by no means the sole grandson. Iago's son, Custennin, had a valid claim to a share of power, and the overthrow of his father to avenge. In 980, he attacked Anglesey, the heartland of Gwynedd, in alliance with Godfrey Haraldsson, a Viking leader from the Isle of Man. Godfrey had raided Anglesey in 972, while Iago was reigning.

That Custennin turned to Godfrey for assistance suggests that he was unable to gather the support he needed from amongst the native nobility of Gwynedd, which in turn is a measure of the success of Hywel. The confrontation between the two was decisive: Custennin was killed in the battle, and Godfrey fled, taking his band south. The death of Custennin and defeat of Godfrey encouraged Hywel to look south. His successes in the north had brought him a measure of confidence and security. He called upon the English for support, and in 983, in company with Aelfhere of Mercia, he launched his assault on Brycheiniog and Morgannwg. He did not succeed in seizing control there, but his actions undermined Einion ab Owain and laid him open to assassination. The attempt to expand had consequences also for Hywel: in 985, his erstwhile allies, the English, turned on him and killed him. The reason for this is uncertain: perhaps, with his strong position in the north and his ambitions to conquer in the south, he had grown too powerful, and was considered a threat by the new English administration under Aethelred II.[13] Hywel was succeeded in the kingship of Gwynedd by his brother, Cadwallon, who did not reign long (and faced a threat from a cousin, Ionafal ap Meurig ab Idwal Foel). In 986, a king from Deheubarth marched north for the first time in thirty years. This was Maredudd ab Owain ap Hywel Dda. Maredudd attacked and killed Cadwallon, and annexed Gwynedd.

At its height, Maredudd's power would be almost as great as that of Hywel Dda. Yet he would not be remembered to the same degree. His activities have only recently begun to attract the interest of historians,[14] and there is some debate as to the degree of his success. Like Hywel ab Ieuaf, Maredudd is a king about whose powers much must be inferred. His reign coincided with an increase in Viking raids on Wales, and he met problems in the north as a result. He also faced resistance to his expansion from surviving members of the royal family of Gwynedd, who preferred one of their own over this cousin from the south. In 987, the year after Maredudd killed Cadwallon ab Ieuaf and seized Gwynedd, Godfrey Haraldsson returned to Anglesey, forcing Maredudd to retreat back into Ceredigion and Dyfed. Godfrey ravaged widely and took many captives to ransom or sell as slaves. Godfrey had allied with Custennin ab Iago in 980, and Wendy Davies has argued that in 987 he allied with Maredudd to exploit the resources of Gwynedd.[15] The argument is hard to sustain, however, as it implies a strategy unlikely to secure to Maredudd any major long-term advantage in the north (indeed, it was more likely to create resentment). Moreover, in the wake of the raid on Anglesey, the Vikings turned their attention south, ravaging the coast from Ceredigion to Morgannwg in 988, and plundering several major monasteries along the way. These lands were the core of Maredudd's possessions: if he and Godfrey had had any alliance, it had been short-lived and brought Maredudd little or no gain. In 989 he paid a tribute to the raiders to redeem captives. It is more likely that Godfrey's raids in the later 980s were opportunistic, seeking to benefit from the turbulence in the north. Maredudd retained his interest in Gwynedd, and by 991 had restored himself to at least partial power there. In this year, he attacked Maes Hyfaidd in eastern central

Wales, probably to curb the activities of the English.[16] To lead an assault so far from Deheubarth with any confidence, he must have been controlling at least Brycheiniog and parts of eastern and southern Powys (previously under the dominion of Gwynedd). It is likely that between around 989 and 992, he was dominant not only in Deheubarth but also over the north.[17] In 992, however, he encountered a challenge to his power.

Thornton has argued that the challenger, Edwin ab Einion, Maredudd's nephew, had substantial backing from within England.[18] Before this year, Edwin had made no impact in Wales, but as a son of Einion, he had a strong claim to Deheubarth. In 992, with an English army, he raided Maredudd's lands of Ceredigion, Dyfed, Gower and Cydweli. The invasion failed and Edwin fades from Welsh records. Thornton, however, has shown that after 992 he became a client of the English state, holding lands in Herefordshire.[19] He had been unable to dislodge Maredudd, but he remained a useful potential tool for the English. After Maredudd's death he may finally have achieved his ambition of ruling at least part of Deheubarth. It is hard to know how seriously Maredudd took the threat from Edwin, for also in 992, he struck out, not against the central border where Edwin may have been living, but into Morgannwg, hiring a Viking army to aid him. Perhaps this may have been intended to secure his border and prevent the lords of this area from supporting his rival, but it is equally possible that he was over-extending himself. He had defeated Edwin, and he may have believed that his position was completely secure.

It was not. The challenge to him did not go unnoticed in the north, and in the wake of Edwin's raid, the northern branch began to reassert itself. In 993, the sons of Meurig ab Idwal (Hywel's cousins) attacked Gwynedd, forcing Maredudd to meet them in battle the following year. He lost, and while he escaped south, his nephew and ally, Tewdwr ab Einion, was killed. The battle marked the end of his hegemony over the north, and the restoration to power there of the northern branch.[20]

The last years of Maredudd's life are obscure. He died in 999, still king of Deheubarth. At some time, perhaps within a few years of his death, a flattering obituary became attached to his name in the surviving Welsh Chronicles, calling him most famous king of the Welsh.[21] He had achieved a great deal, recreating for a few years the hegemony of Hywel Dda, but unlike Hywel, he did not enjoy it long. The extent of his power disturbed his English neighbours, but Aethelred II was no Athelstan, and moreover faced too many problems within his own kingdom to have time to curb a Welsh king. In later centuries, Maredudd would come to be regarded as a desirable ancestor in pedigrees and two of the most effective kings of the middle eleventh century were his grandsons.[22] For at least the first part of the eleventh century, his reign cast a shadow over the affairs of Deheubarth. Yet his achievements were curiously limited: he was unable to maintain control over the north and to suppress the claims of the northern branch. More seriously, unlike Hywel Dda, he was unable to transmit his kingdom to his children: his son Cadwallon had died in 992. His death created a power vacuum in Deheubarth which would be exploited by Einion's grandchildren, but also by dynasties from the south-east, the former victims of Maredudd's and Einion's expansionist policies.

The eclipse of the Line of Merfyn

The eleventh century is one of the most complex periods in the history of independent Wales. It saw the rise of new royal families, and the dismantling of much of the power of the Line of Merfyn. The central years of the century marked the height of native Welsh power, with the unification of the whole country under a single ruler, Gruffudd ap Llywelyn ap Seisyll, while the last quarter of the century saw the arrival of the Normans and the beginning of the conquest and colonization of Welsh lands by them.

On the death of Maredudd, these developments were as yet unguessed at. The first two decades of the eleventh century are thinly documented. Deheubarth passed into the hands of Maredudd's nephews, Cadell and Edwin, and Cadell's son, Tewdwr.[23] In the north, the sons of Meurig probably continued to rule, being joined or displaced in the period 1000-1003 by Cynan ap Hywel ab Ieuaf. Cynan met his death violently, suggesting that the struggle for dominance over the north was still in progress. Between 1004 and 1018, we have only one notice of any event in Wales, a raid in 1012 as far west as St Davids by a powerful Anglo-Saxon nobleman, Eadric Streona, earl of Mercia. The Welsh context of the attack is unknown: Eadric was a dominant force at the English court who operated almost independently of King Aethelred II, and his invasion may have been driven by personal ambition. The distance involved may suggest that the native kings in southern Wales were weak or divided at this period, perhaps in consequence of internal dynastic friction. When the records become fuller again, throughout Wales a new set of people are to the fore, with few or no connexions to the Line of Merfyn.

This appearance of new dynasties has created some problems of interpretation. The roots of the difficulty lie in the twelfth century, by which time the Line of Merfyn had reasserted itself successfully in Gwynedd and Deheubarth. Having regained power, the line found itself not only still threatened by conflict between its northern and southern branches but challenged by the powerful Anglo-Norman state. One way in which the northern branch responded to this was the promulgation of propaganda claiming that natural sovereignty over Wales was vested only in those descended in the direct male line from Anarawd ap Rhodri Mawr, the founder of the northern branch. This doctrine proved influential, and has tended to dominate modern discussions of medieval Wales. However, it was not current in the eleventh century. Modern accounts of eleventh century political development which speak of kings who did not derive their ancestry from that line as intrusive rulers and pretenders are based on a retrospective model of the nature of legitimate kingship in Wales.[24] The kings in eleventh century Wales whose ancestry lay outside the Line of Merfyn in the male line were not considered in any way anomalous or intrusive by their contemporaries.

In 1018, a king called Llywelyn ap Seisyll is recorded for the first time. Our knowledge of him is limited, but it is clear that he was a figure of some importance: when he died, his death was recorded not only in the Welsh Chronicles, but in several Irish sources.[25] In 1018, he killed the shadowy Aeddan ab Blegywryd and the latter's sons. Where this occurred, and why is not known: Lloyd assumed that Aeddan was a king himself,[26] but there is no way to prove this, and if he was a king, we do not know where or for how long he ruled. From later events, it seems likely that Llywelyn ap Seisyll was already king of Gwynedd (and thus Aeddan may have been the leader of resistance against him, although this can only be speculation), having displaced the sons of Meurig and their heirs. It is possible that he was complicit in the death of Cynan ap Hywel in 1003.

Who was Llywelyn? This problem is one which exercised medieval genealogists as well as modern historians. He was certainly king of Gwynedd, and he had ambitions in Deheubarth also. He was to be the father of the most successful king Wales would ever know, although this son may have been a minor at the time of his father's death. We know that Llywelyn made a clever marriage, to Angharad, daughter of Maredudd ab Owain.[27] This gave him no legal claim on Deheubarth but made his son a member, in the female line, of the southern branch of the Line of Merfyn. This kinship proved important in the eyes of later genealogists and chroniclers, but in the lifetimes of Llywelyn and his son, the main use of the marriage was to help them gain the vital support of the local nobility. The relative late pedigrees in *ABT* claim that Llywelyn's mother was Prawst, daughter of Elise ab Anarawd ap Rhodri, thus affiliating Llywelyn also to the northern branch of the Line of Merfyn.[28] There are a number of problems with this claim, however. The fabrication of a link in the female line was a convenient means to affiliate an outsider, fictionally, to an existing royal dynasty. Neither Prawst nor Elise are recorded outside the genealogies, and their existence must be regarded as uncertain.[29] There is no early evidence for any link between Llywelyn and the Line of Merfyn apart from his marriage to Angharad ferch Maredudd. No material survives regarding his descent in the male line. This leads me to believe that he was a man from an obscure background, perhaps a member of the lesser nobility, who rose to power not through claims – real or fake – to descent from former kings, but through his own ability.

The details of Llywelyn's rise to power are lost to us. But by 1022, he must have been ruling over all north Wales securely, and had ambitions towards Deheubarth. We can infer this from the events of that year. In 1022, a stranger called Rhain came to Deheubarth, claiming to be a son of Maredudd ab Owain. His true identity is not known: according to the *Brutiau,* he was of Irish origin, and his claim to kinship with Maredudd was dubious.[30] Rhain attempted to intrude himself into the kingship of Deheubarth, perhaps gaining some local support.[31] Llywelyn – called by a Welsh Chronicler 'king of Gwynedd and the supreme and most praiseworthy king of the Britons'[32] – came south with an army and inflicted a decisive defeat upon Rhain, who fled. Llywelyn followed up his victory by plundering Deheubarth, perhaps in revenge for an endorsement by some segments of its people of Rhain's claim. He clearly regarded Deheubarth as under his influence, a situation perhaps based in part upon his marriage to Angharad, but doubtless reinforced by military strength. The surviving Chronicles are based upon a text composed at St Davids, in the heartland of Deheubarth: there is in them no hint of any disapproval of this king from Gwynedd operating in the south. From this, we must conclude that Llywelyn's position was in no way considered anomalous or intrusive.

These two events are all we know of Llywelyn, and they occurred towards the end of his career. In 1023, he died, perhaps still a relatively young man.[33] Like Merfyn Frych, he was an outsider who imposed his authority upon a Welsh kingdom, but his achievement outstripped that of Merfyn, for Llywelyn could act confidently in Deheubarth as well as Gwynedd. His son was probably still a minor in 1023, and Gwynedd passed back into the hands of a member of the northern branch of the Line of Merfyn, Iago ab Idwal ap Meurig. But while Llywelyn could not transmit his kingdom intact to his son, he did leave him a legacy of ability and ambition. Iago proved neither forceful nor ambitious: for the duration of his reign, he was content to restrict himself to Gwynedd, making no impact on wider Welsh political life. His accession did not go unchallenged: Llywelyn's son was underage, but he had left a brother, Cynan, who in 1027 launched an attempt to install himself in Gwynedd. He failed, dying in battle. Cynan must have had a power-base: while there is no certain evidence for this, I suggest it may have been Powys. From the mid-eleventh century, Powys would play an increasingly important role in the control of and access to power over north Wales. Llywelyn's widow Angharad had married a Powysian nobleman, Cynfyn ap Gwerystan, and with him would found a major new royal line (the second dynasty of Powys) who became close associates of Gruffudd ap Llywelyn ap Seisyll. It is possible that Llywelyn and Cynan themselves had come from Powys originally, and likely that Powys was one of their core territories.

While the north passed back into the hands of the Line of Merfyn, the south took a different course. At some point in the early part of the century, a new family had come to the fore in Morgannwg, under one Rhydderch ab Iestyn. Like Llywelyn ap Seisyll, Rhydderch is a man of obscure background and, like Llywelyn, he presented an enigma to medieval Welsh genealogists. By the time of the composition of the earliest pedigree to mention him, *ABT*, his father Iestyn (who must have lived in the later tenth and early eleventh century) had been confused with a later Iestyn ap Gwgan who lived in the 1070s, and who was no relation to Rhydderch.[34] Later tradition made Rhydderch's father Iestyn another son of Owain ap Hywel Dda (and thus a brother of Maredudd and Einion).[35] There is no other evidence for this connexion, however, and it should probably be regarded as spurious, a by-product of the later desire of genealogists to affiliate all successful kings in Wales to the Line of Merfyn.

Rhydderch may have come originally from Gwent, perhaps from its eastern border, Ergyng, and from this base he intruded himself into the kingship of

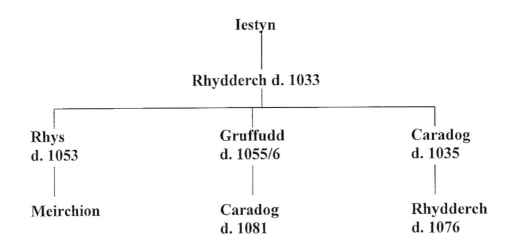

Chart 2: Historically attested descendants of Rhydderch ab Iestyn.

Morgannwg, driving out or subduing (but not destroying) its previous ruling family. We know little about him, but by 1023 he was strong enough to seize power over Deheubarth, reversing the achievements of Einion and Maredudd, sons of Owain. For three generations, his family would play a significant part not only in south Wales but in the politics of Wales as a whole, and in the development of relations between Wales and England. Rhydderch occurs as a donor in the *Book of Llandaff*.[36] While this text is controversial, the fact that Rhydderch's name was included suggests that he was still remembered in the 1130s as a worthy grantor.[37]

Rhydderch died in 1033, killed by the Irish. The Welsh Chronicles give no further details, but it should be remembered that the pretender Rhain was an Irishman, and that although he had been defeated in 1022, he had not been killed. It is possible that a measure of Irish (or Hiberno-Norse) interest in Deheubarth had persisted into the early 1030s. However, it is equally possible that Rhydderch may have fallen victim to an opportunistic raider. Rhydderch left sons, who probably inherited Morgannwg from him. Deheubarth passed back to the southern branch of the Line of Merfyn, in the persons of Hywel and Maredudd, sons of Edwin ab Einion. Their power was challenged almost immediately by the sons of Rhydderch and the two sides met in battle at Irathwy in 1034. The sons of Edwin probably won, as Hywel continued as king of Deheubarth until his death in 1044. Maredudd survived the battle for only a year, being killed in 1035 by the sons of Cynan. The identity of the latter is uncertain: most likely they were sons of Cynan ap Seisyll, with a power-base in Powys, raiding and fighting in the northern borders of Deheubarth and in Ceredigion (control of Ceredigion was to be a long-term goal of the second dynasty of Powys). In the same year, Caradog ap Rhydderch ap Iestyn was killed by the English, suggesting that having lost Deheubarth, the sons of Rhydderch turned their expansionist attention eastwards into the border with England. After Irathwy, the sons of Rhydderch co-existed peacefully with Hywel ab Edwin, but they did not forget their father's domination over all south Wales, and returned to this goal after Hywel's death. But both Hywel ab Edwin and the sons of Rhydderch were to find their ambitions checked and challenged by a third party, arguably one of the most effective rulers Wales ever knew. For the year 1039, the Welsh Chronicles record: 'Iago, king of Gwynedd, was killed. And in his place ruled Gruffudd ap Llywelyn ap Seisyll, and he, from beginning to end, pursued the Saxons and other foreigners and killed and destroyed them and defeated them in a great number of battles'.[38]

Gruffudd ap Llywelyn

1039, the year in which Gruffudd ap Llywelyn came to power, set the pattern for much of the rest of his reign. He engineered a coup in Gwynedd, overthrowing and perhaps killing Iago ab Idwal and driving out the latter's son, Cynan, who fled to Ireland. Almost at once, as if he already knew his control in the north to be secure – which it would prove to be almost to the day of his death – Gruffudd struck against Deheubarth. He attacked and plundered the monastery of Llanbadarn, in the debatable land of Ceredigion, and he drove the king of Deheubarth, Hywel ab Edwin, into temporary exile. Not content with these victories, he moved east, where he won yet another, this time against the English, at Rhyd-y-Gors on the River Severn, killing Edwin, brother of Leofric, earl of Mercia. From the first, it was clear that Gruffudd intended to expand his power and to brook no resistance.

Deheubarth was his first goal, and he devoted much of the first part of his reign to conquering it. The expulsion of Hywel proved short-lived. In 1041, Gruffudd once again struck south, this time meeting Hywel in battle at Pencadair. Once again, Gruffudd won, and he topped the victory by abducting Hywel's wife and taking her for himself. However, he had not succeeded in taking Deheubarth. Hywel remained in control and began to rebuild his strength. The following year, a Viking warband arrived off the southern coast and plundered the fringes of Dyfed. Hywel defeated the marauders at Pwlldyfach. In the same year, Gruffudd suffered his first setback. A Viking band also appeared in Gwynedd, and Gruffudd was temporarily captured. Nothing in our sources explicitly connects these two events but it is possible that, in the wake of his victory, Hywel bribed or persuaded the Vikings to attack Gruffudd. Hywel certainly had ties to the Vikings who had settled in Ireland, for in 1044, by which time he was again facing aggression from Gruffudd, he hired a fleet of them. He had been expelled once again from Deheubarth, and fled overseas. He arrived at the mouth of the River Tywi with his mercenaries, and met Gruffudd in battle. Once again, Hywel was defeated: this time, the defeat cost him his life.

The events of the following year, 1045, are of particular interest in this context, for the Welsh Chronicles speak of a great treachery between Gruffudd ap Llywelyn and Gruffudd and Rhys, sons of Rhydderch ab Iestyn, then kings in Morgannwg.[39] After the death of Rhydderch ab Iestyn, the old native line of Morgannwg had regained some power in that kingdom, under Hywel ab Owain and his son Meurig. Meurig had been captured by Vikings in 1039, and although apparently ransomed back and still active in the mid-1040s, he was not an effective figure, sharing power with his father. Hywel ab Owain died in 1043, and no member of his dynasty is known to have any power again until the 1070s. It is likely that during the 1030s and early 1040s the sons of Rhydderch established themselves in the south-east: by 1045, they secured control of Morgannwg and had time and resources to spend on operations elsewhere. Like Gruffudd ap Llywelyn they had an eye to Deheubarth. The reference in the Chronicles to treachery between the sons of Rhydderch and Gruffudd ap Llywelyn, combined with their mutual interest in Deheubarth, makes it possible that there had been some form of co-operation or collaboration between the two sides against Hywel ab Edwin, but after Hywel's death, one side or the other reneged. It was Gruffudd ap Llywelyn who encompassed the death, and who must be held responsible for undermining Hywel beforehand, yet it was the sons of Rhydderch who stepped into the void as the new kings of Deheubarth. In 1047, Gruffudd ap Llywelyn's warband was attacked and defeated in eastern Deheubarth (Ystrad Tywi), probably by the sons of Rhydderch. He retaliated by ravaging both Ystrad Tywi and Dyfed, perhaps with English assistance.

For several years after this, Gruffudd ap Llywelyn left the south, and the sons of Rhydderch, alone. In 1049, a large Hiberno-Norse fleet landed in Deheubarth and raided widely. Gruffudd ap Rhydderch (and perhaps his brother Rhys) came rapidly to terms with them, and with them launched an attack on the English border. The local levy was mustered by the Anglo-Saxon bishop of Worcester, Ealdred, but it was betrayed to Gruffudd ap Rhydderch by Welshmen serving in it, and defeated. This action by the sons of Rhydderch was doubtless opportunistic, but it would have consequences for them from both England and north Wales.

In 1052, the English border was once again raided by the Welsh, led probably by Gruffudd ap Llywelyn.[40] The following year, Rhys ap Rhydderch was killed by the English (perhaps in reprisal), leaving his brother, Gruffudd ap Rhydderch, in sole control of Deheubarth and Morgannwg. He did not enjoy the position long: in 1055 or 1056, after a long respite, Gruffudd ap Llywelyn marched south and met Gruffudd ap Rhydderch in battle. The result was the latter's death, and this time, no new figure emerged to challenge Gruffudd ap Llywelyn. He held Deheubarth, along with his existing northern lands, until his death: he also extended his influence over Morgannwg, the sole king known to have united all Wales under his direct rule. It was a great achievement, but for Gruffudd, it was

1. A medieval portrait possibly of Macsen Wledig, Magnus Maximus.

2. Roman remains at Caerleon.

3. Wiston, formerly Wizo's, castle, part of the Flemish settlement in Dyfed.

4. Medieval cross from Carew.

5. Medieval cross from Llandough.

7. Worcester Cathedral.

8. The later medieval castle at Rhuddlan.

9. Talacharn Castle.

10. Talyllychau Abbey.

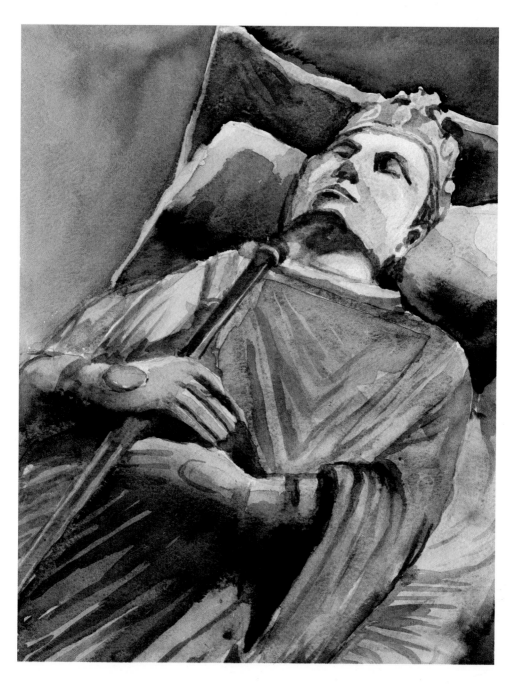

11. Henry II from his effigy in the Abbey of Notre-Dame de Fontévraud.

12. Effigy, probably the Lord Rhys, from St Davids.

13. Effigy of King John, from Worcester Cathedral.

14. Seal of Gwenwynwyn.

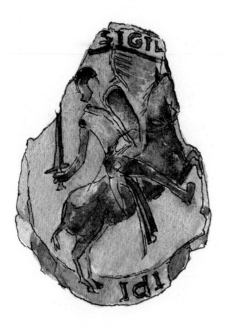

15. Seal of Llywelyn ap Iorwerth, 1208.　　　　　　　*16. Seal of Llywelyn ap Iorwerth.*

17. Bronllys Castle.

*18. The death of Gruffudd
ap Llywelyn.*

19. Wigmore Castle, property of the Mortimer family.

20. Ludlow Castle. Llywelyn and his army passed through Ludlow on their way to aid Simon de Montfort at Bridgenorth.

21. Effigy of Henry III in Westminster Abbey.

22. Graves at Strata Florida, probably of the descendants of the Lord Rhys.

23. Castell-y-Bere.

not enough. As he had done in 1039, he turned east, focusing his attention on the border with England.

Gruffudd initiated a new phase of Anglo-Welsh relations. It is significant that it is with his reign that English sources begin to take interest in Welsh affairs, which testifies to his status and influence. There had been raids from Wales into England, and vice versa, throughout the early medieval period, and there had been intermittent alliances between the two sides, but between Cadwallon in the seventh century and Gruffudd in the eleventh, no Welsh king intruded himself so forcefully and so effectively into English politics, and Gruffudd was to build an alliance which would span two generations.

He seems to have formed the idea of brokering an alliance with an English magnate at some point after the sons of Rhydderch had excluded him from Deheubarth. In 1046 or 1047, he allied with Earl Swegen Godwinesson, who held lands in the border of Wales and England. Swegen was a potentially useful contact: he was the eldest son of Earl Godwine of Wessex, the most powerful man at the court of the English king, Edward the Confessor, and a major landholder in his own right. Both Swegen and Gruffudd stood to gain from their alliance, as both were under threat of raids and attacks from the sons of Rhydderch. However, although they combined to strike at the sons of Rhydderch, and took a fair amount of plunder, their alliance did not last beyond the year. Swegen was an opportunist, and on his way back to England, kidnapped the abbess of Leominster, for whom he had formed an attraction. This action, understandably, attracted royal disfavour, and he was exiled. He was erratic and unreliable, unsuited to the purpose for which Gruffudd wanted an alliance: the connexion was severed. Swegen had been seeking short-term advantage and plunder: Gruffudd needed a reliable friend and ally who might represent his interests at the English court and help secure his borders.

The reign of Edward the Confessor was characterized by court factions and rivalries, and three families in particular dominated its political life: those of the earl of Wessex, Godwine and his sons, Swegen, Harold, and Tostig; the earl of Mercia, Leofric, his son Aelfgar and grandsons Edwin and Morcar; and Earl Siward of Northumbria.[41] The lands of the earls of Mercia corresponded at least in part to the old kingdom of Mercia, and had borders with Wales. Mercia, more than any other area of England, had had dealing with Welsh kings since the Anglo-Saxon settlement age, and the population of the border was mixed English and Welsh. Gruffudd had come into contact with Leofric's family in 1039, when he slew the earl's brother in battle. Leofric was an important figure at court, but the growing power of Earl Godwine, and in particular the ambitions of Godwine's sons, disturbed Leofric's son and heir, Aelfgar. Godwine's sons were seeking lands and position for themselves and had their eyes on Leofric's lands: Aelfgar needed an ally to support him against his rivals. He found one in Gruffudd ap Llywelyn.

Their alliance is mentioned explicitly in our sources only twice during the lifetime of Gruffudd (in 1055 and 1058), but its traces are detectable over a much longer period. In 1055, Aelfgar, who at the time was holding the earldom of East

Detail of Leominster Priory.

Anglia, a rank which had previously belonged to Harold Godwinesson, was deprived of his position and outlawed. The rank had been bestowed on him as a sign of royal distaste for the ambitions of the sons of Godwine. He fled England, looking for aid. The reasons for Aelfgar's exile are unknown: the three versions of the ASC (the C- D- and E-texts) give conflicting accounts. The E-text, written by a supporter of the faction of the Godwinessons, states that Aelfgar was guilty of an unspecified act of treason, to which he is said to have confessed. The C-text, written by an enemy of the Godwinessons, makes no mention of any treason, and states that Aelfgar was exiled even though he was innocent of any crime. The D-text, written after the Norman Conquest and aware of the other two versions, attempts to rationalize the two variant accounts and thus writes that Aelfgar was only slightly guilty.[42] On being expelled, Aelfgar journeyed to Ireland, where he hired Hiberno-Scandinavian mercenaries. He then sailed to Wales, where he met with Gruffudd ap Llywelyn. Together, they attacked Herefordshire. An opposing force under a local magnate, Ralf the Timid, was routed by them, and they marched onto the city of Hereford which they burnt and looted. Harold Godwinesson, who had succeeded his father as earl of Wessex in 1053, was despatched against them with an army, which he led into parts of north Wales. But Gruffudd and Aelfgar eluded him and eventually Harold's force dispersed. It was clear that military force would not be sufficient to deal with the allies. Edward the Confessor arranged a meeting with them at Billingsley. There, a peace was agreed between the two sides, and Aelfgar was reinstated to his earldom. Gruffudd also made gains, for it seems that at this meeting, certain lands in the border, notably Ergyng, which he had overrun were confirmed to him by Edward.

Three years later in 1058, Aelfgar was again exiled, and this time there is no hint in our sources as to why (although it probably had its roots in the rivalry between him and the sons of Godwine). He went directly to Gruffudd, and, together with the unexpected help of the king of Norway, Magnus Haraldsson,[43] the allies once again forced Edward to reinstate Aelfgar. No details of this campaign survive, but it likely that the same tactics of border raiding were used. The alliance had served both sides well, securing Gruffudd's borders and bringing to him English recognition, and protecting Aelfgar from the manoeuvrings of the sons of Godwine. But how and when had it been forged?

Lloyd argued that it began in 1055, a by-product of Aelfgar's first exile. As I have shown elsewhere, however, this explanation is unsatisfactory.[44] Gruffudd's effectiveness as a military leader had been ably demonstrated to the English by 1055, and Aelfgar would have been taking a very great risk indeed by arriving on his shores with a Hiberno-Scandinavian fleet, unless the two had had some prior contact. The raids of 1039 and 1052 had shown that Gruffudd could take on and defeat English levies: for Aelfgar, his father ageing and surrounded by ambitious rivals, Gruffudd might have appeared as a very useful potential friend.[45] In my view, Aelfgar had already approached Gruffudd before his first exile, and, indeed, it is very likely that the treason of which he was accused was precisely this opening of private negotiations with this dangerous neighbour.[46] In 1051-2, there had been a civil war in England between the king and the family of Earl Godwine, and for a short period Godwine and his sons had been expelled: Gruffudd took advantage of this to raid the border. During the exile of the family of Godwine, Aelfgar held Harold's earldom of East Anglia. When Harold, his father, and brothers were reinstated in 1052, Aelfgar lost his new earldom. He was re-granted it in 1053 when Harold became earl of Wessex on Godwine's death, but the events of the previous three years showed Aelfgar the insecurity of his position. In 1055, Tostig Godwinesson became earl of Northumbria on the death of Earl Siward, with Siward's son Waltheof (a minor) being passed over. Aelfgar's own father was ageing: he may have feared he would lose his Mercian patrimony to the ambitions of the Godwinessons. In my view, these circumstances led him to seek an alliance with Gruffudd, to help counterbalance the faction of Earl Harold and his brothers. Gruffudd too stood to gain. In 1055, he was newly king of Deheubarth as well as Gwynedd and Powys, and probably also of Morgannwg. This gave him power and resources undreamed of by his predecessors, and it was unlikely that his new position would be viewed with equanimity by the English. Earl Harold had lands in the border which Gruffudd's status threatened. He could probably expect aggression from England in the near to medium future. A supporter at the English court, who could express his views, justify his status, and protect him from attack, would be of great value. At some time between 1052 and 1055, negotiations were opened between them for an alliance of mutual support and friendship. Once formed, it lasted throughout their lifetimes, and beyond.

It was immediately recognized as a threat by Harold. I have already suggested that the alliance was the cause of Aelfgar's exile. However, when this measure failed Harold resorted to military means. In 1056, he arranged for the appointment as bishop of Hereford of one Leofgar, a prelate more renowned for martial skills than piety and encouraged him to attack Gruffudd. Leofgar gathered an army, which Gruffudd defeated, and the bishop was killed in the battle.[47] So decisive was Gruffudd's victory that the English once again sought a formal peace with him. Earl Harold, together with Aelfgar's father, Earl Leofric, and Bishop Ealdred of Worcester, were sent to meet him. If Gruffudd had not been assured tenure of his conquests in the border in 1055, he was now. In return, he made a token submission to Edward. Unlike the submissions of the ninth- and tenth-century Welsh kings to Alfred the Great and his heirs, this submission carried with it no known obligations. Gruffudd was not required to visit Edward's court nor to assist with Edward's wars. It was a face-saving move, no more. Edward and his envoys doubtless knew that no duties could be enforced on Gruffudd, and the oath was aimed at regularizing Gruffudd's position *vis à vis* the English polity.

The alliance of Gruffudd and Aelfgar is at its most visible in joint military action, but it can be traced in other ways also. According to the Anglo-Norman historian, Orderic Vitalis, writing in the early twelfth century, Gruffudd married Aelfgar's daughter, Ealdgyth.[48] The late-twelfth-century writer, Gerald of Wales, recorded that the Norman conqueror of Brycheiniog, Bernard of Neufmarché, married Nest, the daughter of Osbern Fitz Richard and his wife Nest, daughter of Gruffudd ap Llywelyn.[49] Osbern Fitz Richard was a Norman lord who had come to England before the Norman Conquest with Edward the Confessor.[50] Edward had granted him lands in Herefordshire: the remains of his stronghold at Richard's Castle still remain. It is likely that Nest was Gruffudd's daughter by Ealdgyth, on the evidence of Domesday Book.[51] The latter records that in 1086 Coventry Abbey, founded by Ealdgyth's grandfather Earl Leofric, held Binley, which it had bought from Osbern Fitz Richard but which had belonged in the time of King Edward to Ealdgyth wife of Gruffudd. Binley was probably part of Ealdgyth's dower land. It is likely that Ealdgyth was Nest's mother, as under Welsh law women could not inherit land. They could under English law: Binley lay in England and was passed by Ealdgyth to Nest, again probably as dowry. We do not know precisely when Gruffudd married Ealdgyth, but 1057 must be likely, as this was when Aelfgar succeeded his father as earl of Mercia, making him Gruffudd's neighbour as well as ally.

Aelfgar died in 1062 or early 1063, leaving Mercia to his young son Edwin. Almost immediately, Harold Godwinesson took advantage to strike at Gruffudd. By this time, Gruffudd too was no longer young, and some friction may have been developing within his large kingdom. An English army reached his

Richard's Castle, Herefordshire.

stronghold of Rhuddlan and burnt it, but Gruffudd evaded them. Later in 1063 or early in 1064, Harold launched a two-pronged attack by land and sea, leading an army while his brother Tostig led a fleet. Again, they had considerable successes, but were unable to lay hands on Gruffudd. They did, however, break his hegemony, forcing large numbers of the Welsh to foreswear him. Finally, beleaguered by English attacks, and perhaps bribed by the English, Gruffudd's household turned on him and killed him.

Harold tried to take the credit for Gruffudd's death. He imposed submission of some kind upon Gruffudd's successors, Bleddyn and Rhiwallon, sons of Cynfyn, who were Gruffudd's maternal half-brothers. He took Ealdgyth for himself and married her. This move was designed to placate her brothers, Edwin, earl of Mercia, and Morcar. However, while Harold's pressure on Wales contributed to Gruffudd's downfall, it may not have been the sole reason. Folk-tales recorded in the mid-twelfth century by Walter Map recall Gruffudd as a forceful and ruthless ruler, who brooked no rivals, and took swift and fatal action against any potential threat.[52] In the wake of Harold's campaign, old enmities came home to Gruffudd to roost.

His wide kingdom did not survive him. Deheubarth passed into the hands of Hywel, Maredudd and Rhys, sons of Owain ab Edwin, the nephews of Gruffudd's old enemy, Hywel ab Edwin. Morgannwg was dominated by Caradog, son of Gruffudd ap Rhydderch, who had an eye to Deheubarth, too. Powys and

69

Gwynedd passed to Gruffudd's half-brothers, Bleddyn and Rhiwallon, as mentioned above. Harold Godwinesson made some attempt to prevent the alliance surviving Gruffudd. He tried to secure the loyalty of Bleddyn and Rhiwallon for himself, and, as has been mentioned, he married Ealdgyth. In 1065, he went so far as to support Morcar, Ealdgyth's younger brother, against his own brother Tostig, when the latter was driven out of the earldom of Northumbria by its resentful inhabitants, who then chose Morcar as their new earl. The policy did not work, and Harold would shortly have other things to think about.

Gruffudd ap Llywelyn is unique in the history of Wales: no other ruler, not even Llywelyn ap Gruffudd, enjoyed such wide power and influence throughout Wales. His kingdom did not survive him, but it set a pattern which later rulers tried to emulate. That he initially had been king of Gwynedd had a formative influence on the development, in the later twelfth century, of the ideology of the natural supremacy of north Wales over south, which would be fostered by the northern branch of the Line of Merfyn. A hundred years after his death, he was remembered as a powerful king, a great warrior, and a hero.[53] His alliance with Aelfgar created a new active approach towards the English which his brothers continued, and his marriage to Ealdgyth is the first known marriage of a Welsh prince to a foreigner. His border successes were to cost Wales dear, as their fresh memory contributed to Norman aggression towards the Welsh. He was undoubtedly one of the greatest leaders Wales has ever known.

But he failed to found a dynasty. He left two sons, Maredudd and Ithel, who were not old enough to seize power on his death. In 1069 they rose up against their uncles and sought to regain Gwynedd. Battle ensued, and neither of the sons of Gruffudd survived. Rhiwallon ap Cynfyn also died, leaving as sole ruler in north Wales another extraordinary man, Bleddyn ap Cynfyn, founder of the Second Dynasty of Powys.

4 From Bleddyn ap Cynfyn to Owain ap Cadwgan:
1069 - 1116

Bleddyn ap Cynfyn, Caradog ap Gruffudd and Trahaearn ap Caradog

When Bleddyn ap Cynfyn and his brother Rhiwallon became kings of north Wales, they were already men of great importance. Both had probably been part of Gruffudd ap Llywelyn's warband, and involved in his councils. It is possible – although not provable – that one or both may have acted as deputies for Gruffudd in parts of his territories, most likely in Powys, their homeland. Gruffudd's former ally, Earl Aelfgar, was known to them, and while Harold Godwinesson tried to bring them into an alliance with himself, the brothers were not willing to let go of the existing relationship with Mercia. When in 1065, Aelfgar's younger son Morcar became earl of Northumbria, after the exile of Harold's brother Tostig, Bleddyn and Rhiwallon lent him Welsh troops with which to secure the new earldom. It is possible that some part of this Welsh force was involved in the battle of Stamford Bridge the following year. The exiled Tostig allied with the king of Norway, Harald Hardrada, who had a claim to the throne of England, and the two launched an invasion of northern England in 1066, after the death of Edward the Confessor and the accession to the throne of Harold Godwinesson. The English won at Stamford Bridge, and Morcar, his elder brother Edwin, and their forces were left holding the north when Harold Godwinesson marched south to meet yet another invasion, that of William of Normandy. As a result, both Aelfgar's sons escaped the battle of Hastings, and were amongst the Anglo-Saxon nobility who made submission to the victorious William. Their submission would not last long, however, and this had consequences for Wales.

From the dawn of the Norman Conquest, Bleddyn showed himself ready to help rebels against the new king. In 1067, a Shropshire landholder, Eadric *Cild,* rose against William and attacked Herefordshire, which had been entrusted to a new Norman earl, William Fitz Osborn. Bleddyn and Rhiwallon lent their forces to Eadric. Like Gruffudd ap Llywelyn before them, they stood to gain territorially and politically should the rebellion succeed: they must also have been concerned with protecting their lands and rights. In 1069, Edwin and Morcar rebelled, and again Welsh troops were made available to them. By this time, Bleddyn was sole ruler of north Wales. He needed secure borders in order to consolidate his position in Wales. The alliance with Mercia was crucial to this: it is likely that he aided Edwin, Morcar and Eadric in order to try and

Chepstow Castle, founded by William Fitz Osborn.

safeguard himself. But by 1071, both rebellions were over. Eadric had come into the king's peace, and Edwin and Morcar had been dispossessed and defeated. Edwin was dead: Morcar remained a prisoner until his death. Henceforth, Bleddyn turned his attention away from England, but the memory of the alliance with Mercia remained, effecting both Norman attitudes to Wales, and, in the early twelfth century, the plans of Bleddyn's sons.

While Bleddyn consolidated himself in the north and helped English rebels, control of south Wales was under dispute. The two main claimants were Maredudd ab Owain ab Edwin, a nephew of the former King Hywel ab Owain; and Caradog ap Gruffudd, son of the other great rival of Gruffudd ap Llywelyn, Gruffudd ap Rhydderch. Caradog's power-base lay in the south-east: in August 1065, on the eve of the Norman conquest, he came to blows with Harold Godwinesson, who had attempted to build a hunting lodge at Portskewett in Gwent, to which he intended to invite the king, doubtless to show his new power in Welsh lands. Caradog waited until Harold had gathered all the resources and supplies that were needed for a royal visit, then launched a raid. He killed Harold's men and took the goods as plunder, putting an end to Harold's ambitions there. He may around the same time have made further raids across the border, for Domesday Book records the destruction of villages in Gloucestershire by a certain King Caradog, who can only have been Caradog ap Gruffudd.[1] Caradog would be the first native Welsh king to deal with Norman troops within his own lands: in 1072, we find him allied with a band of Normans and pursuing his rivalry against Maredudd ab Owain.

There had probably already been some Norman expansion into south-east Wales, and particularly into Gwent, before 1072, but no details of this survive. Although Caradog ap Gruffudd was active in the south-east, he was not the only king there: Cadwgan ap Meurig, the last scion of the old line of Morgannwg, was still ruling in at least part of that kingdom. Cadwgan may have ruled under the dominance of Caradog: after the latter drove out Harold Godwinesson, he devoted much of his energy to the attempt to seize Deheubarth, and may therefore have been secure in the south-east. The early Norman raiders do not seem to have been regarded by him as a serious threat. Rather, he viewed them much as his father Gruffudd had the Vikings: as a convenient source of useful military assistance. In 1072, supported by Norman troops, Caradog met and killed Maredudd in battle on the banks of the river Rhymni. This was a long way east, suggesting that Maredudd may have been emulating his tenth-century predecessors, Einion and Maredudd, sons of Owain ap Hywel Dda, and attempting to impose himself on Morgannwg. Alternatively, he may have been attempting to check the power and ambitions of Caradog. It has been argued that the presence of the Normans at this battle suggests that Caradog was a client or subordinate of the Normans,[2] but apart from his use of Norman troops in 1072, there is no evidence to show him acting in the Norman interest, and we do not know the identity of the leader of his Norman allies in 1072.[3] The Normans did not pursue any major invasions into south-east Wales until the later 1080s, after Caradog's death, and it seems more likely that he negotiated some kind of temporary alliance for mutual gain with a Norman neighbour. Indeed, the evidence of Domesday Book for Caradog raiding into Gloucestershire may, if it does not refer to his actions after expelling Harold in 1065, refer to resistance to Norman neighbours between 1067 and 1081.

For the next ten years, Deheubarth would be a battle ground. In 1073, Norman forces raided Dyfed and Ceredigion, and in 1074 they raided Ceredigion alone. At this time, Ceredigion may have been under the control of Bleddyn ap Cynfyn. In 1075, Bleddyn came south, attacking Ystrad Tywi. It seems, that like his half-brother, Gruffudd ap Llywelyn, he regarded the south with an envious eye, and sought dominion there. He was not to succeed, but there is some possibility that his presence in Ystrad Tywi in this year was more than simple aggression. The Welsh chronicles record that 'Bleddyn ap Cynfyn was killed through the evil-spirited treachery of the princes and nobility of Ystrad Tywi...and it was Rhys ab Owain who killed him'.[4] Rhys ab Owain was the brother of Maredudd ab Owain, and one of the contenders for control of Deheubarth. The reference to treachery suggests the existence of some prior relationship between Bleddyn and Rhys. Perhaps Rhys had appealed to Bleddyn for assistance against the Norman raiders, or against Caradog ap Gruffudd. Perhaps the chronicler assumed that Bleddyn had an overlordship of some kind over Rhys. While it cannot be determined with any certainty, it is likely that

Bleddyn came south in response to an appeal, only to meet his death at the hands of Rhys, who was to prove himself to be both cunning and dangerous over the next years. What is clear from our surviving evidence is that Bleddyn would be remembered as a just and honourable ruler, with hegemony over all the Britons. His obituary reads:

> ...the gentlest and most merciful of kings...who wrought good to all and who did harm to no-one...terrible in war, beloved and meek in peace and a defence for all.[5]

This claim that Bleddyn was king of all the Britons reflects on his position as successor to Gruffudd ap Llywelyn, but the title is used very rarely by our sources and only of rulers whose influence extended outside their own original lands. Bleddyn certainly ruled Powys and Gwynedd, he may have held Ceredigion and perhaps Brycheiniog. His description as king of the Britons may further suggest that he had overlordship over Rhys of Deheubarth, and in the later-eleventh and early-twelfth centuries, his sons and grandsons would seek repeatedly to take and rule Ceredigion and Dyfed, perhaps in emulation of Bleddyn's status. Bleddyn's reign coincided with the early years of Norman expansion, but his involvement in English rebellions went unpunished. Later tradition claimed that he, like Hywel Dda, revised the way in which certain aspects of Welsh law was practised. As with Hywel, we cannot be sure that any of the emendations attributed to Bleddyn were in fact made by him, but what is clear is that he was remembered as a king who had the necessary security to devote time to administrative reform, as well as to war, and whose reign was peaceful – perhaps the last major native Welsh ruler to rule without harassment or interference from the Norman kings and lords.

Bleddyn never succeeded in ruling all Wales directly, but in one way he surpassed the achievement of Gruffudd ap Llywelyn. Gruffudd's line died out with his sons in 1069: Bleddyn founded a new royal house, the second dynasty of Powys. This family removed Powys from the hands of the Line of Merfyn and recreated it as an independent kingdom, parts of which remained in the hands of Bleddyn's heirs down until the early fourteenth century. Owain Glyndŵr, the great Welsh leader of the early fifteenth century, was a direct descendent in the male line of Bleddyn ap Cynfyn.

In 1075, however, Bleddyn's sons were too young to rule. Control over Gwynedd and Powys passed instead to his cousin, Trahaearn ap Caradog, a member of a noble family from Arwystli. It is at this point that the Line of Merfyn Frych reappeared in north Wales, for also in 1075 comes the first mention of one Gruffudd ap Cynan ap Iago. Gruffudd was an outsider: he had been raised in Ireland, and at this time derived all his support from the Hiberno-Norse mercenaries of the Viking kingdom of Dublin. But his grandfather, Iago ab Idwal, had been king of Gwynedd 1022-1039, and Gruffudd had a claim to its throne. In 1075, he made his first move, raiding Anglesey, perhaps the most valuable part of Gwynedd. Later in the same year, he came to blows with Trahaearn. The details are not certain: Gruffudd was to be the sole Welsh king

Chart 3:
The second
dynasty of
Powys.

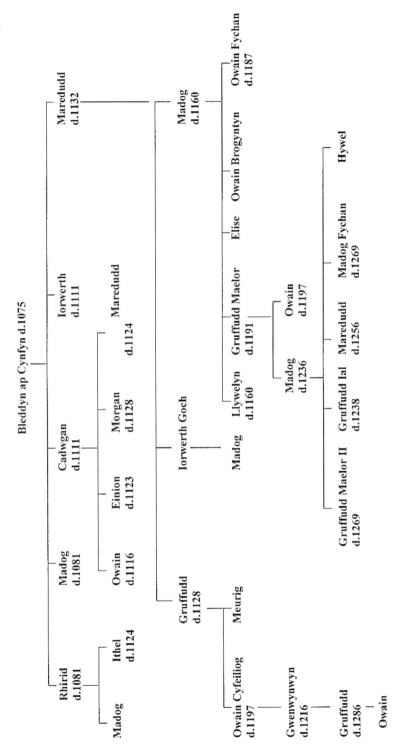

ever to be recorded in a medieval biography, the *History of Gruffudd ap Cynan* (*HGK*), and as a result we are well-informed about him.[6] However, the biography was not written until after his death, and may not have been official: many of the details it contains are suspect, designed as dynastic propaganda, and it is undeniably biased in its account of other Welsh leaders. Trahaearn in particular suffered at the hands of the biographer, and care must be taken with its description of his dealings with Gruffudd. In 1075, at the start of his reign, he found himself facing opposition from Gruffudd, who at this time had little or no support inside Gwynedd. According to *HGK*, Gruffudd landed at Abermenai, and dispatched messengers to the leading men of Anglesey, Arfon and Llŷn, representing himself as the rightful heir to the kingdom. He rapidly gained their support and proceeded to Rhuddlan, then in the hands of a Norman colonial lord, Robert: Robert too offered him support. Two men opposed him: Trahaearn, and one Cynwrig ap Rhiwallon, described by *HGK* as a petty king of Powys.[7] Gruffudd met and killed Cynwrig in battle and then marched on Trahaearn, defeating him in the battle of Gwaed Erw in Meirionydd, driving him back as far as Arwystli. Gruffudd straight away began to consolidate his hold on Gwynedd, and to attempt to drive out Robert of Rhuddlan, burning the latter's castle. But his allies from Llŷn turned against him and killed some of his Irish guardsmen. Trahaearn heard of this and gathered an army from Powys: with the help of the turncoat men of Llŷn, and of another Powysian dynast, Gwrgenau ap Seisyll, Trahaearn invaded Gwynedd, defeated Gruffudd in battle at Bron-yr-Erw, and expelled him from Wales.[8]

Only certain aspects of this account can be verified from sources other than *HGK*. In particular, the Welsh Chronicles, which are contemporary records for the later eleventh century (which *HGK* is not) make no mention of the battle of Gwaed Erw, or of the presence of Normans as far west as Rhuddlan. There is nothing in our surviving material to suggest that Bleddyn ap Cynfyn had faced any threat from the Normans, so any Norman settlement would have been small and insecure in 1075. The Chronicles do refer to the death of Cynwrig ap Rhiwallon but do not associate it with Gruffudd: they record rather that the men of Gwynedd killed him. Certainly, it cannot be proved that the leader of these men was not Gruffudd, but it might equally have been Trahaearn, or any member of a local noble family. Cynwrig is obscure: he seems to have belonged to the nobility of Gwynedd, but beyond that we cannot be certain.[9] Gwrgenau ap Seisyll may have been a distant cousin of Bleddyn ap Cynfyn – there is some late pedigree evidence which hints that his great-grandfather may also have been Bleddyn's grandfather.[10] It is thus probable that he was a Powysian aristocrat who supported Trahaearn. He was killed in 1081 shortly after Trahaearn's death by members of a noble family from Gwynedd, which may be further grounds for viewing him as an associate of Trahaearn with a presence in Gwynedd which was resented by some of the local population.

What of the battle of Gwaed Erw? The chronicles omit it, but it is named in one other source, and one associated with Gruffudd ap Cynan. This is the *Elegy* composed after Gruffudd's death by his poet Meilyr Brydydd.[11] But the *Elegy* notes this battle simply as one in a series of victories, without giving any clear indication as to when in Gruffudd's career it occurred, or against whom it was fought. The account of the events of 1075 as given in *HGK* should not be accepted as certain, given the disparity between its version – which is late and biased – and that of the Chronicles. What can be said is that in 1075, Gruffudd ap Cynan made his first bid for power, but met with only limited success against the better-placed Trahaearn.

Trahaearn is an interesting figure, and one whose reputation has suffered at the hands of the author of *HGK*. By the later twelfth century, when *HGK* was written, his family had lost its power and influence: it was thus easy for its author to present Trahaearn in a negative light without fear of reprisal.[12] However the Chronicles, whose underlying text was probably compiled closer to his lifetime, betray no disapproval of him. Indeed, if anything, he is portrayed positively, as the avenger of the respected Bleddyn ap Cynfyn.

Bleddyn's death had been a consequence of the on-going struggle for control over Deheubarth, and within three years, Trahaearn too was involved. This demonstrates that he must have possessed a secure power-base in the north – had he been beleaguered by resentful Venedotian nobility and ambitious Norman knights, as *HGK* would have us believe, it is unlikely that he would have had resources to spare for the south, nor would it have been safe for him to leave his kingdom for a campaign.[13] Rhys ab Owain had kept hold of Deheubarth since 1072, despite the ambitions of Caradog ap Gruffudd, and raids by Norman forces (perhaps encouraged by Caradog), but his position was far from secure. In 1075, after he killed Bleddyn ap Cynfyn, he was attacked by Goronwy and Llywelyn, sons of Cadwgan ap Elystan, an aristocratic family from Buellt, who were allied in 1075 with Caradog ap Gruffudd. Buellt lay in the border country between England and Wales and had long been subject to attempts at domination from Deheubarth. It had common boundaries with Morgannwg, where Caradog had his stronghold, and the two families may have been natural allies. The sons of Cadwgan ab Elystan may also have been interested in avenging Bleddyn: according to a pedigree in JC 20, their grandmother, Lleucu, was a daughter of Maredudd ab Owain ap Hywel Dda, and a sister of Bleddyn's mother, Angharad ferch Maredudd.[14] In addition, the brothers may have had a more distant kinship with Trahaearn ap Caradog, as both their family and his seem to have traced their ancestry back to one Iorwerth Hirflawdd.[15] The battle in 1075 against Rhys known as the battle of Camddwr had a further complication. Rhys too had an ally, one Rhydderch ap Caradog, a first cousin of Caradog ap Gruffudd. It seems that the struggle for control in the south had spread, and that Caradog now had a rival for Morgannwg. Camddwr was a victory for Rhys and Rhydderch, but it did not put a stop to Caradog's ambitions. A year later, Rhydderch was killed by yet another member of his family, Meirchion ap Rhys ap Rhydderch (who may perhaps have belonged to Caradog's faction). In 1077, the sons of Cadwgan attacked Rhys a second time, and suffered a second defeat in the battle of

Gweunytwl. In 1078, Trahaearn decided to intervene. He met Rhys, and Rhys's brother Hywel, in battle at Pwllgwdig and defeated them heavily. The *Brutiau* record that through this victory he avenged the blood of Bleddyn ap Cynfyn, through God's grace.[16] Rhys fled the battle, only to be attacked by Caradog ap Gruffudd: this time, Caradog finally succeeded in killing his rival (Hywel ab Owain also fell in this encounter). It is hard not to suspect that the activities of Trahaearn and Caradog in 1078 were coordinated. Caradog was one of the most aggressive kings of the period, yet at no point do we have a record of him involved in warfare with Trahaearn, Bleddyn, or any of the clients and supporters of these kings (which may have included the sons of Cadwgan ab Elystan: certainly by the 1090s this family was staunchly allied with Bleddyn's son, Cadwgan). Both Trahaearn and Caradog stood to gain by the removal of Rhys. Caradog had long aspired to control Deheubarth while Trahaearn may have wished to secure his southern borders, and Rhys had, by killing Bleddyn in 1075, shown himself no friend to the rulers of the north. The murder of Bleddyn may also have left Trahaearn with a personal score to settle. Rhys ab Owain's reign had lasted only three troubled years, and he was to be one of the few Welsh leaders of whom the account of the *Brutiau* was almost entirely hostile. A scion of the Line of Merfyn, he was a valid candidate for kingship, but his conduct and perhaps his dealings with Bleddyn (whom the annalist whose work underlies this section of the *Brutiau* seems to have favoured) seem to have won him scant popularity. Once again, however, on the death of Rhys, Caradog ap Gruffudd found himself unable to win control of Deheubarth. It would seem that he possessed insufficient support in the south-west to install himself as king. The new king of Deheubarth was one Rhys ap Tewdwr – like Rhys ab Owain, a member of the southern branch of the Line of Merfyn. He was the first member of his sub-section of that family to reign, but his would be the line that would continue as lords in the kingdom down until the end of native dominion in Wales in 1283.

Caradog had spent almost a decade trying to seize Deheubarth, and the elevation of Rhys ap Tewdwr did not put an end to his ambitions. His alliance with Trahaearn survived the death of their common enemy, Rhys ab Owain, and this had consequences both for them and for Wales as a whole. In 1081, Caradog launched a final assault on Deheubarth, and unwittingly changed native politics forever.

The consequences of Mynydd Carn

This turning point was the battle of Mynydd Carn, the last act in the long internal struggle over Deheubarth. Accompanied by Trahaearn, Caradog struck against Rhys ap Tewdwr. Since becoming king, Rhys had faced no recorded aggression from his fellow Welsh, but his kingdom had suffered a Viking raid in 1080, which may have weakened him. Further support was provided to Caradog by Meilyr, son of Rhiwallon ap Cynfyn and kinsman of Trahaearn.[17] Faced with this combination, Rhys ap Tewdwr sought outside assistance, and found it in the form of Gruffudd ap Cynan. Between 1075 and 1081, Gruffudd seems not to have been active in Wales: probably he had returned to his birthplace, Dublin, or had been operating with the various Viking fleets active in the Irish Sea. In 1081, leading a mercenary Hiberno-Norse fleet, he reappeared in Wales, and joined with Rhys. In the pitched battle that ensued, Trahaearn, Caradog and Meilyr all fell. Perhaps more than any other battle, Mynydd Carn would have a long legacy for Wales. The death of Caradog put an end to effective Welsh native leadership in south-east Wales, which the Norman lords of Hereford and Gloucester exploited in the later 1080s and 1090s. The deaths of Trahaearn and Meilyr cleared the way for the succession in Gwynedd of Gruffudd ap Cynan, and in the wake of the battle, he marched north to seize his new lands, plundering and ravaging as he went. But on his arrival in Gwynedd, he fell into the hands of Robert of Rhuddlan, and was imprisoned in Chester, where he remained for more than ten years. Trahaearn's sons – and Bleddyn's – may still have been young and unable to muster support in Gwynedd proper. The earl of Chester and his men quickly took advantage of the power vacuum that followed, and overran much of Gwynedd. (Powys, conversely, may have remained at least partially intact, under the sons of Bleddyn). The sole true victor at Mynydd Carn was Rhys ap Tewdwr, who found himself suddenly the strongest native leader in Wales, a position which would be ratified later in the same year when William I of England visited Wales, met with Rhys, and drew up an agreement with him. The details do not survive, but according to Domesday Book, in 1086 Rhys of Wales in theory owed the king £40 per annum for his lands.[18] It is likely that in 1081, Rhys made some kind of submission to William, accepting him as his overlord, and in return received assurances of non-aggression and protection.

As a result of its long-reaching effects, Mynydd Carn has long occupied an important role in the historiography of medieval Wales. The most reliable accounts of it are to be found in the Welsh Chronicles, but a long section in *HGK* is also devoted to it, and this description – which is dramatic and detailed – has rather coloured modern understanding. *HGK* treats it as concerned almost wholly with the rights of Gruffudd to Gwynedd: Rhys is presented as the junior partner in the alliance and great care is taken to show him making formal statements of submission to Gruffudd as his lord and leader. In the context of the period in which *HGK* was composed – the last quarter of the twelfth century at the earliest – this is understandable. At this period, another Rhys from Deheubarth, Rhys ap Gruffudd, grandson of Rhys ap Tewdwr, was in a position of considerable power and influence in Wales and represented a threat to the power of the kings of Gwynedd. By presenting Rhys ap Tewdwr as submitting to Gruffudd ap Cynan in 1081, the author of *HGK* probably hoped to undermine, subtly, the position of Rhys ap Gruffudd. But, despite the dramatic descriptions in *HGK*, Mynydd Carn was fought primarily over Deheubarth, between the rivals Caradog ap Gruffudd and Rhys ap Tewdwr.

Both Gruffudd ap Cynan and Trahaearn ap Caradog were there as allies of the main combatants, and Trahaearn's death in the battle was pure serendipity for Gruffudd. The exact location of the battle is not known, but even *HGK* states that beforehand Rhys's and Gruffudd's troops mustered at Porth Clais, near St Davids, and met their opponents after around a day's march. It is likely, therefore, that the battle occurred somewhere in Ceredigion or Ystrad Tywi, both lands subject to Deheubarth.

The truce with William I bought several years peace for Rhys. We know little of his activities in this time, but it is likely that he took advantage of the death of Caradog ap Gruffudd to expand his interests eastwards, as in the early 1090s, he would be found operating in Brycheiniog. While Norman lords moved into Gwynedd, the south was left alone. But the death of William I in 1088 changed all this. Several Norman lords with lands in the Welsh border, including Roger of Montgomery, earl of Shrewsbury, Roger de Lacey, Ralph Mortimer and Bernard of Neufmarché, went into rebellion against the new king, William's second son, William Rufus. With Welsh assistance, perhaps from Powys, they attacked Worcestershire. This distraction of Norman power away from Wales provided an opportunity for native Welsh lords. In Powys, three of the sons of Bleddyn ap Cynfyn – Madog, Rhirid, and Cadwgan – had come of age. To the north and the east, they were threatened by Norman colonies; to the south and the west lay Deheubarth under Rhys ap Tewdwr. Bleddyn had enjoyed a wide-ranging hegemony, which his sons had not forgotten: the three struck south, driving Rhys out from Deheubarth and seeking to impose their own dominion. Rhys retreated to Ireland, where he hired a mercenary fleet of Hiberno-Norse, and invaded his kingdom. His fleet defeated the invaders, and killed two of them, Madog and Rhirid: Cadwgan fled back to Powys. But Rhys's power-base was being slowly eroded. William Rufus bought off the rebels with permission to renew expansion into southern and central Wales, and the conquest of Glamorgan (under Robert Fitz Hamo, earl of Gloucester) and of Brycheiniog (under Bernard of Neufmarché) began.[19] Rhys ap Tewdwr represented a threat to this process. It is perhaps no coincidence that in 1091, the sons of Cedifor ap Gollwyn, a leading nobleman of Dyfed, deserted him and turned instead to his distant kinsman, Gruffudd ap Maredudd, son of that Maredudd ab Owain, who had been killed by Caradog ap Gruffudd and the Normans in 1072. Gruffudd had been living in England, where he had been granted various lands in Herefordshire by William I. A client of the Norman kings, he may have been encouraged to move into Deheubarth at this juncture with the express purpose of destabilizing Rhys. Rhys fought off and killed Gruffudd in battle at Llandudoch, but the invasion exposed weaknesses in his control over his nobility, and revealed that he could no longer expect immunity from Norman interference. In 1093, he was forced to confront this. During the late 1080s, Bernard of Neufmarché had begun the conquest of Brycheiniog, and had backed up his military activities with marriage to the granddaughter of Gruffudd ap Llywelyn. By 1093, he was well ensconced and looking to move

Brecon Priory, founded by Bernard de Neufmarché.

further west: he probably received support in this from his overlord, Roger of Montgomery. In 1093, Bernard's men met Rhys's army near Aberhonddu, where Bernard was in the process of building a castle. In the ensuing battle, Rhys met his death, and then, wrote a Welsh chronicler, 'the kingdom of the Britons fell'.[20]

Rhys would be the last king of Deheubarth: arguably, he was also the last Welsh king in all of Wales to rule in a wholly native manner, for later kings in Gwynedd and Powys were inevitably influenced and shaped by Norman practices and requirements. All the later native princes and lords in Deheubarth would trace their descent from Rhys, yet none of them would use the title king. Rhys himself is something of an enigma: he cannot have been a young man when he became king in 1081, yet he seems to have become a claimant for kingship only after his cousins, the sons of Owain, had all been killed, suggesting either a lack of ambition or a lack of support.[21] Between 1081 and 1088 he reigned unchallenged, but he was readily driven out by invaders from Powys and required overseas, rather than local, aid, to reinstate himself. In 1091, members of the Dyfed nobility readily deserted him for the English-raised Gruffudd ap Maredudd. His military record is patchy. As Babcock has pointed out, this does not indicate a king whose power was secure or whose personality was dominating.[22] Yet the annalist remembered him, perhaps retrospectively, as the last true king in Wales, and

William I identified him as the key figure in native Wales with whom a truce was necessary to create a stable border. We should picture Rhys, perhaps, as a man more gifted in diplomacy than military strategy, more clever than charismatic, capable of retaining his lands through negotiation, but perhaps less able to create a secure network of power and support to sustain him over time. More crucially, at his death, his two sons were underage, while the internal strife of the 1070s had resulted in the deaths of many of his adult kinsman. No-one remained, on Rhys's death, to protect Deheubarth from the new pressure of Norman colonialism, and none of his descendants would ever succeed in fully recreating the old kingdom in its fullest form.

The first anti-Norman rebellion

The death of Rhys opened Deheubarth up to invasion not only from the Normans but from fellow Welsh. Within the year, Cadwgan ap Bleddyn of Powys raided the south, plundering widely through Deheubarth in an attempt to establish his position as leading native ruler. His attack was followed up by an invasion from England, spearheaded by Roger of Montgomery. Ceredigion and Dyfed were overrun and encastellated. But this new wave of expansion did not go unchallenged: Cadwgan ap Bleddyn, who had first entered our records in 1088, had had time to consolidate his power in Powys and to expand his network of alliances within Wales. From 1094 down to his death in 1111, this king from Powys would be the focus and centre of Welsh politics, pursuing a policy of considered and sometimes devious resistance to the Norman kings while attempting to exploit the growing power of the Norman border lords. He and his elder brothers Madog and Rhirid may have been the leaders of the Welsh who had joined in Roger of Montgomery's rising against William Rufus in 1088, and his raid on Deheubarth in 1093 may have in part been designed to open up the region for Roger, with whom he may have had some form of alliance. Cadwgan was, however, by no means Roger's puppet, and, as subsequent events would show, he had ambitions of his own, particularly in respect of Ceredigion (formerly subject to Rhys) and its northern neighbour, Meirionydd (usually subject to the kings of Gwynedd), together with other territories bordering his native Powys. In 1094, William Rufus left England for Normandy, taking some of his lords with him, and Cadwgan took advantage of his absence. There was an uprising against the Normans in Gwynedd, almost certainly masterminded by Cadwgan.[23] A Norman attempt to quell the revolt was defeated in battle at Coedysbys. From there, rebellion spread to Deheubarth, where all the Norman strongholds, with the exception of Pembroke castle and Rhyd-y-Gors, were razed. In 1095, William Rufus, now back in England, led an army into north Wales to try and control the Welsh: simultaneously, Norman forces struck at Gower, Cydweli and Ystrad Tywi in the south. Neither was able to extinguish the rebellion, and by 1096, it had spread into the south-east. A Norman army, which had forced submission on the

Pembroke Castle.

inhabitants of Brycheiniog, Gwent and Gwynllŵg, was ambushed on its way home and defeated at Gelli Tarfawg. A second defeat was inflicted at Aberllech. This Welsh action was led by the sons of Idnerth ap Cadwgan from Buellt. Meanwhile, Cadwgan's warband, accompanied by two noblemen from the north, Hywel ap Goronwy and Uchdryd ab Edwin (the latter related to Cadwgan by marriage), attacked and despoiled Pembroke castle. Nearly everyone involved in the rebellion was connected to Cadwgan: both the sons of Idnerth ap Cadwgan and Hywel ap Goronwy were his distant kin, as well as being members of the southern aristocracy. Hywel additionally claimed descent in the female line from Hywel Dda, and may have represented a possible new source of leadership in parts of Deheubarth. Uchdryd ab Edwin was not only Cadwgan's first cousin, but also cousin to the sons of Idnerth, and held strategically important lands in north Wales.

The rebellion continued through 1097, and William Rufus led a second, equally unsuccessful, expedition into the north, while Gerald of Windsor, steward of Pembroke castle, made reprisals in the south. At around this time, Gruffudd ap Cynan escaped or was released from prison. The exact date is unclear: *HGK* gives the length of his captivity as twelve years in one place and sixteen in another.[24] We know he had been captured in 1081 after Mynydd Carn, so his earliest date of freedom would have been 1093, around the beginning of the rebellion. Lloyd accepted twelve years as the length of his imprisonment, and indeed, ascribed the rebellion from 1093 to him.[25] However, it should be noted that Gruffudd does not reappear in the Welsh Chronicles before 1098, and these texts represent an earlier layer of recording than *HGK*: the latter moreover ascribes no action to him after Mynydd Carn which can be securely located earlier than 1098. Furthermore, while the Welsh chronicles do not mention Gruffudd as involved in the rebellion before 1098, they repeatedly refer to the activities of Cadwgan ab Bleddyn, and all the other leaders of the rebellion were Cadwgan's kin and allies. These leaders were, moreover, largely based in mid-Wales, the centre of Cadwgan's power and some of them continued under his influence after the end of the rebellion. Non-Welsh sources also serve to confirm that Cadwgan was the leader of the rebellion: he is the sole Welsh king to be named in the account of the E-text of the Anglo-Saxon Chronicle *s.a.* 1097 of William Rufus's second expedition, where he is described as the finest of them.[26] If anything, the arrival on the scene of Gruffudd seems to have destabilized the rebellion, for it is when we find Gruffudd among the leaders of the Welsh that we also see the signs of a change of fortune. This in turn raises the possibility that he may have been released deliberately (or that his escape was colluded in by his captors) in order to undermine Cadwgan by providing an alternate source of leadership. Initially, at least, Gruffudd joined up with Cadwgan in 1098, but this may have been an alliance of expediency: thereafter the two seem to have enjoyed only distant relations and to have avoided each other's society.

By 1098, the Welsh rebellion had lost its momentum in south Wales: the failure of the Welsh to destroy Pembroke castle had left Gerald of Windsor, a vassal of the earl of Shrewsbury, with a secure base from which to coordinate Norman response, while the local Welsh probably lacked consistent leadership. Cadwgan and his allies were in a sense aliens. Rhys ap Tewdwr's sons were young and in exile, while his brother Rhydderch seems never to have possessed the drive for rule: it would not be until the central part of the twelfth century that Welsh lordship in Dyfed and Ystrad Tywi would make any substantial and lasting headway. In the north, too, 1098 proved a turning point. The earls of Chester and of Shrewsbury, both called Hugh,[27] combined their forces and drove Cadwgan, by this time accompanied by Gruffudd ap Cynan, almost all the way across north Wales, until they were besieged on Anglesey. The earls were aided in this by a leading Welsh nobleman, Owain ab Edwin, brother of Uchdryd ab Edwin. This family held their main lands in Tegeingl, which lay directly in the hinterland of Chester: as a result, Owain was vulnerable to the ambitions of its earl. There may, however, have been more than fear behind his decision to help the Normans: his family would prove a powerful but often unreliable and even destabilizing force in north Welsh politics in the first two decades of the twelfth century, and both Cadwgan and Gruffudd ap Cynan were to take steps to secure their allegiance. Uchdryd, in the 1090s, was aligned with Cadwgan's faction, and would later benefit from Cadwgan's generosity with the receipt of a substantial grant of lands in Meirionydd and Cyfeiliog.[28] Owain later formed a marriage alliance with Gruffudd ap Cynan, although this did not to prevent him and his sons from troubling Gruffudd and Gruffudd's sons. Owain was probably the elder brother, and he may perhaps have felt threatened not just by the power of the earl of Chester but by the favour his brother Uchdryd was receiving from Cadwgan. He may also have seen himself as potential new ruler in north-east Wales: and one whom the earls may have considered more controllable, and hence more desirable, than the resourceful and intelligent Cadwgan, or the – to date, anyway – belligerent Gruffudd.

Gruffudd, after escaping from prison, had appealed to his old allies, the Vikings of Dublin, and he and Cadwgan were provided with a fleet to assist with their defence of Anglesey. Such fleets, however, were never wholly trustworthy.[29] The Norman earls bribed the Viking leaders into giving them access to the island. Cadwgan and Gruffudd fled to Ireland, where they took sanctuary, leaving the Normans in possession. They did not enjoy it long, however, for while they were ravaging, the king of Norway, Magnus Bareleg, happened past. He was in the Irish Sea with a fleet of his own, attempting to bring under his control the Viking lord of the Isle of Man. Seeing the forces arrayed around Anglesey, however, he came to investigate and came to blows with the Norman invaders. In the ensuing battle, Hugh of Shrewsbury was struck in the face by an arrow, and killed. The Norman forces, deprived of one of their leaders, withdrew, taking at least some of the population with them as captives. In the wake of this defeat, their erstwhile guide, Owain ab Edwin, rebelled, leading the men of Gwynedd against the remaining Norman lords and colonists.[30]

An official resolution was required. In 1099, Cadwgan and Gruffudd returned from Ireland. The rebellion was over, but its leaders might not be ignored. The earl of Chester made peace with them, probably on behalf of the king, and recognized their rights to hold certain lands. The division that was made clearly shows the greater importance placed by the Normans upon Cadwgan: he received central Powys, together with Ceredigion. This was at the expense of the new earl of Shrewsbury, Robert, but may be a reflection of political reality. Earl Hugh of Chester was more loath to reduce his own lands, and Gruffudd received Anglesey alone. Owain ab Edwin does not seem to have been mentioned in the settlement, but he retained his lands in Tegeingl.

The rise of Powys

Earl Hugh and King William II may have intended these arrangements to be enduring: it is impossible now to know. In 1100, William was killed hunting, and his youngest brother Henry became king. As had occurred at William's accession, a section of the Norman nobility rose in favour of his elder brother, Robert of Normandy. A key figure in this was Robert de Bellême, the new earl of Shrewsbury. In 1102, together with his younger brother Arnulf, lord of Pembroke, Robert rebelled against the king. According to the *Brutiau*, they summoned to them the Welsh who were subject to them, with their leaders, 'that is Cadwgan, Iorwerth and Maredudd, sons of Bleddyn ap Cynfyn'.[31]

During the 1090s, the earl's family had spread west across Wales as far as Ceredigion: Cadwgan must have been well-known to them. When he was confirmed in his lands in 1099, Robert was newly earl, and needed to come to terms quickly with Cadwgan. The testimony of the *Brutiau* for the early years of the twelfth century is problematic: it is based on a single narrative, written after the events it describes, and with certain clear biases. One of these is towards the new dynasty of Powys. Another is towards the power of the Normans, particularly Henry I.[32] *AC* represent an earlier layer of recording but are much thinner for these years. When the *Brutiau* describe Cadwgan and his brothers as subject to Earl Robert, it should be remembered that the terminology may reflect the period in which the narrative was written rather than 1099-1102, and that Cadwgan at that time was not only the most influential and powerful of the Welsh leaders, but the author of a rebellion which had considerably reduced Norman power in Wales. His relationship with Robert was probably closer to an alliance than to subservience, and the *Brutiau* admit that Robert paid for his aid in 1102 with gifts and promises. Robert, in 1099, had few ties to Wales, and needed to secure his new borders quickly: a truce with Cadwgan would have been the most expedient solution. In 1102, Cadwgan and his brothers brought their warbands to Robert's aid, helping him against the king's party in the borders of Wales, and providing shelter within Wales for the flocks, herds and goods of Robert's men.

If Cadwgan's younger brothers had participated in the earlier Welsh rebellion, no record survives. Maredudd, at least, was to prove loyal both to Cadwgan and to Cadwgan's son Owain, accepting both as his overlords. Iorwerth was more ambitious. Henry I had gathered forces against the rebels and seized Robert's castle of Bridgenorth, and was seeking for a means of undermining Robert. On the advice of his counsel, he sent messengers to Iorwerth with offers of reward. He promised to grant him everything held by Robert and Arnulf in Wales.[33] Iorwerth accepted and turned on Robert, allowing his own men to plunder Robert's lands. The *Brutiau*, at least, represented this as the turning point for Robert: it may be that Iorwerth had been particularly close to the earl, and was regarded by him as a key ally.[34] Under pressure from Henry's armies, Robert's rebellion collapsed. He forfeited his earldom to the king, and returned to Normandy, where he had other lands. Arnulf likewise surrendered his lands and departed. This left Henry in control of a key belt of lands, including Pembroke castle, part of Dyfed, Shropshire, plus Herefordshire, which had been in royal hands since 1075. It also left Iorwerth with considerable expectations from the king. It is not clear how relations stood between the Powys brothers: according to the *Brutiau*, Iorwerth at first made peace with Cadwgan and Maredudd and shared his lands with them, but soon seized Maredudd and had him incarcerated in a royal prison.[35] He then made peace with Cadwgan again, giving him Ceredigion and part of Powys. Iorwerth then went to the king, seeking fulfilment of his promises.

What can be made of this story? The lands which Cadwgan is said to have been given are the same as those he held in 1099. It is likely he had continued to hold them: Iorwerth's actions, if genuine, simply confirmed a *status quo*. The only parts of the sequence of actions to be confirmed in *AC* is the capture and imprisonment of Maredudd, and Iorwerth's journey to the king: it is probable that after the collapse of Robert's rebellion, Iorwerth found himself at odds with his brothers, and sought royal help. It was not forthcoming. Both the *Brutiau* and *AC* agree that in 1103 Iorwerth met with Henry at Shrewsbury, where instead of a reward, he found himself captured and imprisoned. Henry is said by the *Brutiau* to have granted Dyfed and Pembroke castle to a trusted knight, and Ystrad Tywi, Cydweli and Gower to Hywel ap Goronwy, probably the most powerful Welsh lord in that area.[36]

The imprisonment of both his brothers left Cadwgan as the sole power in Powys. It may be in the early years of the twelfth century that he made his agreement with Uchdryd ab Edwin, whereby the latter received Cyfeiliog and Meirionydd from him. Uchdryd, by 1105, was the head of his family, his brother Owain having died of an illness. At some time, Cadwgan also married, or took as a concubine, Gwenllian, a daughter of Gruffudd ap Cynan, which may have secured him friendship with Gruffudd – a situation probably more desirable from Gruffudd's point of view than Cadwgan's.[37] He was not without potential rivals, however, and from 1106 began to take steps to impose his authority over his wider kin-group, including not only his nephews, the sons of his late brother Rhirid, but his more distant cousins, the sons of Trahaearn ap Caradog. In this, he was assisted by his eldest son, Owain, and by his brother Maredudd, who escaped from prison in 1107.

In 1106, the sons of Trahaearn ap Caradog, Meurig and Griffri, came to blows with Owain, and were defeated and killed in battle. It is likely that they were attempting to impose their authority over some part of northern central Wales, probably Arwystli. Cadwgan, however, was not willing to permit this. He had ambitions to dominate considerable territories outside Powys itself, including Arwystli, along with Eifionydd, Ardudwy, Penllyn, Cyfeiliog, Ceredigion and Cydweli. Trahaearn's sons may have refused to recognize his overlordship, or may have been trying to reclaim some of the power held by their father. As such, they were a threat to Cadwgan, and action was taken against them.

Cadwgan's position was strong and he had a history of resistance to Norman domination. Henry I rapidly realized that he was a potential threat, and the imprisonment of his brothers may have been intended as a lever on him. It was not in Henry's interest to have a strong leader in Wales, especially one who had shown himself ready to ally with forces rebelling against the king.[38] Henry had substantial lands in Wales and the border, and he wished to maintain firm control there. He introduced Flemish settlers into Dyfed, to help consolidate Norman control. He also attempted to interfere with native Welsh politics, and to impose dominion over Cadwgan in particular.[39] To some extent, Owain was a complicating factor in this. He is one of the more colourful characters in Welsh history, and opinions on him have varied greatly. To the author of the *Brutiau* narrative, he was a hero, but modern scholars have been more cautious.

To Lloyd, he was a loose cannon, while R.R. Davies has seen him as a major contributing factor in the decline of Powys.[40] Like Trahaearn ap Caradog in the 1070s, Owain's reputation has suffered at the hands of comparisons with Gruffudd ap Cynan. He is not mentioned in *HGK*, but that text's brief account of Gruffudd's rise to supremacy (which is debatable) in the early part of the twelfth century, together with the statements of the *Brutiau* about the power of Henry I, have been relied on perhaps overmuch, given the retrospective nature of both (and their biases). The earliest witness to Owain, and indeed to Cadwgan's actions in 1102-1111, is the *AC* and the present writer has made a case elsewhere for the adoption of this text in interpreting events in Powys in this period.[41]

Cadwgan had shown interest in Deheubarth as far back as 1088, and in the first decade of the twelfth century, he continued to try and impose himself over at least parts of it. It lacked a clear native leader, and much of it was in Norman hands. One of the key Norman leaders was Gerald of Windsor, who held Pembroke castle and surrounding lands for the king. In 1109, Owain embarked on a campaign in the south. The details of this have become bound up with legend. *AC* gives a basic outline: Owain attacked and burnt the castle at Cenarth Bychan (probably Cilgerran).[42] As a result, he was obliged to flee temporarily to Ireland, but had returned to Wales by the year's end. His raid was probably launched from Ceredigion, which was in Cadwgan's hands, and its target was Gerald. The *Brutiau* give a far more elaborate account, relating how, at a feast given by his father, Owain was told of the beauty of Gerald's wife, Nest, daughter of Rhys ap Tewdwr and Owain's cousin. He decided he had to see her for himself, and went to Cenarth Bychan where she was staying with her husband. Overcome by her charm, he resolved to carry her off, and returned at night with a small force. He broke into the castle, setting it on fire: Gerald fled, but Nest was captured and carried off with her children to Ceredigion. Cadwgan urged him to restore her to Gerald, but Owain refused (he did return the children). Reprisals were not long in coming. The king's commander in Shrewsbury, Richard de Beaumais, bishop of London, summoned to him Madog and Ithel, sons of Rhirid ap Bleddyn. These two were Cadwgan's nephews, and, through their father (killed in 1088) had a claim to power in Powys. Bishop Richard bribed them to attack Cadwgan and Owain. There were joined in this by Llywarch ap Trahaearn, whose brothers had been killed by Owain in 1106, and perhaps by Uchdryd ab Owain. While Madog and Ithel attacked, Uchdryd offered refuge to any who fled Powys, and served as a brake on the ambitions of the brothers.[43] Owain fled to Ireland while Cadwgan opened negotiations with Bishop Richard. The king granted him peace, but deprived him of almost all his lands. Madog and Ithel seized part of Powys, where they rapidly showed themselves harsh rulers. Perhaps to limit them, Henry restored Ceredigion to Cadwgan, on condition that he would not communicate with Owain and that he pay a fine of £100. Owain shortly returned to Wales, where he leagued with Madog ap Rhirid. The two embarked

Cilgerran Castle.

on a widespread campaign of raiding and plundering. The repercussions ran on into 1110, when Henry I released Iorwerth ab Bleddyn from prison, while Owain and Madog continued their attacks on Norman colonial lands in Wales, using Powys as a base. Iorwerth, fearing royal reprisal, sent his warband after them, and drove them into the territory of Uchdryd ab Edwin in Meirionydd. Uchdryd, likewise, moved to drive them out, but instead his army was put to flight. In the wake of this, Madog and Owain parted, Madog going to Powys, Owain to his father in Ceredigion. From there, he resumed his attacks on Dyfed, with the help of ships he had brought with him from Ireland, and of the younger nobility of Ceredigion. In reprisal, Henry I offered Ceredigion to Gilbert fitz Richard in an attempt to undermine Cadwgan. Hearing of this, Owain, together with Madog, retreated once again to Ireland, although Madog returned shortly thereafter. (Cadwgan, according to the *Brutiau*, was during this time at Henry's court, engaged in negotiations with the king.) Madog sought the help of Iorwerth ab Bleddyn, but finding him uncooperative, turned to his old ally Llywarch ap Trahaearn, and together they plotted the downfall of Iorwerth. Early in 1111, Madog ambushed and killed Iorwerth near Caereinion. This left Henry I without an ally in the Powys royal house: he made peace with Cadwgan, who returned to Powys. Henry also sent messengers to Owain in Ireland, offering peace. Apparently before Owain could return, Madog ambushed and killed Cadwgan near Welshpool. He appears to have been relying on his old agreement with Henry I, but this would prove to be of no benefit to him. Instead of recognizing him as king in Powys, Henry continued his overtures to Owain, with Maredudd ab Bleddyn acting as their intermediary. By the end of 1111, Owain was back in Wales, no longer a rebel but the acknowledged king of Powys. The *Brutiau* provide a long and complex account of these events, and it is not certain that the details they provide are reliable. What is clear from the earlier account of *AC* is that in the period 1109-1111, Owain was engaged on a consistent campaign against the Norman colonies in Wales, with the knowledge and backing of his father, and that the king had relatively few sanctions against them. Cadwgan was deprived of Ceredigion, at least officially, and Gilbert fitz Richard embarked on an attempt at settlement (which would eventually succeed). Henry further sought to weaken Cadwgan by interfering in the politics of the Powys royal line, by offering incentives to the ambitious but unreliable Madog ap Rhirid, and by releasing Iorwerth. The *Brutiau* provide considerable detail about Henry's manoeuvrings, down to supposed conversations between him and Cadwgan, but even this narrative cannot conceal that Henry was unable to prevent Owain's raids or to destroy Cadwgan, and ultimately had to come to terms. The picture of the king in the *Brutiau* is a curious one: he is at once threatening and oddly powerless. The text, written after the events, may have been attempting to fit a model of the king of England as a determined and far-reaching overlord (modelled perhaps on Henry II) with a native record of a period in which the king's writ did not, in fact, yet run so widely into Wales. Despite the activities of Madog and the release of Iorwerth, Cadwgan remained securely king of Powys throughout all these events. If *AC* is given priority, Henry's actions – the attempt to undermine Cadwgan, the opening of Ceredigion to colonization, and the eventual recognition of the troublesome Owain – show increasing desperation in the face of a determined resistance centred on Cadwgan, a man with a thirty-year history of rebellion.

Throughout his lifetime, Cadwgan retained his hold on Powys, and, with the help of his son, made considerable attempts to expand his power outside it. He dominated mid-Wales, had a strong claim on Ceredigion (and had he not been murdered in 1111, Gilbert fitz Richard's colony may have faced serious, perhaps fatal, opposition), and through his relations with the equivocal Uchdryd ab Edwin, had considerable influence in north Wales also. Lloyd accused him of failing to control his kin,[44] but in fact, he suppressed the ambitions of his cousins from Arwystli, kept his brothers under his control (*AC* shows no friction between him and Iorwerth 1110-1; both *AC* and the *Brutiau* confirm that there was nothing but amity between him and Maredudd), and until 1111 seems also to have overawed his nephew, Madog ap Rhirid. He had at least six sons by various women: however Owain seems to have been the recognized heir, a situation Cadwgan was able to enforce without strife or conflict.[45] It is probable, moreover, that all of Owain's actions were undertaken with Cadwgan's full agreement, and most of these were aimed at removing and weakening Norman power in Wales. Cadwgan's death in 1111 was the result of family conflict. Certainly, he was ageing, and Madog, ambitious and excluded from power, seized an opportunity. However, it would do him no good. The core of the royal house – Owain and Maredudd – were quite clear as to where right-to-rule lay. In 1112, Maredudd captured Madog and handed him over to Owain for punishment. He was blinded, effectively ending his public career, and he and his descendants (if any) vanished for good from the kingship of Powys.

Owain ap Cadwgan survived his father by five years, and, like Cadwgan, enjoyed considerable influence. He did not forget his family's claims to Ceredigion, and in 1114 Henry I was obliged to lead an army into Wales to check his raids. In the north, Gruffudd ap Cynan, whose career between 1099 and 1114 is largely obscure, and Goronwy ab Owain ab Edwin had also been harassing their Norman neighbours, and likewise incurred Henry's wrath. Initially, the three Welsh leaders formed an alliance against the king, led by Owain. However, Gruffudd and Goronwy entered into negotiations with Henry's army. Owain remained reluctant, retreating into Snowdonia to evade the royal army. His chosen place of refuge is interesting: it suggests either that Gruffudd ap Cynan had not yet extended his authority into this area, traditionally part of Gwynedd, or that Gruffudd was insufficiently powerful in his own lands to prevent or influence Owain's movements. Gruffudd was cautious in his attitude towards the Norman king, and would prove himself no friend to those in rebellion: it is unlikely that he colluded in Owain's behaviour in 1114. Henry, however, could not force a battle on Owain (and perhaps did not want one) and negotiations were opened, with Maredudd ab Bleddyn acting as intermediary. Eventually, Owain agreed to make terms. The king received him with honour, confirming to him his land free of liability, and promising to knight him. The terms offered to Gruffudd and Goronwy were far less generous, despite their less provocative behaviour, and they had to pay heavy tributes. Once again, for any detail, we are dependent on the *Brutiau*, raising problems of reliability: the narrative is biased in favour of Owain, and may be exaggerating his status *vis à vis* the other leaders. But what seems clear is that the men of Powys represented the greatest threat to Norman dominion and were the focus of Henry's actions in Wales.

We do not know if the events of 1114 put an end to Owain's aggression against the colonists. For the last two years of his life, the *Brutiau* depict him as enjoying royal favour and operating as a royal agent against another Welsh rebel, Gruffudd ap Rhys ap Tewdwr, the heir to Deheubarth. Nevertheless, even this narrative concedes that he met his death at Norman hands in 1116. His death may have been due to Gerald of Windsor, whose wife Owain had stolen in 1109, and whose lands had suffered considerably from Owain's raids. The *Brutiau* describe the killing as an act of revenge: Gerald and Owain were both acting for the king against Gruffudd ap Rhys but Gerald took advantage of the confusion to kill his old enemy. *AC* simply notes that Owain was killed by Flemish settlers near Ystrad Rwnws. It was a period of considerable disorder in Deheubarth: Gruffudd ap Rhys, who had been raised an exile in Ireland, had come to Wales the previous year in search of his patrimony. In 1115, with the help of younger members of the local nobility, he had burnt Carmarthen and plundered Arberth. Owain is perhaps more likely to have exploited this and joined in the rebellion in 1116 than he is to have been acting on behalf of Henry I.[46] Gerald of Windsor, if he did instigate Owain's death, met with no royal reprisal, which suggests that Owain was not, in fact, a royal agent in 1116. Owain had left no sons: his brother Einion succeeded as king of Powys, supported by their younger brothers and their uncle, Maredudd. For almost forty years Powys had dominated native politics. Changes in Wales, particularly in the north, would gradually erode this supremacy, but in Cadwgan and Owain, the Welsh had found leaders who maintained consistent and often effective resistance to the new Norman neighbours. Subsequent rulers of Powys would enjoy influence over events in Wales, but from the 1120s a new force would come to the fore in Welsh politics, as the sons of Gruffudd ap Cynan embarked on recreating the power and dominance of Gwynedd.

5 From Owain Gwynedd to Rhys ap Gruffudd:

1137 - 1197

The last years of Gruffudd ap Cynan and the revival of Gwynedd

While Cadwgan ab Bleddyn and Owain ap Cadwgan prosecuted their policy of resistance to the Normans in mid-Wales, their northern neighbour, Gruffudd ap Cynan, was playing a more temperate game. He had been politically active since 1075 and was probably in his middle years when he became ruler of Anglesey in 1099. His route to power had been shaky, and the men of Gwynedd, on whose support he depended, had shown themselves uncertain subjects during his years of freedom before 1081. He had spent most of the 1080s and 1090s as a Norman captive, cut off from his patrimony, and had escaped into a context of rebellion and conflict centred on Cadwgan of Powys, and in which the more powerful nobles of Gwynedd, like the brothers Uchdryd and Owain sons of Edwin, had grown increasingly independent. It is likely that in his early years as king, Gruffudd's position was insecure. He took some steps to improve it, forming one alliance by marrying Owain ab Edwin's daughter, Angharad, and another by giving his own daughter, Gwenllian, to Cadwgan. The kings of Powys seem largely to have left him alone: apart from his brief alliance with Owain ap Cadwgan against Henry I in 1114, Gruffudd is absent from the Welsh Chronicles in the first decade-and-a-half of the twelfth century. *HGK* is equally vague as to his career after he became king, describing his reign in general terms: 'for many years, [he] ruled with deliberation and peace, and with customary neighbourliness with the kings nearest to him...and he was renowned and famous both in kingdoms far away from him and in those close to him'.[1] It seems likely that he slowly expanded his power out from Anglesey at least into Arfon, but no details survive. The sons of Edwin, especially Uchdryd, were a power to be reckoned both in the north-east and in Meirionydd. Owain died in 1105, but in 1114 his son, Goronwy, is spoken of as Gruffudd's equal, suggesting that Gruffudd did not yet dominate all – or even most – of Gwynedd. Meirionydd to the immediate south lay in the hands of Goronwy's uncle, Uchdryd ab Edwin, the ally and perhaps vassal of Cadwgan ab Bleddyn. Down to the early 1120s, Gruffudd kept his head down, concentrating on his own small land, playing no part in the wider political scene. He was anxious, understandably, to avoid incurring Norman attention, coming rapidly to terms with Henry I in 1114. In 1115, he had an opportunity to court royal favour. Gruffudd ap Rhys ap Tewdwr had returned to Wales in 1113 and begun a campaign to install himself as king in the south. He found little support: the *Brutiau* speak scathingly of his supporters as 'young hotheads',[2] suggesting that the established lords of Deheubarth refused him aid, leaving him reliant on the help of younger men – brave, but probably landless and poor.[3] He did a fair amount of damage with his raids, but gained little political advantage, and in 1115 he fled north to Gwynedd, seeking refuge against accusations of sedition. He sought help from Gruffudd ap Cynan,[4] who was his distant kinsman and who had had a brief alliance in 1081 with his father, Rhys ap Tewdwr. Gruffudd ap Cynan initially received him kindly and offered shelter, but seems quickly to have realized that this was unlikely to please Henry I. It was less than a year since Henry's expedition to Wales, which had resulted in Gruffudd's having to enter an expensive peace with the king. It had taken Gruffudd almost twenty-five years to gain even part of Gwynedd: he did not, it seems, want to risk it. Offered incentives by the Norman colonists, he agreed to hand Gruffudd ap Rhys over to them. But someone – presumably one of Gruffudd ap Cynan's unreliable nobles – warned Gruffudd ap Rhys. The young southern prince took refuge in the church of Aberdaron. Gruffudd ap Cynan brought his warband to try and drive him out, but the clergy, jealous of their privilege of sanctuary, resisted, and Gruffudd ap Rhys was able to escape south. The incident does not show Gruffudd ap Cynan in a favourable light, but it does demonstrate his careful approach to his Norman neighbours. He was less a warrior than a diplomat, concerned to retain his hold over his lands by the most expedient and least costly means. Moreover, he was no longer young in 1115 and his lands were still small: he could not afford to risk a war with the earl of Chester, or the Norman lords of the south.

Gruffudd ap Rhys continued his rebellion into 1116, ranging across Deheubarth, and attacking Arberth, Llandovery and Swansea. Henry I took his activities seriously, sending considerable forces against him. By the end of the year, the rebellion was over, and Gruffudd's pretensions to kingship were at an end. He came to terms with Henry, and received one commot of land in Cantref Mawr, a tiny fraction of his father's kingdom. He would remain lord there until the mid-1130s, a minor figure, but one who never forgot his ancestral claims. We know very little of him between 1116 and 1136: he seems never to have been fully accepted or trusted by his new overlords, for in 1127 he was temporarily deprived of his land after an accusation of betrayal.

Part of the reason for our ignorance of both Gruffudd ap Cynan and Gruffudd ap Rhys in the first two to three decades of the twelfth century lies in the nature of our sources. The Welsh Chronicles show little interest in either of them (indeed seem actively hostile to Gruffudd ap Rhys, 1115-6). After Owain ap Cadwgan's death, his uncle, Maredudd, seems to have taken over the role as leader of the royal house of Powys, with the support of Owain's younger brothers Einion, Madog, Morgan and Maredudd, as well as of his own son, Gruffudd. The line continued to press its claim to overlordship in Meirionydd, and Cyfeiliog, where on the death of Owain, Uchdryd ab Edwin seems to have made a bid for independence. The Powys family made swift work of his rebellion. Einion ap Cadwgan and Gruffudd ap Maredudd led an army into his lands, seized and burned his castle at Cymer and took his lands for themselves. Uchdryd himself escaped east into Tegeingl, the land of his nephews, where he continued to promote resistance. In 1118, his nephews, the sons of Owain ab Edwin, made a treacherous attack upon their neighbour, Hywel ab Ithel of Rhos and Rhufoniog, a client of the royal house of Powys. Hywel appealed to Maredudd ab Bleddyn and his kinsmen, who came at the head of a large force to support him. A pitched battle ensued somewhere in Dyffryn Clwyd, which at that time was also subject to Powysian overlordship: the Powysian side won the day, but at great cost. Hywel survived the battle, but with mortal wounds, dying within weeks, and the victorious forces of Powys were unable to retain control of his lands. The sons of Owain ab Edwin gained the support of their Norman neighbour, the earl of Chester, who took advantage of the battle to try to expand his own overlordship into Tegeingl and Dyffryn Clwyd. The more easterly lands of Rhos and Rhufoniog may have passed into the sphere of influence of Gruffudd ap Cynan.

The strength of the line of Powys had received a check, but it was still perceived as a threat. In 1121, Henry I again found it necessary to invade Wales, to cow Maredudd ab Bleddyn. Maredudd sought an alliance with Gruffudd ap Cynan, but Gruffudd already had a peace with the king and did not wish to endanger it. He refused Maredudd's request and threatened war should Maredudd or his kin approach the boundaries of Gruffudd's lands. Maredudd determined on an essentially defensive course of action. Having taken counsel with his leading men, he despatched a small raiding party to harass the royal army on its route, and a lucky shot with an arrow struck Henry himself. Clad in mail, he was uninjured, but was greatly shocked by the accident, and stopped the advance. He offered a truce to his attackers, under which he requested a meeting with Maredudd and the sons of Cadwgan. The latter came to meet him, and made peace, although Henry demanded a heavy tribute from them. The description of this in the *Brutiau,* as with the account of Owain ap Cadwgan, was probably written some time after the event and embellished by its author both to show the power of Henry and the heroism and intelligence of Maredudd's resistance (it additionally casts a negative light on Gruffudd ap Cynan): its details cannot be accepted as certain. The outline, however, is clear from other sources: ten years after the death of Cadwgan ap Bleddyn, Powys remained the leading force within Wales, and the main threat to Anglo-Norman ambition. In 1124, Einion ap Cadwgan died, and Henry again tried to undermine Powysian power, this time by releasing Ithel ap Rhirid ab Bleddyn, another nephew of Maredudd ab Bleddyn, who had been a captive since 1110. Henry's idea seems to have been to provoke internal feuding within Powys, by encouraging Ithel to lay claim to part of Einion's lands (which were partly in Powys and partly in Meirionydd). Maredudd ab Bleddyn, however, did not intend to allow any feud. He claimed Einion's lands himself, repelling not only Ithel, but Maredudd ap Cadwgan, Einion's younger brother and heir.

The death of Einion proved a setback to Powysian ambitions. Gruffudd ap Cynan had largely avoided confrontation within Wales since securing control over

Anglesey in 1099. It had taken him twenty-five years to gain even that toehold, and he was no longer young. However, he had ambitious and effective sons, who sought to restore the old bounds and power of Gwynedd. By 1124, at least two of these, Cadwallon and Owain, were adult, and had considerable influence over their father's policies and resources. The death of Einion ap Cadwgan, and the expansion into Meirionydd of Maredudd ab Bleddyn provided the sons of Gruffudd with an opportunity. Maredudd, like Gruffudd, was no longer young, and his resources were now quite stretched. By excluding his nephew Maredudd ap Cadwgan from Einion's lands, moreover, he may well have reduced his support amongst his own kin. Owain and Cadwallon, with their father's backing and encouragement, were swift to take advantage. They invaded Meirionydd with the help of Llywarch ap Trahaearn, the lord of Arwystli, who had an old grudge against the line of Powys.[5] They took great plunder back with them into Llŷn. This initial onslaught did not expel Maredudd ab Bleddyn from Meirionydd, but it weakened him there. He and his nephews struck out in revenge at Llywarch, and did considerable damage to his lands. It was, however, the beginning of the end for the hegemony of Powys: their influence in the north had received a major blow with the death of Hywel ab Ithel; their influence in the west was waning. Maredudd ab Bleddyn himself would continue to rule securely over Powys itself, and on his death in 1132, would be commemorated by the *Brutiau* as 'the splendour and defence of the men of Powys',[6] but amongst his nephews and sons, relations had become strained. In 1125, Maredudd's son, Gruffudd, had disposed of the inconvenient Ithel ap Rhirid, in Maredudd's presence and probably with his consent. But in the same year, two other nephews, Maredudd and Morgan, sons of Cadwgan, had quarrelled and Maredudd ap Cadwgan had been killed as a result. The murder weighed on Morgan's conscience, and he went on a penitential pilgrimage to Jerusalem, dying in 1128 in Cyprus on his way home. Gruffudd ap Maredudd may have been Maredudd's chosen heir, but in 1128 he also died, and his death provoked some of Maredudd's younger kinsman into making their own ambitions overt. To retain his control, he seized Llywelyn ab Owain ap Cadwgan, and sent him into captivity in England. Llywelyn did not remain long in prison, and by 1129 was back in Wales, where he embarked on a violent campaign against the lords of Arwystli, the sons of Llywarch ap Trahaearn. The form this took – a series of expulsions and mutilations – was unpleasant in the extreme, and hardly conducive to peaceful and harmonious overlordship. Llywelyn's actions also seem not to have been sanctioned by Maredudd ab Bleddyn, and in 1130, Maredudd had Llywelyn blinded and castrated. The feud in Arwystli continued, however, and would eventually result in the destruction of its old ruling line, the descendants of Trahaearn ap Caradog.[7]

Throughout the 1120s, the sons of Gruffudd ap Cynan were on the offensive. The death of Hywel ab Ithel in 1124 opened the way for Venedotian expansion into Rhos and Rhufoniog. Dyffryn Clwyd to the east was in the hands of the surviving sons of Owain ab Edwin, Goronwy, Rhirid and Meilir. These three could claim a tie by marriage to the line of Gwynedd, for Gruffudd ap Cynan had married their sister Angharad. The sons of Owain ab Edwin, like their uncle Uchdryd, proved uncertain allies, alternating allegiance between native Welsh kings and Anglo-Norman border lords, according to their own advantage. In 1125, Cadwallon ap Gruffudd, perhaps influenced by his uncle's history of treachery, killed all three of them, annexing their lands to Gwynedd. The kingdom of Gwynedd was beginning to regain its old shape and bounds. The sons of Gruffudd then turned their attention to lands subject to Powys. By 1132, Cadwallon had pushed his way into Nanheudwy, intending to push the boundary of Gwynedd even further eastward. His ambitions threatened Powys and had made him enemies: he was met by his cousin, Cadwgan ap Goronwy ab Owain, and killed. This put an end – for the time being – to the eastward expansion of Gwynedd. Owain ap Gruffudd and his younger brother Cadwaladr continued careful expansion southwards. Before 1136, they seized Meirionydd. It is not known exactly when this occurred, but it may have been a consequence of the death of Maredudd ab Bleddyn in 1132. After 1132, the Welsh Chronicles are noticeably less informative on the fortunes of the Powysian royal house, and their interest in the line of Gwynedd increases. The increase in the size of Gwynedd led in turn to an increase in its resources, making further expansion easier to fund and support. Venedotian expansion received a further boost in 1135, when, on the death of Henry I, a dispute arose over the succession to the throne between Matilda, Henry's daughter, and Stephen, his nephew. The Anglo-Norman lords with lands in Wales and the March were greatly involved in the ensuing civil war, and had little time or resources to spare for their Welsh lands, or for curbing the activities of native Welsh kings. In 1136 a rebellion against the Norman settlers broke out in Wales. Cadwaladr and Owain, sons of Gruffudd, invaded Ceredigion, burning and destroying Norman settlements and castles. They were supported in this by the native nobility of the so-called Middle March (the lands along the central midland border between England and Wales). When they made a second invasion later in the same year, they were joined by Gruffudd ap Rhys ap Tewdwr, who had been living in relative obscurity in the small territory granted him by Henry I since *c.*1116. This second campaign focused on the Norman stronghold at Cardigan, and resulted in a Welsh victory. Fighting also occurred in the vicinity of Cydweli castle. The area was under the control of Maurice de Londres. The wife of Gruffudd ap Rhys, Gwenllian, a daughter of Gruffudd ap Cynan and sister of Owain and Cadwaladr, launched an attack on Maurice, together with her young sons Maelgwn and Morgan. At the end of the twelfth century, the Cambro-Norman cleric and scholar, Gerald of Wales, who was himself partly of the blood of the old royal line of Deheubarth, and thus a distant kinsman of Gruffudd ap Rhys, wrote of how she rode forth at the head of an army, 'like some second Penthesilea, queen of the Amazons'.[8] Gwenllian's expedition met with defeat, and with the deaths of herself and her son Morgan. She is the sole Welsh woman known from surviving records to have entered the martial arena, and her reasons are obscure. Perhaps she hoped to further the cause of her husband and brothers through conquest, or through offering a distraction to the Norman forces.

Cydweli Castle.

By the end of 1136, the Welsh had made considerable gains in Ceredigion, having taken almost all the major Norman strongholds there. Most of the momentum for this came from Owain and Cadwaladr: both Gruffudd ap Cynan and Gruffudd ap Rhys were ageing, and in 1137 both of them died. The sons of Gruffudd ap Rhys were still young: this left the way open for the sons of Gruffudd ap Cynan, and in particular for the elder of them, Owain.

Owain Gwynedd

Owain ap Gruffudd is better known to history as Owain Gwynedd, a name he acquired in his own lifetime to distinguish him from another mid-twelfth century Owain ap Gruffudd – Owain ap Gruffudd ap Maredudd of Powys, who held Cyfeiliog after 1149 and was thus known as Owain Cyfeiliog. Owain Gwynedd succeeded Gruffudd ap Cynan as king of Gwynedd, and ruled it until 1170. It is likely that he had been the architect of the expansion of Gwynedd in the 1120s and 1130s, and he was to dominate Welsh politics throughout his reign. In 1137, in the wake of the death of Gruffudd ap Rhys, Owain renewed the onslaught on Ceredigion, burning castles at Ystrad Meurig, Lampeter, Humfrey's Castle and Carmarthen. This seems to have allowed him to annex Ceredigion, and before 1143, he had divided it between his brother Cadwaladr and his son Hywel. The sons of Gruffudd ap Rhys

98

Manorbier Castle, childhood home of Gerald of Wales.

made no resistance, perhaps occupied by the continued rebellion in the south-west.

Other factors combined to aid Owain's rise to power. In Powys, Maredudd ap Bleddyn left several sons, of whom Madog seems to have been the most senior. Like Owain, Madog took advantage of the disruption in England to expand his own borders. Fighting occurred all along the Welsh-Shropshire border, resulting in the death at Welsh hands of the sheriff of Shropshire, Payn Fitz John, in 1137. In 1140, the Norman stronghold of Bromfield was destroyed by the men of Powys. But internal friction may have continued within Powys in 1138-9, Madog was obliged to kill one Cynwrig ab Owain, and in 1142, Madog's brother, Hywel, was killed by his own men. This weakness in Powys contributed to Owain Gwynedd's rise to prominence.

Gwynedd itself was not immune to internal dissent. In the lifetime of Gruffudd ap Cynan, his sons coexisted peacefully, but Cadwaladr was ambitious, and unwilling to remain subordinate. In 1143, he attacked and killed Anarawd ap Gruffudd, probably the eldest son of Gruffudd ap Rhys, and Owain Gwynedd's ally. At the time of the murder, a marriage was being arranged between Anarawd and Owain's daughter: Owain was infuriated. He deprived Cadwaladr of all his holdings, and within the year, Hywel ap Owain Gwynedd had launched a campaign against Cadwaladr in Ceredigion. By the beginning of 1144, Cadwaladr was forced to flee. He took refuge in Ireland, where he hired a mercenary fleet. Landing at Abermenai, he prepared to fight, but instead, Owain opened negotiations with him. Peace was arranged between the brothers. The exact terms do not survive, but it seems Cadwaladr was restored: his Irish hirelings, deprived of battle and loot, kidnapped him in order to secure payment, but instead were driven out by Owain. Some compensation must have been paid to Anarawd's brothers, also, for they remained at peace with Owain. The main focus of action remained the rebellion against the Anglo-Normans, several of whom were making efforts to sustain or rebuild their lordships. In 1145, Owain's sons, Hywel and Cynan, ravaged Cardigan. In 1146, the sons of Gruffudd ap Rhys, Cadell, Maredudd and Rhys, took the castles of Dinefwr and Llanstephan, and, with the help of Hywel ab Owain, overran Carmarthen. In the north, Owain Gwynedd seized Mold in the wake of the capture in England of the earl of Chester,[9] and of a preliminary raid into the territory by the men of Powys. In 1147, Hywel, Cadell, Maredudd and Rhys turned against the Flemish colonies in Dyfed, taking Wiston castle. Hywel by this time was an experienced battle leader, and he had ambitions of his own. In the same year, along with his brother Cynan, he launched an attack on his uncle, Cadwaladr. It is likely they sought to exclude him, and more importantly his sons, from power in the north. Owain Gwynedd had a number of sons by several different women, and all of these were potential heirs to his kingdom. Cadwaladr and his heirs represented another possible source of division and loss of land. Moreover, Cadwaladr was an uncertain ally, and known to be ambitious. Hywel and Cynan launched a simultaneous invasion of his lands, seizing his castle at Cynfael. This seems to have ended Cadwaladr's tenure of lands in Meirionydd. The Chronicles do not make it clear if Owain himself was complicit in this: certainly his sons escaped punishment and Cadwaladr was not restored. It is not impossible that Owain intended Meirionydd as an appanage for Hywel, and was content to look the other way. For the time being, however, Cadwaladr remained at peace with his brother. Owain was probably occupied with his campaigns in north-east Wales. The capture of Mold had placed him in a position to embark on the conquest of Iâl, an area to which Madog ap Maredudd of Powys also had a claim. Owain began building a castle on the border, which not only provided him with a defence against any Anglo-Norman attack, but also with a base from which he could resume expansion at the expense of Powys. This may have been facilitated by the fact that Madog in 1149 was preoccupied with his eastern borders, where he had overrun and seized Oswestry and its environs. Like Owain, Madog was operating over a wide area, and in the same year installed his nephews Owain (Cyfeiliog) and Meurig, sons of Gruffudd, in Cyfeiliog as his subordinates. In 1150, however, confrontation finally arose between Owain Gwynedd and Madog over Iâl. Madog allied with Earl Ranulf of Chester and met Owain in battle at Coleshill. Owain emerged victorious, and would remain in control of much of the north-east until his death.[10] He had succeeded in rebuilding the wide hegemony which Gwynedd had enjoyed before the coming of the Normans.

He had not, however, succeeded in totally controlling his family and his allies. Cadwaladr still had lands in the north-west, and in 1149 had given his share of

Dinefwr Castle.

Ceredigion to his son Cadfan – a move which threatened Hywel ab Owain Gwynedd. The following year, Hywel seized Cadfan and appropriated his land. This may have been done without Owain's consent. An arena of conflict had been created in Ceredigion, and this provided an opening to the sons of Gruffudd ap Rhys, who, later in 1150, took possession of Ceredigion south of the river Aeron. It was the first stage in a new conquest. In 1151, the sons of Gruffudd drove Hywel – and thus the line of Gwynedd – out of almost all of Ceredigion (he retained his castle at Llanfihangel). In their early years, the sons of Gruffudd had relied heavily on Hywel for extra troops and support, but now they served notice that they would hold their own lands without interference from Gwynedd. Later in that year, they moved into Gower, and also established themselves at Dinefwr, the legendary centre of Deheubarth. Owain Gwynedd had little attention to spare for this, however, for matters within his family had deteriorated. He had already, in 1150, had to imprison his son Cynan. In 1152, he mutilated a nephew, Cunedda,[11] excluding him from the succession. He also turned on Cadwaladr, and drove him out of Gwynedd. Why is not known, but it is likely that the combination of pressure from his now adult and ambitious sons and awareness of

101

Cadwaladr's history of conflict and untrustworthiness were major factors. Cadwaladr fled into England, where he had relations by marriage.[12] It is likely that Owain spent the next two or three years consolidating his hold in the north-east: the Chronicles tell us little of his activities, concentrating on the expansion in the south of the sons of Gruffudd, who by 1153 were raiding and conquering as far east as Aberafan and as far north as Cyfeiliog. One of them, Cadell, had suffered serious and permanent injury in 1151, and as a result surrendered his share of power. Another, Maredudd, died in 1155, as lord of Ceredigion, Ystrad Tywi and Dyfed – most of the former kingdom of Deheubarth. He was succeeded by the last brother, Rhys, who would rise to be one of the most powerful leaders south Wales had ever known. Rhys's position was now a potential threat to Owain, and in 1156, Owain raised an army and came south into Ceredigion. Rhys was ready for him, and constructed defences near Aberdyfi: the two sides did not come to battle. It may be that this confrontation would have developed into outright war in subsequent years, but in 1157, a new threat presented itself in Wales, and caused Owain and Rhys to abandon their mutual hostility.

The death of Henry I and the ensuing war in England had provided the Welsh with twenty years in which to reclaim their lands and rebuild their sovereignty, but the war was now over. In 1154, a new king had come to the throne, Henry II, son of Matilda. Henry spent the first years of his reign settling English affairs, but by 1157, he had attention to spare for Wales. He sought allies amongst the Welsh, giving shelter to the exiled Cadwaladr, and negotiating with the royal house of Powys. Madog ap Maredudd had laid claim to considerable parts of Shropshire as well as Powys, and his brother, Iorwerth Goch, had coordinated raids along the border. Both stood to lose from poor relations with the new English king. Some of these Welsh leaders joined Henry when he led an army into north Wales against Owain in 1157.[13] He fought a battle against troops under Owain's sons, Cynan and Dafydd, and penetrated as far west as Rhuddlan by land. He had also brought a fleet, which attacked from the west. The latter suffered defeat in Anglesey, however, and Henry decided to offer peace to Owain. Under its terms, Owain accepted Henry's overlordship, gave him hostages, reinstated Cadwaladr in Gwynedd, and restored Tegeingl to its former Anglo-Norman lords. He retained his sovereignty over Gwynedd, but he had been forced to recognize the existence of a determined new power in England. Rhuddlan was put into the hands of Hugh de Beauchamp, weakening Owain's influence in the east: after Henry had departed, Iorwerth Goch of Powys took advantage of this to descend on Iâl and burn Owain's castle there, restoring the Powysian claim to that land. The terms were not favourable to Owain, but he, like his father, seems to have had strong political sense. Henry II had more resources and more manpower; he was secure in his power in England; he had allies in Powys, the old enemy of Gwynedd. Antagonizing him would probably, in the long run, be more damaging than productive both for Owain and for Gwynedd. For the next few years, Owain played a waiting game, avoiding confrontation with English power. Indeed, in 1159, his sons Hywel and Cynan, along with Cadwaladr, aided royal forces against the rebellious Rhys ap Gruffudd in the south, perhaps with Owain's approval.[14]

Owain had been forced to reinstate Cadwaladr and he had lost lands in the east, but he still looked for opportunities to expand. One presented itself in 1160, on the death of Madog ap Maredudd of Powys. Madog is a shadowy figure, less well documented than Owain or Rhys of the south, but what evidence we do possess suggests a ruler of intelligence as well as a warrior. He had gained from the rebellion of the 1130s and 1140s, but had shown himself willing to compound with Henry II when it became necessary, and restored Oswestry apparently without conflict. He had been unable to exclude Owain from Iâl, but he retained the core lands of Powys and also maintained the loyalty of his under-kings in the border lands of Arwystli and Cyfeiliog. He was a patron of the church, and also of literature, and his activities in the border form the background to the middle Welsh prose tale The Dream of Rhonabwy, which describes him as ruling Powys 'from one end to the other, that is from Porffordd as far as Gwavan in the highlands of Arwystli'.[15] Madog had probably intended his kingdom to pass to his son Llywelyn, but Llywelyn was killed shortly after Madog's death. Powys was divided between several rival claimants – Madog's brother Iorwerth Goch, his nephew Owain Cyfeiliog (who already held Cyfeiliog) and his sons, Gruffudd, Owain Fychan and Owain Brogyntyn.[16] This disunity opened the way for a new wave of annexation by Owain Gwynedd. In the early years of the 1160s, he invaded Arwystli, driving out its ruler, Hywel ab Ieuaf: he probably also opened hostilities against Owain Cyfeiliog. This brought territorial gains to Owain without attracting the displeasure of Henry II.[17] He avoided direct personal involvement in the continued war in south Wales. However, it seems unlikely that he was happy with the status quo: later events suggest that he was awaiting a new chance.

It came in late 1163, when Henry II quarrelled with Thomas Becket, archbishop of Canterbury, an event which led to Becket's exile and a division of loyalties throughout Henry's lands. In 1163, Henry caused both Owain and Rhys ap Gruffudd to do homage to him at Woodstock, an act which marked a significant development in Anglo-Welsh relations, for it formalized the claims to feudal overlordship of the English kings.[18] Its significance was quickly realized by the Welsh leaders. Rhys ap Gruffudd had been in rebellion against Henry almost continually since 1158: by the end of 1164, all the other Welsh leaders, including Owain, had joined him, attacking Anglo-Norman lordship throughout Wales and the border. In the north, Owain's son Dafydd raided Tegeingl and Dyffryn Clwyd. Henry assembled a great army at Oswestry and, in 1165, marched towards Rhuddlan. He was met by a pan-Welsh force. The *Brutiau* record: 'Owain Gwynedd and Cadwaladr sons of Gruffudd ap Cynan came to meet him and all the host of Gwynedd with them, and the Lord Rhys ap Gruffudd and all Deheubarth with him, and Owain Cyfeiliog and Iorwerth Goch ap Maredudd and the sons of Madog ap Maredudd and with them all Powys, and the two sons of Madog ap Idnerth and all their strength with them'.[19] As with earlier campaigns, Henry was unable to force a pitched battle on the Welsh, but rather suffered a series of ambushes and raids. This, combined with bad weather and difficult terrain, demoralized his army, and he retreated back into England, where he mutilated the Welsh hostages who were in his hands. The Welsh leaders continued their rebellion. Owain Gwynedd razed Basingwerk castle for the final time (thereafter the site became a monastery), while Rhys ap Gruffudd attacked Cardigan and Cilgerran. The coalition of all the native leaders did not last, however. By 1166, internal feuding had resumed in Powys, resulting in the expulsion of Iorwerth Goch, and in 1167, Rhys and Owain turned on Owain Cyfeiliog, whose power was becoming dangerous to them in central west Wales. They expelled him from Caereinion and gave it to his kinsman Owain Fychan, operating a policy of divide and rule. This drove Owain Cyfeiliog into the hands of the English: within the year he was reinstated in his lands with English help, and the unity of Welsh against English was at an end.

The political climate in England was still favourable to the Welsh rebellion, however. The rift with Becket had provided opportunities to many of Henry's enemies, and Henry had gone to France, where he faced a considerable threat from its king, Louis VII. Owain sought to exploit this in other arenas than simple warfare. Since the coming of the Normans, the churches in Wales had faced continued efforts from Canterbury to dominate and control their offices and rights. At the time of Becket's exile, the Venedotian see of Bangor was vacant, and Owain tried to use Becket's absence to free it from English control. He wrote to Becket suggesting that the new bishop be consecrated by someone other than the archbishop of Canterbury, perhaps in Ireland. This would create a useful precedent, and pave the way for detaching the Welsh bishoprics from dependence on Canterbury – a move which both Becket and the Pope resisted. Owain found himself excommunicated, ostensibly on the ground of incest (his wife Cristin was his first cousin: under Welsh practice, this was perfectly legitimate, but under canon law, it was an unacceptably close degree of kinship). Despite this he sent his choice of bishop to Ireland for consecration. He also opened negotiations with Louis VII, the first Welsh king known to have operated on a European stage.[20] He wrote to Louis proposing an alliance between them against their mutual enemy, Henry II, probably in 1164/5. He may also have sought Louis's help with the issue of the consecration of the bishop of Bangor. While no formal treaty was agreed, both parties stood to gain by friendship, and it was very much in Owain's interest for hostilities in France to be prolonged. The communication set an important precedent for future kings and princes in Wales (and particularly of Gwynedd) to place themselves on an international stage and to seek recognition of themselves and their lands as independent principalities subject to rulers of status equal or near equal to that of other European rulers. The negotiations seem to have extended to include Rhys ap Gruffudd as well as Owain, as the two offered military help to Louis against Henry in July 1168. The Welsh rebellion and Owain's negotiations with France were still ongoing when, in November 1170, Owain died 'the bulwark of all Wales, after uncountable victories and unconquered from his youth'.[21] He was still excommunicated, but despite that, the clergy of Bangor accorded him burial in their church.

Owain should be regarded as the architect of the revival of Gwynedd, and the dominant force in Wales throughout the central years of the twelfth century. He was an effective military leader, but perhaps his greatest skills lay in governance and diplomacy. He was swift to respond – and respond appropriately – to changes in the English state and in other parts of Wales. He made intelligent use of his resources, relying on the skills and loyalty of his family to control lands in Meirionydd and Ceredigion, which may have increased the stability of his rule. He could not always control the ambitions of his sons and brother, but he seems to have been able to recognize problems and take quick action to prevent escalation. By and large, he enjoyed good relations with fellow Welsh rulers, particularly Rhys ap Gruffudd. Most importantly, he left as a legacy an enlarged and strong Gwynedd with a developing profile as a leading player in the Angevin state. His sons would make little of this, but his grandson, Llywelyn ab Iorwerth, would benefit greatly from the policies and precedents of Owain.

The Lord Rhys

Throughout the reign of Owain in the north, Deheubarth had been enjoying a resurgence, coordinated by the sons of Gruffudd ap Rhys. Much of their activity has been described above, and by 1154, the Welsh once more held nearly all of the former kingdom. Gruffudd had left four sons who cooperated and collaborated with each other loyally, but accident and death meant that by 1155, Rhys was sole ruler of the rebuilt lands.[22] He was probably the youngest of the brothers, but he was an experienced and talented war-leader, committed to a policy of expansion and independence which he would pursue throughout his long life. Where Owain Gwynedd showed himself willing to accept the dominion of Henry II, for almost the first twenty years of Henry's reign, Rhys remained resolutely inimical. Henry had settled matters with Gwynedd, Powys and the rest of Wales in 1157; in 1158, he turned his attention south. Rhys initially was willing to negotiate, but the terms imposed on him by the king were harsh. Henry required him to surrender almost all the lands he and his brothers had gained since 1137, including Ceredigion (to be restored to the Clares) and Cantref Bychan (to be restored to the Cliffords). Rhys was left with Cantref Mawr and a few outlying places, a situation he was unwilling to accept. The reinstated Marcher lords rapidly proved themselves unfriendly, moreover, and in the summer of 1157, Walter Clifford raided Rhys's lands near Llandovery. Rhys retaliated, seizing Llandovery himself and sending his nephew to attack Humfrey's Castle. Rhys then marched into Ceredigion, burning and raiding Anglo-Norman settlements. Henry II was obliged to return to Wales with an army and make new terms with Rhys. The details are not known, but peace endured only two years. In 1159 Rhys attacked the Marcher strongholds in Dyfed, besieging Carmarthen. Anglo-Norman forces, assisted by the sons of Owain Gwynedd, drove him back to Cantref Mawr but were unable to achieve a decisive victory. Another truce was arranged, and this one lasted until 1162. In that year, Rhys again took Llandovery castle. Henry II had been absent in his French lands since 1158: he returned to England in January 1163 and set in motion a campaign to deal with Rhys. He led an army into Wales, marching through Glamorgan, Gower and Carmarthen, to meet with Rhys at Pencader, near the border of Ceredigion. Rhys came to meet the king in good faith, but found himself seized and carried off into England as a prisoner. In July 1163, after much deliberation by Henry, Rhys did homage at Woodstock. He was not alone in the act, as was described above, and the ceremony had immediate and violent consequences in Wales. Rhys, returning to his lands, launched a new invasion of Ceredigion, seizing nearly all of it. As has been shown, Henry led an army to suppress the Welsh, but with little or no success. Rhys consolidated his hold over Ceredigion by taking its last stronghold, Cardigan, then moved south to take Cilgerran and Cantref Bychan, driving out the hated Cliffords.

In 1171, after nearly a decade of continued conflict, Henry II finally returned to Wales, but this time without hostile intent. He needed peace in Wales and the support of its leaders, of whom Rhys was now the most prominent, following the death of Owain in 1170. Henry was still facing troubles in his French lands, and over his quarrel with Becket: he was also facing a new, and dangerously independent initiative from some of his nobility. Since 1169, members of the Anglo-Norman nobility of south Wales had been engaged in new colonization, this time in Ireland, whither they had been invited by one of its kings, Diarmait Mac Murchada of Leinster.[23] Foremost amongst this group was the powerful Richard de Clare, whose family laid claim to Ceredigion, and whom Henry distrusted. Richard had married Diarmait's daughter and stood to inherit Leinster upon Diarmait's death, making him a king in his own right. This new circumstance was threatening to Henry, who was already faced with considerable disloyalty amongst his nobility, and he determined to go to Ireland himself and impose his direct control over his errant lords. Rhys was an old enemy of Richard, and occupied much of his lands: peace and friendship between Henry and Rhys would create a power-bloc which would both threaten and restrict Richard's resources. In the autumn of 1171, Henry met with Rhys in the Forest of Dean, where the groundwork was laid for an entirely new relationship between them, and a tribute imposed on Rhys. Henry then came into Wales, en route for Ireland, and held a second meeting with Rhys at Pembroke. At it, he confirmed Rhys in his possession of not only Cantref Mawr, but of Ceredigion, Ystrad Tywi, Cantref Bychan and Emlyn – all the lands he had seized from the Anglo-Normans. Additionally, Efelffre and Ystlwyf were granted to Rhys, leaving him holding almost the whole of Deheubarth. This was not all: Henry eased the terms of the tribute payment, and restored to Rhys his son Hywel, who had been the kings hostage. In return, Rhys acknowledged Henry as his overlord.

This agreement, it has long been recognized, was a turning point for Rhys. It ended his long enmity with Henry and transformed him from distrusted rebel to

Strata Florida Abbey.

honoured ally, a status he would retain until Henry's death. Moreover, the death of Owain Gwynedd had led to a succession dispute in Gwynedd between his sons. As a result, from 1171-2, Rhys emerged as the supreme leader within native Wales. In 1172, Henry returned from Ireland and met with Rhys again at Talacharn. The king appointed him Justice of south Wales – a position of great honour and responsibility – conferring upon him jurisdictional control over all the native nobility and petty royalty of southern Wales (including the south-east). Rhys was now the highest effective power in south Wales, in the eyes of the Welsh and English alike. He established two centres of power. One was at Dinefwr in the Tywi valley on the site of an old Iron Age hillfort with strong legendary associations, serving to tie Rhys's dominion explicitly to ancient native traditions and beliefs, and to emphasize its roots in antiquity. The other centre served equally important ideological functions. It was at Cardigan, which had been one of the first Norman bridgeheads in Wales, and which Rhys himself had worked long and hard to seize from its settlers. By identifying himself and his rule with it, Rhys reasserted his key role in the Welsh revival, and his triumph over the invaders, and reminded his Marcher neighbours of his new status and rank. He had the castles on these sites rebuilt in stone, and, in 1176, he held a major cultural and social gathering at Cardigan, which included national competitions in music and poetry, and which is often regarded as the first Eisteddfod. Certainly, the meeting served to mark his standing, being attended by people from throughout

Aberystwyth Castle.

Wales. The long period of stability which followed the agreement of 1171-2, allowed Rhys to pay attention to other civil matters also. He became a notable patron of the church, favouring not only those churches with a long established position in Wales, but also the new monasteries which had been established by Norman settlers earlier in the twelfth century. He founded the two houses, the Premonstratensian monastery of Talyllychau, and the Cistercian nunnery of Llanllyr; and made grants to the Benedictines of Cardigan, the Knights' Hospitallers of Slebech, and the Cistercians of Strata Florida, amongst others. It is likely, also, that he instituted administrative reforms within his own lands, transforming the way in which renders due to him were paid from dues paid in goods and food to money payments.[24] It has been recently suggested that he may have fostered the development of native towns at Aberystwyth and Rhayader.[25] Although no original documents issued by Rhys survive, later copies show that he used the title 'prince', rather than 'king'.[26] This does not necessarily imply, however, that he considered himself to hold a lesser status than his forebears: it has been argued that by his time, the title king had become somewhat dilute in Wales, used by a series of petty chiefdoms whose power and rank did not compare with the powers wielded by Anglo-Norman and continental kings. 'Prince' may have come to symbolize an individual with more defined and clear dominion, and whose status and rank was recognized by external powers as well as by native Welsh.[27] To later generations, he has come to be known, however, as 'The Lord Rhys', a title not certainly used by him in his lifetime, and which may reflect on the assumptions and ideology of the thirteenth century and later – in at least parts of Wales, the idea developed that only the rulers of Gwynedd could properly be called princes.[28]

Despite royal favour and despite the long period of relative peace, Rhys's position was not completely secure. His principality lacked strong natural boundaries, and confrontations continued between Welsh nobility and Marcher lordships in the Welsh March. To defend both his own lands and Welsh rights, Rhys needed strong alliances and good relations with his neighbours, Welsh and English. He cultivated a complex network of marriage ties with native Welsh lords throughout southern Wales. The lord of Meirionydd was his first cousin, the lords of Elfael and Gwrtheyrnion were his sons-in law, the lords of Aberafan and Senghenydd were his nephews, and the lord of Upper Gwent was his brother-in-law. In 1175, he brought all of them to a meeting with Henry II at Gloucester, where they reconfirmed their allegiance both to prince and to king. Rhys also sought to build relations with the Anglo-Norman lords: he married two daughters to Marcher barons in Cemais, a territory key to the defence of Cardigan, and he betrothed his son Gruffudd to the daughter of William de Braose, one of the most powerful Marcher lords. It fell to Rhys to try to regulate and control relations between native lords and Marchers, a task which cannot always have been easy. There were a series of murders and feuds in the border lands of Maelienydd and Elfael in the 1170s, which threatened stability in Wales. Rhys intervened with the king and restrained his fellow Welsh. To some extent, he received help from Henry in this: in 1179, Henry imprisoned Roger Mortimer, a member of a powerful Marcher family, in punishment for the latter's persecution of the Welsh lords of Maelienydd and Elfael. But king and prince could not completely prevent the feuds, and in 1182 the long-running feud between the de Braose family and the Welsh lords of Upper Gwent escalated to a point where Henry's justiciar in England, Ranulf Glanville, had to restore peace to the territory by force. In 1184, Rhys met with Henry at Worcester and the feud was discussed: Rhys promised to put an end to the problems, buying off a possible new invasion. He left a son with Henry as a hostage for his performance of this pledge. At a further meeting in 1185, Rhys was unable to report favourable progress, but it seems that despite this he retained the king's trust. Their relationship was doubtless often uneasy, and subject to considerable strains. Yet despite this, both men demonstrated a continued commitment to maintaining and upholding it – Rhys going so far as to send his son, Hywel Sais, to join Henry in France in 1173, when the latter was facing a serious rebellion from his own sons. And in the spring of 1174, Rhys himself led a troop of Welshmen to help royal forces against the rebels at Tutbury. The relationship between Rhys and Henry may not have been overly friendly, but it was important enough for both men to be willing to work at sustaining it.

Their meeting in 1185 was their last, but Rhys continued in contact with Henry's representatives. In 1186, he met with Glanville and with Archbishop Baldwin of Canterbury at Hereford, and in 1188 he hosted the archbishop on his journey through Wales to preach the crusade. More so even than Owain Gwynedd, Rhys had become a part of the wider political life of the Angevin Empire.

Llanstephan Castle.

Henry died in 1189, and his death provided Rhys with a new opportunity. The period 1171-1189 had allowed him to consolidate his pre-eminence in native Wales: now he had a chance to recommence the expansion of his direct territorial control. The new king, Richard I, was preoccupied with affairs overseas, and he and his government had little attention for or interest in Welsh matters. On Henry's death, Rhys launched a new offensive against the Anglo-Norman colonies in south Wales, attacking the castles of Talacharn, Llanstephan, and Carmarthen. Quite why he resumed expansion is not known: it has been suggested that he was offended by the attitude of Richard's new government, or that he was under pressure from his numerous, ambitious, and now adult sons.[29] It may equally have been that he had not lost his old ambition, and, as in his earlier career, was ready to take advantage of the new circumstances. Richard's brother, Prince John, met with the Welsh princes at Worcester to try and make peace, and later in the same year, Rhys went to Oxford, hoping to meet with Richard. Richard, however, did not come, and Rhys, returning to Wales, returned to the attack. By December 1189, Richard had left England with no agreement made with the Welsh. Rhys seized and strengthened Cydweli in 1190, in 1191 he moved into Cemais, in 1192 he attacked Deugleddyf and Swansea, and in 1193, he seized Wiston castle.

By now, however, a new difficulty had arisen. Rhys had many sons, amongst whom rivalries ran high. Several of them had been involved in the rebellion, and were operating with their own interests in mind. In 1189, Rhys had imprisoned

Chart 4: Descendants of
the Lord Rhys.

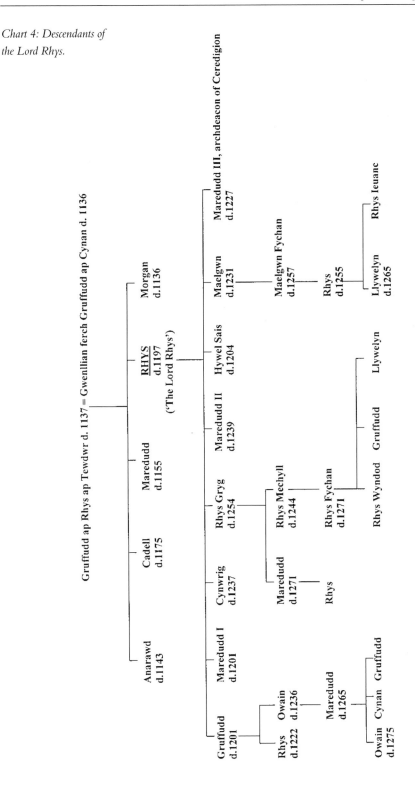

one of them, Maelgwn, at the instigation of another, Gruffudd, and Maelgwn was then handed over to William de Braose. He was released in 1192 and returned to south Wales, where he continued to work against Gruffudd. In 1194, Gruffudd and a third son, Hywel Sais, captured and imprisoned Rhys himself. His sons were preparing the way for war over his lands: Gruffudd seems to have been his favoured heir, but under Welsh law, all the sons were potential princes, and each sought the advantage of himself or his faction. Rhys was released before the end of 1194, but in 1195 faced an attack from two more sons, Rhys Gryg and Maredudd. These two seized Llanamdyffri and Dinefwr: Rhys captured and imprisoned them at Ystrad Meurig in Ceredigion, far from Cantref Mawr and Cantref Bychan where they had built up a following. The troubles within his family were not over, but this event seems to have given Rhys at least a temporary respite, and time to resume his activities against the Anglo-Normans. In 1196, he burnt Carmarthen and annexed the important territory of Buellt. From there, he struck out against Radnor, defeating an Anglo-Norman force there, and invaded Lower Elfael, where he came to terms with William de Braose. These border lands were crucial to the defence of Deheubarth, and the legacy of feuds in the 1170s and 1180s had left Rhys with the knowledge that he must dominate them to be secure.

Rhys ap Gruffudd died on 28 April 1197 and was buried at St Davids, prince of a vastly expanded Deheubarth and head of all the native rulers of southern Wales. He had built up a network of alliances which protected his borders and had used the long peace of 1171-1189 not only to foster the church and the arts but to institute reforms which served both to bolster his authority and to simplify the administration of his lands. He had acquired and maintained the respect of Henry II, and may have been the first native ruler to have his powers and status recognized and formalized by the English state. His contemporary and kinsman Gerald of Wales, who knew him, described him as 'open in his behaviour and of such great natural kindness',[30] while the *Brutiau* included in their obituaries for him two Latin poems, describing him as the 'glory of Wales' and the 'noble diadem of Welsh grace'.[31] He was respected both in Wales and in England, and his reign would be the last great peak of southern Welsh power. Yet, like so many other Welsh rulers, he was unable to transmit his lands and his status intact to any one of his sons, and as a result, the rebuilt Deheubarth he had created did not endure. The reason for this lay partly in geography: it lacked strong natural boundaries, and contained a number of Anglo-Norman enclaves, leaving it vulnerable to attack and annexation. But the main reason was the disunity amongst his many sons. None of them was willing to submit to any of the others; none of them were strong enough to dominate or control the others. The result was, on Rhys's death, new divisions and conflicts erupted, which dismantled Deheubarth for the final time.

6 Llywelyn ap Iorwerth:

c.1194 - 1240

The succession to Owain Gwynedd

The death of Owain Gwynedd in 1170 was a set-back for Gwynedd. He had had several sons of whom the eldest was Hywel. In Owain's lifetime, Hywel had enjoyed considerable success as a military leader, and had been established in Ceredigion. He had played an important part in the internal conflict between Owain and the latter's brother Cadwaladr, and probably enjoyed Owain's full confidence, as well as being well connected with the influential nobility of both Gwynedd and the other lands subject to it.[1] He may well have been Owain's chosen candidate for successor, and certainly was well-placed to make a bid for power. Owain, however, had sons by several women and unity by no means reigned amongst them. The most determined cabal was that centred on Owain's widow, Cristin ferch Goronwy ab Owain, and her two sons, Dafydd and Rhodri. Cristin came of a powerful family – none other than that line from Tegeingl which, in the persons of the brothers, Owain and Uchdryd, sons of Edwin, had caused so much trouble to Cadwgan ab Bleddyn and Owain ap Cadwgan. She was Owain Gwynedd's first cousin, and pressure had been brought to bear on him towards the end of his life to divorce her on grounds of consanguinity. This Owain had refused to do, perhaps motivated by the need to resist interference from England, but perhaps also by an attachment to Cristin herself. As a result of her position and family, Cristin possessed intimate knowledge of the workings of the Venedotian court, perhaps greater than that possessed by Hywel, who spent long periods away from his family's heartland. Hywel was in Gwynedd shortly after Owain's death, but within months he too was dead, killed in battle at Pentraeth in Anglesey against his half-brothers, the sons of Cristin. Once Hywel was removed, the kingdom was divided between some or all of the surviving sons of Owain Gwynedd, with Dafydd perhaps taking the lead amongst them. Relations between Owain's remaining sons were, for a time, peaceful. Dafydd, however, was ambitious, and within a few years he turned on another half-brother, Maelgwn, who had been holding all or part of Anglesey. Dafydd attacked him, driving him into temporary exile in Ireland. Maelgwn returned in or by 1174, only to be captured and imprisoned by Dafydd, who by now was embarked on a full-scale campaign to control all Gwynedd. One of his half-brothers, Cynan, who had been holding Meirionydd, Eifionydd and Ardudwy, died of natural causes during 1174, but he left two sons, Gruffudd and Maredudd, who inherited his lands. Dafydd's full brother, Rhodri, was also still living and ruling part of the kingdom, but during the course of 1174, Dafydd expelled all three of them at least temporarily.[2] He imprisoned Rhodri, who had returned to make a bid to regain his lands in 1174, but his position was

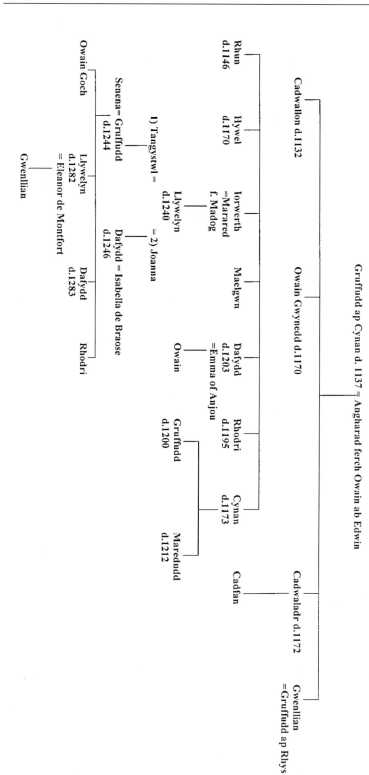

Chart 5: The royal line of Gwynedd in the twelfth and thirteenth centuries.

insecure. Dafydd stood to benefit from finding a powerful ally outside Gwynedd, and during 1174, opened negotiations with Henry II. At this time, Henry was facing problems in England, and in need of peace in Wales. He therefore acceded to Dafydd's request for permission to marry Emma of Anjou, Henry's illegitimate half-sister. Dafydd was a far less useful potential ally for Henry than Rhys of Deheubarth, and his influence was much smaller, but his lands abutted the English border, and he might well cause trouble in the March. The marriage of Dafydd and Emma took place before the end of 1174. However, also before the end of 1174, Rhodri escaped from prison, and effectively turned the tables on his brother. Very swiftly, Dafydd found himself driven out not only of Anglesey but of all of Gwynedd west of the River Conwy. Restricted to eastern Gwynedd, he agreed to come to terms with his brother. The division of Gwynedd was reinstated, Rhodri holding Anglesey and Gwynedd uwch Conwy, Dafydd Gwynedd is Conwy (including Tegeingl) and the sons of Cynan being restored to their father's lands of Meirionydd, Ardudwy and Eifionydd. This division endured for some years to come. Dafydd had gained less than he had hoped from his marriage, and in 1177, at a meeting of all the rulers and lords of native Wales with Henry II, Dafydd persuaded the king to grant him the manor of Ellesmere in Shropshire. In return, Dafydd swore homage. The division and lack of unity amongst the sons and grandsons of Owain Gwynedd contributed to the rise to supremacy in native Wales of Rhys ap Gruffudd, and at the same meeting, Henry showed that he valued Rhys far more than Dafydd or Rhodri, granting to Rhys the right to Meirionydd, despite the sons of Cynan ab Owain (who had not come to the meeting). Henry clearly saw that Rhys was far more effective than any of the line of Gwynedd. After the 1170s, Dafydd would make little impact, and his attempts at domination of the north ended. He had not inherited Owain Gwynedd's gift of leadership, but perhaps he did possess at least one of the qualities of his paternal grandfather, Gruffudd ap Cynan: Gerald of Wales noted of him that he demonstrated 'good faith and credit by observing a strict neutrality between the Welsh and the English'.[3] His marriage alliance had not brought him the royal support he may have wanted, but he was adept at avoiding confrontation with the king and the Marcher lords, a skill for which he would have cause to be grateful later in life.

The rise of Llywelyn ap Iorwerth

Amongst the sons of Owain Gwynedd was one who seems to have played little or no part in the struggle for control of Gwynedd. This was Iorwerth Drwyndwn (flat-nosed), who had been born to Owain by Gwladus ferch Llywarch ap Trahaearn of Arwystli. Llywarch's father, Trahaearn, had been king of Gwynedd 1075-1081, and while it is unlikely that Llywarch himself ever had any hopes of obtaining that kingdom, he had forcefully asserted his independence from the kings of Gwynedd and of Powys in the early decades of the twelfth century. His lands in Arwystli were a key zone in the route south from Gwynedd into Ceredigion and Ystrad Tywi, and his goodwill would have been of great use to the rulers of Gwynedd in their rivalry with Powys. By the mid-1120s, Llywarch was found amongst the allies of Gruffudd ap Cynan and his sons, opposed to Maredudd ab Bleddyn and his nephews of Powys. Owain's marriage to Gwladus may have been a consequence or even a condition of this alliance,[4] and Iorwerth may have been among his elder sons. Unlike Hywel ab Owain, Iorwerth seems to have played no part in Welsh political life. Later tradition insisted that Iorwerth had been in some way disfigured or disabled, and this had excluded him from power. Lloyd suggested that Iorwerth may have held lands in Arfon, perhaps the commot of Nanconwy, on the basis of a line in a poem of Seisyll Bryffwch.[5] If this is so, however, we do not know when he was there, or for how long, or, indeed, even if his lordship post-dated his father's death. Just as Hywel and Cadwaladr held lands in Ceredigion in Owain's lifetime, and Dafydd seems to have had influence in Tegeingl, Iorwerth may have been provided with lands closer to the heartland by his father, particularly if he was in some way debarred from warfare. Iorwerth made no impact on the historical record, being noted only in reference to his famous son, and he seems to have been dead by or before the mid-1170s. He married Marared ferch Madog ap Maredudd of Powys, and it is possible their son Llywelyn was brought up largely outside Gwynedd (which in the 1180s may not have been a safe environment for a child with a claim to a share of land and power). Charter evidence suggests that Marared remarried into a Shropshire Marcher family, the Corbets of Caux.[6] The Corbet lands abutted on Powys, and a Corbet might have seemed a suitable husband for a widowed Powysian princess. If Marared did marry into the Corbets, then Llywelyn may have received part of his upbringing and education in the March. Throughout his life, Llywelyn would show himself adept both at dealing with the Marcher lords, and with negotiating the complex world of English court politics. This could well be a by-product of an education in the mixed Anglo-Welsh world of the March.[7]

Llywelyn launched his bid for power in Gwynedd by the early 1190s at the latest. Gwynedd was still divided, with the east subject to Dafydd ab Owain, the north-west to Rhodri ab Owain, and Meirionydd to the sons of Cynan ab Owain. Rhodri and the sons of Cynan had been engaged in disputes over the control of western Gwynedd in the early 1190s, with Rhodri at one point being expelled by his nephews, and reinstated in 1193 with the help of the king of Man, whose daughter he had married. By the end of the year, the sons of Cynan had once again driven him out. The situation was volatile, and the nobility divided in their loyalties. The young Llywelyn formed an alliance with his cousins, Maredudd and Gruffudd, sons of Cynan, who were at the time in the strongest position within Gwynedd, and together they struck east against Dafydd, defeating him heavily in or near Aberconwy, and capturing much of his territory. Rhodri may also have been involved in this battle, perhaps out of expedience, on the side of Llywelyn and the sons of Cynan. Rhodri by now was ageing, and died the following year, in 1195. His lands at first seem to have passed to the sons of Cynan, while Llywelyn established himself in some or all of Dafydd's territories.

1197 saw a major change in the political map of Wales, with the deaths both of the Lord Rhys and of Owain Cyfeiliog of Powys. In the north, in that same year, Llywelyn finally encompassed the complete defeat of Dafydd ab Owain. After a period of captivity, Dafydd left for England with his wife and son, and established himself in his manor of Ellesmere. He remained there until his death. Llywelyn now held a substantial block of territory in the north-east, and began to look for new routes of expansion. He formed a brief alliance with the new king of southern Powys, Gwenwynwyn ab Owain Cyfeiliog, assisting him in a major, but unsuccessful campaign in the Middle March in 1198. Gwenwynwyn had just annexed Arwystli, had made a series of attacks on the March, and was involving himself in the civil war which had broken out between the sons of the Lord Rhys in south Wales: he was this time rather stronger than Llywelyn, and better connected into the network of native alliances, kinship and patronage. In the north-west, the sons of Cynan ab Owain were still strong, but in 1200 one of them – Gruffudd – died. Down to this point, Llywelyn had made no moves towards their territories, but this death presented him with a new opportunity. In 1201, he moved west, seizing Eifionydd and Llŷn from Gruffudd's brother, Maredudd, leaving the latter with no more than Meirionydd. But Gruffudd had left a son, Hywel, who in 1202 attacked and expelled Maredudd from this final area. Hywel would prove to be a loyal supporter and ally of Llywelyn, who now had the whole of Gwynedd under his control.

Despite this, Llywelyn's position in the first years of the thirteenth century was not unassailable. He had driven out or subjugated his rivals in Gwynedd, but the history of the last twenty years had shown that these same rivals were able and willing to continue to pursue their claims by war even after expulsion. Moreover, he had a powerful neighbour to the south and east, in the shape of Gwenwynwyn, and the quarrelling heirs of the Lord Rhys in the south were partly within Gwenwynwyn's orbit. He also faced an England under a determined and largely resident king, John, and a ring of powerful Marcher lordships. To survive, and to expand, Llywelyn needed not only peace and control at home, but secure relations with his neighbours. In 1201, he entered into negotiations with John, and as a result, a treaty was drawn up between them in July. The text of the treaty still survives: Llywelyn and his leading men swore service and promised homage to the king, while John conceded that either Welsh or English law might be employed in lands subject to Llywelyn, thus giving royal recognition to the existence of a separate legal practice in Wales. As R.R. Davies has pointed out, law and rights to homage of the native nobility were to be perhaps the two dominant themes of Anglo-Welsh relations in the thirteenth century.[8] Four years later, the relationship between Llywelyn and John was further cemented when Llywelyn married John's illegitimate daughter, Joanna.

The marriage was of considerable significance. Other Welsh rulers had married into Anglo-Saxon or Anglo-Norman nobility, and partly as a result of this, the society of the March of Wales had developed complex networks of kinship, blood-ties and alliance. Llywelyn's uncle, Dafydd, had sought royal favour and protection by his marriage to Emma. Llywelyn had been seeking for a politically advantageous marriage for some time – in the years down to 1203, he negotiated to marry a daughter of the King of Man. Such a marriage would require papal dispensation, as the daughter in question had previously been married to his uncle

Rhodri. This dispensation was granted in April 1203, but Llywelyn did not act on it. The reason lies in his dealing with England. By this time, he was securely in possession of Gwynedd, and, having gained his treaty with John, had begun to move against Welsh rivals outside Gwynedd. In 1202, after the expulsion from Meirionydd of his cousin Maredudd, he gathered a force to strike against Gwenwynwyn. The *Brutiau* present this almost as an act of necessity, provoked by the (albeit undetailed) hostility of Gwenwynwyn.[9] Apart from their brief alliance in 1198, we know almost nothing of the relations between Llywelyn and Gwenwynwyn in this period, but Gwenwynwyn had ambitions to power in the south and the west, and might have perceived Llywelyn's expansion into Meirionydd as threatening. Similarly, Gwenwynwyn's influence in Ceredigion and Arwystli threatened the security of Llywelyn's borders. Gwenwynwyn himself is something of an enigma. He had considerable political influence in the mid-1190s, and, like Llywelyn, enjoyed the favour of John in the early years of the thirteenth century. On the basis of an entry in the *Brutiau,* it has been suggested that in his early years, he may have looked to make himself the leading political force in Wales.[10] His activities in 1196-98 concentrated on the expansion of his power into those areas bordering Powys – western Shropshire (parts of which he annexed at least temporarily), Arwystli and Ceredigion. In 1198, he formed an alliance with a number of other native leaders and invaded English holdings in Elfael. It is not clear, however, that he sought in any way to intervene in Gwynedd, or to re-annex northern Powys: as R.R. Davies has argued, he seems rather to have seen himself as the successor to the position of the Lord Rhys in south and central Wales, a position he continued to try to retain down to around 1208.[11] His major problems, however, were the demands of John, who proved an unreliable overlord, and the ambitions of Llywelyn, who would continue the long-established history of intermittent conflict between Powys and Gwynedd.[12] In 1202, Llywelyn summoned to him all the leading nobility of his lands. One of them, Elise ap Madog, lord of Penllyn, was loath to become involved in war with Gwenwynwyn, raising questions of his loyalty. Penllyn lay between the lands of Llywelyn and Gwenwynwyn, and probably on the intended route of Llywelyn's army. His support was thus key to Llywelyn, but his reluctance, given his vulnerable position to the rulers of both principalities, is easy to understand. Deprived of this particular ally, Llywelyn decided instead to make peace with Gwenwynwyn, via the mediation of the clergy. However, Elise's reluctance did not go unpunished – Llywelyn did not wish to give the impression that his actions might be overly influenced by the behaviour of any one of his lords. Llywelyn drove Elise from most of Penllyn, probably taking most of it into his own hands, and thus giving himself an important foothold on Gwenwynwyn's borders. His behaviour cannot have gone unnoticed by the English court. A marriage between Llywelyn and the daughter of the king of Man would give him support and a potential source of military aid from outside the lands controlled by John. It was thus in John's interest to entice the increasingly powerful Llywelyn into his own circle. Llywelyn also stood to gain from a marriage into John's family. John was attached to his children, far more than Henry II had been to his half-sister. The marriage to Joanna brought not only royal support for Llywelyn and potential security for his lands. It gave him a chance to enter the network of blood- and marriage-ties which bound the leading rulers throughout western Europe. Llywelyn's children by Joanna would be grandchildren of the current king of England, and first cousins of the next – a considerable advantage. By granting the marriage of Joanna to Llywelyn, John was in effect recognizing Llywelyn's status and position as prince of north Wales and as a ruler of lesser, but still not inconsiderable, power. The exact date of the marriage is not known, but Llywelyn received as Joanna's marriage portion the manor of Ellesmere in Shropshire. Dafydd ab Owain had died in 1203 and the manor had reverted to the king.

Llywelyn's relations with John remained largely good throughout the first decade of the thirteenth century. In 1208, Gwenwynwyn fell foul of the king, and, at a peace meeting in October at Shrewsbury, was taken into royal captivity. Llywelyn was quick to exploit this. Gwenwynwyn's lands had been declared to be in the hands of the king, but Llywelyn quickly launched an invasion, and seized possession of them. His movement threatened the native lords of Deheubarth, and one of them, Maelgwn ap Rhys, burnt the castles of Ystrad Meurig, Dineirth and Aberystwyth to prevent them falling into Llywelyn's hands. Llywelyn, however, having annexed southern Powys, now had designs on Ceredigion. He occupied the cantref of Penweddig, and reconstructed Aberystwyth.

Up to this point, he had played no part in the complex politics of the south, where the sons and grandsons of Rhys were still engaged in a struggle for power. Now, however, Llywelyn was in a position to interfere. Northern Ceredigion was in his hands. He kept Penweddig, closest to Meirionydd, for himself, but gave the rest – the area between the rivers Aeron and Ystwyth – to the sons of Gruffudd ap Rhys, nephews and rivals of Maelgwn, thus seeking to create a client lordship in the south.

His power was now growing noticeably, and it was necessary to defuse potential royal suspicion. Llywelyn made a show of his loyalty to the king in 1209, accompanying John north on his expedition against the king of Scots. For a Welsh ruler to go so far from his lands in support of a neighbour or overlord was almost unprecedented: earlier kings and princes of Wales had lent troops for campaigns away from the Welsh to Anglo-Saxon and Anglo-Norman kings and noblemen,[13] or had supported royal or noble activity in the March,[14] but before Llywelyn ap Iorwerth, only Owain ap Cadwgan and Hywel Sais may have travelled so far in the company of the king of England.[15] Llywelyn was, however, determined to retain his independence within Wales, as his actions towards Powys and Ceredigion showed, and he resisted interference in Welsh affairs. During the period of his marriage negotiations he had involved himself in the campaign to reduce the influence of Canterbury over St Davids. It appears that he was willing to deal with John but in return he expected recognition of his full status as a ruler with separate powers.

In 1210, relations between the two deteriorated. John had been in Ireland trying to curb the power of the de Braose and Lacey families. The expedition was a success, and the rebellious William de Braose fled to France. The absence of the king, and the uncertainty created in the March by the rebellion of two of its major families, however, had created new opportunities. The earl of Chester rebuilt Degannwy castle, perceived by Llywelyn as a threat. Llywelyn retaliated by ravaging the earl's lands. In the south, Rhys Gryg, son of the Lord Rhys, allied with royal troops, attacked and seized Llandovery castle. Llandovery belonged to Rhys and Owain, young sons of Gruffudd ap Rhys who were allies of Llywelyn. Rhys Gryg's action, supported by the king, was more than just another stage in the complex battle for control of the south. It was a move against the influence of Llywelyn. It was only the first sign of a new hostility on the part of John. Royal troops were lent also to Gwenwynwyn, who had been living in England as the king's dependent since 1208, and with their help, he was reinstated in southern Powys. Maelgwn ap Rhys, another of the sons of the Lord Rhys, and Gwenwynwyn's ally, sought terms with the king and then took the field against Rhys and Owain, sons of Gruffudd. Llywelyn's position as the premier ruler within Wales was under threat: he moved to protect it. By 1211, he was leading regular raids in the March.

The same year, John prepared an expedition against Gwynedd, planning, says *Brut y Tywysogyon,* 'to dispossess Llywelyn and destroy him utterly'.[16] John summoned to him at Chester all the major native Welsh leaders – Gwenwynwyn, Maelgwn ap Rhys and his brother Rhys Gryg, two of the claimants to the south, and, most seriously, two of Llywelyn's allies, Hywel ap Gruffudd ap Cynan of Meirionydd and Madog ap Gruffudd Maelor of Powys Fadog. Only the sons of Gruffudd ap Rhys held aloof. John was bound on the total subjugation of Llywelyn. Llywelyn retreated into the uplands of Gwynedd ahead of the advance, but although reaching Degannwy, John's army was forced back by problems with supplies. He was not deterred, however, and by August had returned with a new, larger army. This time, the royal forces crossed the Conwy into the heartland of Gwynedd, burning Bangor and even penetrating Snowdonia. Llywelyn, almost his whole principality overrun, had no choice other than to come to terms. He sent Joanna to her father to sue for peace on any terms. Those imposed were harsh: John deprived Llywelyn of all of the Perfeddwlad, demanded twenty hostages, and required a heavy tribute in cattle and horses. In the south, the sons of Gruffudd were likewise forced to come to terms, and to surrender to John the land between the rivers Dyfi and Aeron.

John's triumph was short-lived. The terms were too severe, and created a backlash of resentment against him. In 1212, a cabal of native leaders formed under Llywelyn's leadership. With his new allies – who included Gwenwynwyn, Maelgwn ap Rhys, and Madog ap Gruffudd Maelor – Llywelyn besieged and took all John's castles in Gwynedd apart from Degannwy and Rhuddlan. In Powys, the royal castle at Mathrafal was besieged, and although the Welsh did not take it, John was forced to burn it to prevent it falling into their hands. John was facing rebellion within England, also, and his resources were over-stretched. He executed several of the Welsh hostages, and planned a new campaign in Wales. But this was abandoned when he was warned of a plot by his nobility to assassinate him. Llywelyn was able to retake the Perfeddwlad, including Rhuddlan and Degannwy, by the end of 1213. He sought help from the other enemies of John, and in the summer of 1212 sought an alliance with Philip Augustus of France.[17] By now, John was faced with considerable conflict within England, and was powerless against the Welsh resurgence. By the end of 1215, Llywelyn and his Welsh allies had captured Shrewsbury, Carmarthen, Emlyn, Trefdraeth, Cilgerran, and Cardigan. Cemais had been plundered, Cydweli and Carnwyllion subdued, the castles of Arberth, Maenclochog, Loughor, Tal-y-Bont, and Oystermouth, burnt, and Llanstephan, St Clears and Talacharn razed in campaigns in the south by Rhys ap Gruffudd, Maelgwn ap Rhys and Llywelyn.

Their successes were due in part to the conflict in England. In June 1215, John was forced to compound with his nobility. The ensuing agreement, recorded in Magna Carta, had consequences for Wales as well as England. Under its terms, John had to release Llywelyn's hostages and restore to the Welsh the privileges withdrawn from them in 1211. In 1216, after the successes of the campaigns of the previous year, Llywelyn held a meeting at Aberdyfi at which he shared out the new conquests amongst his allies from south Wales. Maelgwn was granted Cantref Gwarthaf, Cemais, Emlyn, Peuliniog, and Cilgerran castle in Dyfed, Hirfryn, Mallaen and Llandovery castle in Ystrad Tywi, and Gwynionydd, and Mabwynion in Ceredigion. The sons of Gruffudd received three cantrefs in Ceredigion, and the castles of Nantyrarian and Cardigan. Rhys Gryg received Dinefwr, Cydweli, Carnwyllion and most of Cantref Bychan and Cantref Mawr. It is likely that at the same time, Llywelyn received the homage of these lords: what is clear is that by 1216 he was widely accepted as the pre-eminent ruler in Wales.

1216 saw the removal of two major enemies. Gwenwynwyn had participated in the rebellion, but in 1216 he made terms with John, renouncing his former pact with Llywelyn. Llywelyn invaded Powys Wenwynwyn with the help of his southern allies, and expelled Gwenwynwyn for the final time. Gwenwynwyn died shortly afterwards in England, leaving underage heirs. Llywelyn entered an agreement with the English government whereby the lands would remain in his hands until the heir was of age: in the event, he was to hold it until his own death. Also in 1216, in October, John died. His heir, Henry III, was a minor, and the minority government was more cautious towards Wales. In March 1218 Llywelyn met the new king at Worcester, and peace was declared. Llywelyn did homage to Henry, and was confirmed in all his lands, including those he had conquered during the civil war.

Having achieved a position of supremacy, Llywelyn moved to secure it. Like Rhys ap Gruffudd, he took steps to create a network of connexions in the March to complement those he had within native Wales. He entered into a series of marriage alliances with various Marcher families. He had married one of his daughters, Gwladus, to Reginald de Braose, who held extensive lands in the former kingdom of Brycheiniog and around Abergavenny, probably in 1215, during the civil war. Reginald was part of the baronial faction which Llywelyn had joined, and the marriage helped reinforce the ties between them in the short term. It had long term implications also: the de Braose family were influential at the

Oystermouth Castle.

royal court as well as in the March, and had long been a problem for the native Welsh lords. By binding Reginald to him through marriage, Llywelyn hoped to reduce the de Braose threat to Welsh sovereignty, and to provide himself with a secure and stable friend in a sensitive area. In the event, Reginald proved an unreliable ally, and Llywelyn gave another daughter, Marared, to Reginald's nephew, John de Braose. John had lands in Gower, and a claim on lands held by Reginald. He thus provided Llywelyn with an ally who might act as a check and even a threat on Reginald. A third daughter, Elen, was married to John, the heir of the earl of Chester, Llywelyn's eastern neighbour. Another daughter, Gwenllian, was given to William de Lacey, who held lands in Ireland as well as the March. When Gwladus was widowed in 1227-8, Llywelyn arranged a second marriage for her to Ralph Mortimer. The Mortimers, perhaps more than any other Marcher family, had proved inimical to the Welsh, and had long been involved in conflict over the control of the key area of Maelienydd in the Middle March. From Maelienydd, routes lay open west, north and south, threatening the lands both of Llywelyn and of his allies. When John de Braose died, Llywelyn arranged for Gwladus to marry another Marcher from south-east Wales, Walter Clifford, lord of Bronllys and Clifford. These marriages were designed to provide Llywelyn with a ring of relations whose lands buffered his own, and who might be called upon to support or protect him.

After the expulsion and death of Gwenwynwyn, Llywelyn faced little or no resistance to his overlordship within native Wales. The southern lords, the descendants of the Lord Rhys, abided by his settlement of their lands and remained largely loyal to him.[18] Indeed, in 1220, at his command, Rhys Gryg surrendered to the English lands he had seized from them in the 1210s. In 1225, Llywelyn arranged a new partition of lands in the south between Maelgwn ap Rhys, and Maelgwn's nephews, Owain ap Gruffudd and Cynan ap Hywel. The lord of Powys Fadog, Madog ap Gruffudd, was a reliable ally until his death in 1236; Llywelyn punished rebellion by one of Madog's sons in 1238 with expropriation. By 1230, Llywelyn adopted a new title, prince of Aberffraw and lord of Snowdon, replacing his older one of prince of north Wales. The new style played on the associations of the court of Aberffraw, legendarily the seat of the hero Bran the Blessed, and – according to the propaganda of Llywelyn's own family – endowing its holder with hegemony over all the other leaders of native Wales.[19] Despite his strength, however, Llywelyn was faced with one major potential problem: the succession to his own lands and power. The roots of the problem lay in his marriage to Joanna. At the time of the marriage, Llywelyn had already had children by a mistress, including a son, Gruffudd, and under Welsh law, illegitimate sons had as much right to inherit from their father's as legitimate sons. When he married Joanna he had undertaken to ensure that only a son by her would inherit from him, despite Welsh practice. This was a pragmatic step, but it should not be seen simply as placating the king. By the early twelfth century, ideas on marriage and legitimacy were changing in native Wales. Llywelyn had, moreover, witnessed the conflict in Deheubarth on the death of the Lord Rhys, with multiple sons by different wives and mistresses each contending for power a conflict which had led to the final destruction of any true independence in the south-west. He himself had had to fight for his rights in Gwynedd with his uncles and cousins. He wished to prevent the same kind of destructive warfare from breaking out in Gwynedd on his own death. His son by Joanna, Dafydd, was younger than Gruffudd, but he was born of a marriage which would be recognized as legal by the king and the lords of the March, and he was the first cousin of Henry III. Llywelyn chose to make Dafydd, and not Gruffudd, his official, designated heir, intending him to succeed not only to Gwynedd, but to the whole of Llywelyn's wide influence and overlordship in Wales. The marriages of Dafydd's sisters were designed as much to provide Dafydd with a network of kinsmen amongst the Marchers as to help Llywelyn himself.

In 1220, he made the first formal move in a long process. He obtained from King Henry formal recognition of Dafydd as his heir and successor. In 1222, Llywelyn obtained formal recognition of Dafydd as heir from the Pope, and in 1226, he caused the leading native lords of Wales to swear an oath recognizing Dafydd. In 1229, Dafydd did homage to Henry III as heir to Gwynedd, and in 1230, Llywelyn arranged a highly advantageous marriage for him, to Isabella de Braose, daughter of William de Braose, son of Reginald, with the promise of Buellt as her dowry.

Initially, Llywelyn tried to make provision for Gruffudd, establishing him in Meirionydd and Ardudwy. However, Gruffudd proved himself to be a harsh lord, and in 1221, Llywelyn deprived him of his lands. Gruffudd did not wholly forfeit his father's favour and in 1223 he led his father's warband on a campaign in Ystrad

Tywi. Hostilities had broken out between Llywelyn and the English, perhaps initiated by problems in the March.[20] Llywelyn seized the fortresses of Kinnerley and Whittington in the Shropshire border. The Crown used this as a pretext to seize the castles of Carmarthen and Cardigan, which Llywelyn had been holding since 1216. Gruffudd was sent to lead Llywelyn's troops to intercept the royal forces in south Wales – a position of some responsibility – although in the event no battle occurred. Royal forces also took possession of Montgomery: the Crown sought to regain control of certain key defences around Wales. The native lords in Deheubarth remained loyal to Llywelyn during this, but it was clear that the English intended to reduce Llywelyn's power in the south and the border. He chose, however, to come to terms, rather than prolonging the conflict, and peace was made in October 1223. The southern Welsh lords were returned those lands which they had lost in the campaign, but Llywelyn had to surrender Whittington and Kinnerley, without any restoration of his losses. It seems likely he preferred peace to a long-running conflict which might endanger his ties with the Welsh lords of the south, and jeopardize his negotiations over the succession to Gwynedd. By placing Gruffudd in charge of the southern expedition, Llywelyn had placed considerable trust in him. It may be that Gruffudd held the position of *penteulu*, leader of the warband, an influential office often occupied by members of the royal kin. He remained in favour until 1228, but he was by no means reconciled to his exclusion from the succession. That year, his resentment erupted into violence, and Llywelyn seized him and imprisoned him at Degannwy, where he remained until 1234. 1228 was the year before the one in which Dafydd received English recognition as heir: control over Gruffudd was necessary to this process.

The imprisonment of Gruffudd was not the end of Llywelyn's family problems. During 1228, Llywelyn had been involved in a campaign in Ceri, designed to discourage the ambition of Hubert de Burgh, who held Montgomery, to expand into that area. Llywelyn had little difficulty in achieving his aims, and by October, Hubert's pretensions were at an end. But during the course of the campaign, Llywelyn had captured the influential Marcher William de Braose, son of his former son-in-law, Reginald. William was held captive for some months, and Llywelyn used this to persuade him to grant the hand of Isabella to Dafydd.[21] The captivity was to have consequences other than marriage, however. Contact between Llywelyn and William continued after William's release, and an alliance was doubtless anticipated.[22] But at Easter 1230, Llywelyn discovered William in highly compromising circumstances with Joanna. Joanna was banished from court; William was hanged for adultery on 2 May 1230. This was not the action of a diplomat: for the only recorded time in his life, Llywelyn acted without thought, in anger and distress.

Fortunately, the king did not use William's execution as a pretext to harass Llywelyn, and their relations remained peaceful. Llywelyn quickly sought to mend affairs with the de Braose family and the marriage of Isabella to Dafydd went ahead. Joanna was restored to Llywelyn's favour during 1231. In 1231, Llywelyn embarked on another campaign to quell the ambitions of Hubert de Burgh, who

White Castle, near Abergavenny, part of the Welsh holdings of Herbert de Burgh.

had assembled considerable lands in Wales and the border. Llywelyn attacked Montgomery, Radnor, Brecon and Hay, destroying castles and towns, then marched south with the support of the Welsh lords of upland Glamorgan to attack Caerleon, Neath and Cydweli. Finally, with the help of the native lords in Deheubarth, he seized back Cardigan. English response was slow and ineffective, and a truce was arranged in November. Henry III had problems amongst his barony, and had little attention to spare for Wales over the next few years. By 1233, he faced a revolt by certain of his aristocracy. Towards the end of 1233, Llywelyn joined in, supporting the baronial side in the March, and as a result acquired control of Buellt as well as Cardigan. By June 1234, the rebellion was over: a truce was negotiated between Llywelyn and the king which left Cardigan and Buellt in Llywelyn's hands. He had successfully used the conflict to increase his own power.

He was once again secure. He released Gruffudd from prison, granting him half of Llŷn. This time, Gruffudd seemed willing to accede to his father's arrangements, and by 1238, he was holding all of Llŷn, together with southern Powys, which Llywelyn may have meant as an appanage for him. Gruffudd,

125

however, had not lost sight of his ambitions, and there was no love between him and Dafydd. Gruffudd was able to attract supporters, building up a block opposed to that of Dafydd (which included Joanna, and Llywelyn's powerful steward, Ednyfed Fychan). In 1237 Joanna died and Llywelyn suffered a stroke. Action to secure Dafydd's succession to Llywelyn's full position was now urgent. Throughout most of 1238, Llywelyn's envoys were in negotiation with Henry III. Llywelyn wanted the title prince of Aberffraw and lord of Snowdon assured to Dafydd, along with control over all Llywelyn's wide hegemony. He wanted all the magnates of native Wales to swear homage to Dafydd as their future lord, a highly significant act. Henry II refused on all points, making it clear he had no intention (despite his earlier pledges) of recognizing Dafydd as anything other than lord of the heartland of Gwynedd. Llywelyn was unable to give Dafydd any more security beyond, in October 1238, having the Welsh magnates swear fealty, which carried with it fewer rights. At the same time, perhaps as a result of his failing health, he seems to have given Dafydd quasi-regent powers. Dafydd at once moved to protect his own interests. The death of Joanna, the failure of Llywelyn's health, and the intransigence of the king had weakened Dafydd's position. Meanwhile, his rival, Gruffudd, was ensconced in southern Powys, a region long a centre of hostility and resistance to Gwynedd. Dafydd deprived Gruffudd of southern Powys and restricted him to Llŷn, intending to reduce his resources. Gruffudd responded violently, and in late 1239 or early 1240, Dafydd tricked him, and imprisoned him at Cricieth castle.

Llywelyn died on 11 April 1240 at Aberconwy. He had carved out for himself a position and powers greater than any other native Welsh ruler in the post-Norman period. He operated on both the national, Welsh stage, and the international one, forming ties of blood and alliance with England and France as well as in Wales and the March. He was widely respected in his lifetime by his neighbours, be they friends, allies, rivals or enemies. His achievements were not without cost, however. His appropriation of Powys Wenwynwyn contributed to the long history of conflict between Gwynedd and Powys and created a legacy of distrust between the heirs of Gwenwynwyn and the princes of Gwynedd which would have damaging repercussions for his successors. His innovations in governance and inheritance practice had led to friction within Gwynedd, and seriously compromised the relations between his sons. He had made great gains from the English Crown in respect of his own status and rights, but was unable to gain a secure promise from Henry III that these would be transferred intact to Dafydd. His achievement was thus flawed. Nevertheless, he possessed a remarkable charisma, which allowed him to attract and create allies throughout Wales. He was a gifted diplomat, able to negotiate successfully with changing English governments, and an equally gifted military leader, able to plan and maintain successful campaigns over large distances. His energy and determination provided a focus for Welsh independence and identity for over forty years: like the Lord Rhys, Llywelyn remains one of the most remarkable leaders of Medieval Wales.

Cricieth Castle.

Dafydd ap Llywelyn

Dafydd did homage for Gwynedd to the king in May 1240, but his claims to wider lordship were already under dispute. Rival claims were brought against him by Marcher lords and native Welsh over Powys Wenwynwyn, Mold, Buellt, and Cardigan, and repeated attempts at arbitration failed. It was becoming clear that Henry III had no intention of allowing to Dafydd his father's full position. By August 1241, war broke out. In the ensuing conflict between king and prince, Gruffudd became a pawn. Henry made an agreement with Gruffudd's wife, Senena, in August 1241, and invaded Gwynedd, using Gruffudd's imprisonment and exclusion from the succession as a pretext. Llywelyn had used English legal models to settle the succession on Dafydd, at least in part in the hope of placating the Crown and protecting the future of Gwynedd. Henry, however, resistant to any form of lasting independent lordship over Wales exercised by the princes of Gwynedd, responded by posing as the protector of native Welsh legal practice, and the rights under it of Gruffudd. Moreover, when Henry launched his invasion in 1241, he had the support of many leading Welshmen, including those who had congregated around Gruffudd, but also including former allies of Llywelyn, Gruffudd ap Madog of Powys Fadog and the southern lord Maelgwn Fychan. Faced with determined opposition, in less than a month Dafydd surrendered to Henry at Gwern Eigron. The terms imposed on him were harsh. He was stripped of all Llywelyn's gains – the disputed lands of Powys Wenwynwyn, Meirionydd and Mold. He was required to hand over Gruffudd to the king, who proclaimed an intention of seeing him established as a prince in part of Gwynedd alongside Dafydd. Native Welsh lords were to do homage to the king, not to Dafydd. He was forced to promise that should he die without an heir of his body, Gwynedd would pass to the king. The rights which Llywelyn had hoped to secure for his heir had been lost in a little over a year.

Henry soon reneged on his agreement with Senena. Far from being restored, Gruffudd ap Llywelyn found himself taken, a captive, to London, where he was imprisoned in the Tower, as a perpetual threat against Dafydd. Henry's position in Wales was now very strong: the Welsh lords in both northern and southern Powys were his allies, as were the new Welsh lords of Meirionydd. The key fortresses of Cardigan, Carmarthen and Degannwy were in the hands of the Crown. Henry took steps to maintain this position, rebuilding castles and enforcing royal judicial power. Dafydd pursued a cautious policy after 1241, but he had not forgotten his wider claims, and in 1244, rebellion broke out anew. Dafydd forged alliances with almost all the native lords, and retook much of the land lost in 1241. He was helped in this by the removal of his rival, Gruffudd. On Saint David's Day, 1244, Gruffudd made an attempt to escape from the Tower, by climbing down a makeshift rope of bed-sheets. The sheets tore under his weight, and he fell to his death.[23] His death left Dafydd secure in control over Gwynedd, and took away one of the levers against him possessed by the king. The rebellion, however, was not an unadulterated success, and by the summer of 1245, major preparations against Dafydd were underway. How his leadership might have endured, faced by a major royal campaign, is unknown: Dafydd died on 25 February 1246, while the revolt was still in progress. A royal campaign in the summer of 1246 reached Degannwy, and by the end of that year, the lords of native south Wales had gone over to the king. Had Dafydd lived, it is possible that resistance might have continued longer, but the difference in available resources between the two sides was very great.[24] Dafydd lacked the ring of reliable allies his father had possessed: he found it dauntingly hard to continue his revolt in the face of determined royal aggression.[25] By the end of 1246, Henry once again had a strong position in Wales.

He did not try to enforce the right granted to him in 1241. Dafydd had died childless, which technically gave the king a legal claim to Gwynedd. Gruffudd, however, had left four sons, Owain, Llywelyn, Dafydd, and Rhodri. Owain had been a captive with his father, and was still in England on Dafydd's death. Dafydd and Rhodri were still children. Llywelyn, however, was a young adult, and present in Gwynedd. On the death of Dafydd ap Llywelyn, Henry made an attempt to stir up support in Gwynedd for the captive Owain, but without result. Escaping from his captors at Shotwick, Cheshire, Owain fled into Wales and rapidly allied with his brother Llywelyn to present a united front. In the spring of 1247, the two sides came to terms, in the Treaty of Woodstock. The treaty was hardly favourable to the two new rulers of Gwynedd, confining them to no more than Gwynedd beyond the River Conwy, but it provided the necessary breathing space, in which a renewed principality of Gwynedd would grow.

7 Llywelyn ap Gruffudd:
1246 - 1282[1]

From Woodstock to Montgomery

The Treaty of Woodstock greatly restricted the territory and rights of the two new young princes, but it did put a stop, for several years, to the conflict between Gwynedd and the king. English rights in Wales had been considerably expanded disputes over lands and inheritance within native Wales were to be heard in the king's courts,[2] and all native nobility owed homage to the king, not to any native overlord. Confined to only part of the old kingdom, and possessing few resources, Owain and Llywelyn were far from the status which had belonged to Llywelyn ap Iorwerth. Nevertheless the treaty and subsequent peace gave them valuable time in which to rebuild structures of lordship and alliance. In 1250, Llywelyn formed an alliance with Gruffudd ap Madog of Powys Fadog. In 1251, he and Owain made an alliance with two of the Welsh lords of Deheubarth.[3] Gwynedd uwch Conwy had been divided, according to native practice on land-rights, between the brothers. Llywelyn and Owain do not seem to have been particularly close – indeed, as Owain had spent some years in prison with their father, they may not have known each other well – but to begin with, they were able to co-exist peacefully. This arrangement benefited royal interest: as in Deheubarth, partition of native lands and lordship provided a rich opportunity for English interference and domination, and Henry envisaged that further partition would ensue, as the two younger sons of Gruffudd, Dafydd and Rhodri, came of age. Llywelyn ap Gruffudd, however, was ambitious.

In 1252, Dafydd reached adulthood, and was granted land in Llŷn. His portion was not large, and certainly not equal to those of his elder brothers. He soon came to resent this. His brother Owain supported him in his discontent, and in 1255, war broke out between the brothers. Henry attempted to impose his own negotiations, but this was ignored. In June 1250, the combined forces of Owain and Dafydd met those of Llywelyn at Bryn Derwin. Owain, it seems, was willing to see a greater share of land and power pass to Dafydd: Llywelyn was not. The resulting victory by Llywelyn was a turning point for Gwynedd. He seized and imprisoned both his brothers, and installed himself as sole ruler. It was a position he was to retain until his death, but his brothers, particularly Dafydd, never surrendered their own claims, and Llywelyn would face several challenges to his authority from within his own family. He was, however, to prove both an effective and a charismatic ruler, and from 1256, the fortunes of Gwynedd began to change dramatically. Having imposed himself as sole prince in what remained of Gwynedd, Llywelyn was in a position to expand his influence. In November

1256, he invaded Gwynedd is Conwy, aided by a southern ally, Maredudd ap Rhys Gryg. They drove the English out of all of the Perfeddwlad, apart from Degannwy and Diserth. It may be at this time that Llywelyn began to build a castle at Ewloe to defend his eastern border.[4] The campaign soon assumed national proportions. In December, Llywelyn marched into Meirionydd, annexing it from its native lord, and using it as a base from which to overrun the king's lands in north Ceredigion. He granted these to another descendant of the Lord Rhys, Maredudd ab Owain, who in return accepted Llywelyn's overlordship. By the end of 1256, Llywelyn had invaded Buellt, Ystrad Tywi and Gwerthrynion, and distributed them amongst his Welsh allies.

Not all those he drove out were English. In addition to taking Meirionydd from his kinsman, Llywelyn ap Maredudd, he deprived a southern lord, Rhys Fychan, of Dinefwr and Carreg Cennen, giving them to Maredudd ap Rhys. Llywelyn clearly intended to become the recognized power within native Wales, and would prove harsh to those who opposed him, Welsh or English. In 1257, he turned his attention to Powys. Gruffudd ap Gwenwynwyn of Powys Wenwynwyn was unwilling to accept his overlordship. The long history of aggression from Gwynedd was not forgotten, and Gruffudd remained loyal to Henry. In 1257, Llywelyn invaded Powys Wenwynwyn, causing Gruffudd to flee into England. Llywelyn turned south, forming alliances with the native lords in the Middle March, and, with Maredudd ap Rhys, heavily defeating an English army in the Tywi valley in June. At this juncture, Rhys Fychan abandoned his loyalty to the king and also joined Llywelyn. Within less than a year, Llywelyn had undermined much of the English position in Wales and reclaimed for himself the loyalty of most of its native lords.

Henry took steps to check him. A royal expedition was sent into north Wales in August, but was unable to proceed beyond Diserth. Llywelyn had harassed Powys Fadog in 1256, despite his earlier agreement with its lord, and in the wake of the failure of this royal expedition, Gruffudd ap Madog openly joined his cause. Henry intended to launch a new expedition in 1258, but events in England interposed, as a powerful part of the English nobility, under the leadership of Simon de Montfort, launched a serious challenge to royal power and rights. Unable to spare resources for Wales, Henry entered into a truce with Llywelyn in June 1258.

Llywelyn now moved to consolidate his status. He held an assembly of all the native lords, who gave to him an oath of allegiance.[5] At around the same time, he adopted a new title, *princeps Wallie*, prince of Wales. Like his grandfather, Llywelyn ap Iorwerth, he recognized the value of allies outside Wales, and in March 1258 made an agreement with the baronial leaders of Scotland, themselves opposed to Henry III. He was determined, too, to ensure the continued recognition of his pre-eminent status within Wales. During 1258, Maredudd ap Rhys had returned his allegiance to the king, perhaps resentful of the position of his nephew and rival, Rhys Fychan. When Rhys joined Llywelyn, Maredudd's power in the south had been reduced, as he was now obliged to share it.[6] On 28 May 1259, Llywelyn

Carreg Cennen Castle.

had Maredudd formally tried in his court in Arwystli. Found guilty of treason, Maredudd was imprisoned. This was a forceful and highly significant statement by Llywelyn of his conception of the nature of his powers. He was not simply an informal overlord, first among native equals: he was a formal, feudal overlord.

His authority now extended throughout much of Wales, and in 1260 he expanded it to cover Buellt, driving out its Anglo-Norman lord, Roger Mortimer. In 1261, he took control of Cydewain and installed his own nominees in Ceri, making it clear that he intended to be recognized as overlord of all native Wales. Despite his aggression, however, Llywelyn recognized that he needed a formal relationship with the Crown to protect his new status and rights. He made several overtures to Henry in the years after 1258, but with little progress: Henry was preoccupied with affairs in England and France.[7] In 1262, frustrated by the failure of negotiations, Llywelyn once again went on the offensive. In November, the Welsh of Maelienydd seized and razed Cefnllys castle from Roger Mortimer. Mortimer's forces, trying to retake it, encountered Llywelyn and were driven back. In a very short while, Llywelyn had taken Maelienydd from Mortimer, overrun Brecon, supported by the local native lords, and was threatening Abergavenny. English response was piecemeal, and did little to check his advance. Llywelyn continued to make gains throughout 1263, and by autumn had seized the last two Crown strongholds in north Wales, Diserth and Degannwy. An expedition had been despatched in April under the king's eldest son, Edward, to aid these fortresses, but had been summoned back into England, where Henry now faced a civil war. Under the leadership of the earl of Leicester, Simon de Montfort, a large section of the English barony had risen against him, seeking to curb royal power, decrease the influence at court of foreign advisers, and to increase the role of the aristocracy in government.[8] Many Marchers joined Simon's faction, although the Mortimers remained loyal to the king. These political divisions greatly weakened English influence and resources in Wales and the March, and provided an arena in which a fair measure of Welsh independence might be reasserted. In spring 1263, Llywelyn abandoned his attempts to reach a negotiated peace with Henry, and instead turned to the rebels led by Simon. Llywelyn sent his army to Bridgenorth in June to assist the rebels besieging it. In May 1264, Henry himself was defeated and captured by Simon, and induced to join Simon's faction. This did not end the war, however, and Llywelyn continued to be active in the March, particularly against Mortimer. In July, with Simon, he ravaged Mortimer's lands in Herefordshire and Shropshire. Later in the year, he supported Simon against the royal faction in battle at Worcester. Both Simon and Llywelyn stood to gain from their relationship, and Simon took steps to reward Llywelyn for his aid. The earldom of Chester had long been a threat to Gwynedd, and was in the hands of Edward: Simon removed it from him, taking it into his own hands, providing Llywelyn with a secure north-eastern border. In January 1265, an agreement was drawn up between them, recognizing Llywelyn's right to hold all he had gained by conquest. By mid-1265, however, Simon was under increasing pressure from Henry's faction, and Llywelyn's support may have increased in importance to him. In June 1265, a treaty was drawn up by Simon in the name of the king, between Llywelyn and the English state, known as the Treaty of Pipton. This granted to Llywelyn the right to use the title prince of Wales, and overlordship over all the native lords of Wales. All earlier treaties which in any way infringed or reduced his rights were withdrawn, and all lands which had been seized from Llywelyn or from Dafydd ap Llywelyn were to be restored to him. His possession of recent acquisitions was confirmed, including the strategically important lands of Painscastle, Hawarden and Whittington. In return, Llywelyn would pay £20,000 to the Crown and give his support to Simon's government. It may be that around the time of the negotiation of this agreement, Llywelyn may have entered also into an arrangement to marry Simon's daughter, Eleanor.[9]

This treaty never came into effect. On 4 August 1265, Simon was killed in battle against the royalist forces at Evesham, and Henry III was restored to power. This presented a potential threat to Llywelyn, as Chester returned to Edward's hands. Llywelyn made it clear he intended to retain what he had gained, attacking Hawarden in September. Henry faced a considerable task in restoring order in England, and chose initially to avoid confrontation with Llywelyn. A truce was agreed between them in November 1265. This was followed in 1267 by a formal peace, negotiated by the papal legate to England, Cardinal Ottobuono.

On 29 September 1267, a meeting was held at the ford of Rhyd Chwima near Montgomery between Llywelyn and the king, at which a new treaty was ratified, and Llywelyn did homage. This treaty – usually known as the Treaty of

Montgomery – had been agreed four days earlier on 25 September at Shrewsbury by the representative of both rulers. Its provisions secured to Llywelyn possession of Gwrtheyrnion, Brycheiniog, Cydewain, Ceri, Buellt, and the Perfeddwlad. He was to receive the service due from Whittington. He and his heirs were granted the title prince of Wales and the right to receive the homage and fealty of all the native lords of Wales, including Gruffudd ap Gwenwynwyn, with the exception of Maredudd ap Rhys, who had requested to remain in the king's fealty. Llywelyn, however, might buy Maredudd's homage from the king for 5,000 marks. Gruffudd ap Gwenwynwyn was to retain all the lands he had held of the king, but to return any recent conquests. In return, Llywelyn was to surrender all other lands and castles, including Hawarden, which he and his men had occupied during the civil war, and to permit Roger Mortimer to build a castle in Maelienydd – if, however, Llywelyn could prove his right to it, the castle and land were to be returned to him. Llywelyn was also required to make provision for his brother Dafydd. He was to do homage and fealty to the king for all this, and to pay 25,000 marks in instalments for his lands and rights.

The treaty represented a major achievement for Llywelyn. It secured to him and his heirs a status and title to which even Llywelyn ap Iorwerth had only been able to aspire. It conceded to him the status as pre-eminent leader of the Welsh, formally subordinating to him all the other native Welsh lords, despite the fact that Wales was a land of separate, distinctive geographical and political regions with local dynasties and leaders and a long history of inter-regional conflict. The rulers of Gwynedd had long claimed mastery over the other regions of Wales, but agreement to this by the native lords of these other regions had proved hard to gain and harder to keep. The territorial grants made to Llywelyn were also important: the Perfeddwlad had proved a major bone of contention between Welsh and English and had been repeatedly used by English kings and lords to launch campaigns against Gwynedd. The other lands similarly served to provide him with a buffer zone against the Marchers.

Yet despite his gains in territory and status, the treaty was not without flaws. He had received his lands and title not by right, but by grant,[10] and grants can be revoked. The sum demanded of him, 25,000 marks, was a large sum, and Gwynedd was, relatively speaking, poor. He possessed feudal overlordship over the other native lordships, but he did not possess the right to levy taxes or fines within them, so his own lands would have to bear the burden of payment. He had not secured his right to Maelienydd; and Mortimer, a consistent enemy and aggressor, had been granted the right to build a fortification there. Strategically, Maelienydd was a key territory in terms of access into and control over, central and south Wales. Hawarden was of similar strategic importance: it guarded the northern coastal route into Wales. The problems of overlapping claims to lordship and power in the March between Welsh and English lords had been largely left unresolved, and this would prove to be a serious source of conflict in subsequent years.

The treaty laid out a pattern of feudal submission by the native lords to Llywelyn, but, as would appear over time, not all these lords would agree with the judgement that they and their lands were subject to the authority of Gwynedd. The expansionism of the kings and princes of Gwynedd had long been seen as a threat by the rulers of Powys and the south, and Gruffudd ap Gwenwynwyn in particular was never more than a reluctant ally of Llywelyn who regarded Llywelyn's interest in his lands with suspicion and distrust. Another potential source of difficulty was Llywelyn's brothers: the provision in the treaty for Dafydd restricted him to lands in the north-east which were particularly vulnerable to English aggression and interference. It also served to distance him from the aristocracy of Gwynedd itself, reducing his chance to build up support among them. This served Llywelyn's interest: Dafydd had, during the course of the civil war, proved an uncertain ally, changing sides between royalist and rebel as best served him, and Llywelyn had little reason to trust him or to want him to gain a following in the Venedotian heartland. But Dafydd was Llywelyn's probable heir, and his good will and support were useful. Llywelyn's support of Simon de Montfort had antagonized both Henry III and his son Edward, and would not be forgotten.

1267 marked the zenith of Llywelyn's power, but the long war – eleven years – he had waged to gain supremacy left marks on his relations with his kin, his nobility, the other native lords of Wales, the Marcher lords and the English royal family. Consequences were to follow.

The Treaty of Aberconwy

Much of Llywelyn's power depended on the goodwill of his countrymen and on his ability to keep the Marcher lords at bay. He had shown himself adept at creating alliances within Wales and skilled as a military leader. But he had not been able to expel the English from Wales totally, and this presented difficulties particularly in mid and south-east Wales. The Treaty of Montgomery had not laid out a specific border and the middle March contained lands which had only recently become subject to Llywelyn and wherein lordship was still, to a degree disputed. Llywelyn took steps to secure this area, not simply taking the homage of the native lords in Brycheiniog and Elfael, but requiring them to give him hostages for their good behaviour. Certain native lords held lands in areas which had a substantial and influential English presence, especially in the south-east, and might be expected, on earlier experience, to be subjected to pressures to submit to the local Marcher lord. Llywelyn gave open support to the Welsh lords of Upper Gwent and Senghenydd, who had long been under threat from the English lords in Glamorgan. He was well aware of the strategic importance of castles in creating and maintaining control, and commenced the construction of a castle at Dolforwyn in Cydewain as both a guard against possible hostility from the Marchers in the area around Montgomery and as a check on the activities of Gruffudd ap Gwenwynwyn, whose main stronghold lay nearby at Welshpool. This new castle proved a potent source of friction between Llywelyn and

Caerphilly Castle.

Gruffudd. Llywelyn may also have constructed a castle at Carndochan and instituted new building works at Clun and Sennybridge castles as well as at castles within Gwynedd.

The need for defence was immediate: certain Marchers had lost out as a result of the treaty, and conflict soon developed. In the south-east, the earl of Gloucester, Gilbert de Clare, sought to reassert his control over the uplands, putting pressures on its native lords. To support this, he commenced the construction of a major new castle at Caerphilly. The result was a series of attacks and counter-attacks: in October 1270, Llywelyn attacked Caerphilly, and destroyed it. Gilbert recommenced construction during 1271, and Llywelyn again brought an army south to attack it, and was only persuaded to desist by the intervention of the bishops of Worcester and Lichfield. He was promised that Caerphilly would be taken into royal hands and further building prevented: in the event, however, Gilbert soon regained it and this time, construction was completed. Around this time, in 1272, Gilbert also successfully reasserted authority over the Welsh lord of Caerleon. Similarly, Llywelyn faced a challenge to his authority over Brycheiniog, from Humphrey de Bohun, heir to the earl of Hereford. Humphrey had a claim to the district through his mother, and by 1275, had achieved lordship there, despite Llywelyn's resistance and attempts by the king to impose peace between the sides. In Maelienydd, Roger Mortimer had recommenced the building of his castle at Cefnllys, threatening Llywelyn's control. Llywelyn complained to the king on several occasions, but received no real redress.[11] The Treaty of

Montgomery was expensive, moreover, and Llywelyn was able to raise revenue only from within Gwynedd: it is likely that his resources were stretched. The conflicts with Mortimer, Bohun and Clare represented a further drain on these. Llywelyn paid the instalments owed to the crown under the terms of the treaty on time until the end of 1269. His payment for 1270 was made late and piecemeal; after this, he made no further payments. All this contributed to a deterioration of relations between Llywelyn and the crown, which increased after the death in 1272 of Henry III and the succession of Edward.

Llywelyn also found himself beginning to face problems from within Wales. Despite his undoubted successes as a military leader and his commitment to the protection of Welsh law, Welsh culture and Welsh independence from the interference of the English state, he did not enjoy total and consistent support within native Wales. Regional loyalties persisted, as did local and dynastic rivalries. He had achieved overlordship over the native leaders, but this did not translate into direct rule over their lands. He had no direct control over the leading aristocracy of any area other than Gwynedd, which reduced the degree to which he could check their immediate lords. He tried, in some instances, to achieve a measure of power over leading regional noblemen: thus, he required Hywel Fychan, a nobleman of Ceredigion, to do homage directly to himself, rather than to Hywel's immediate lord, Owain ap Maredudd from Ceredigion.[12] Llywelyn also tried to increase his level of control over the senior native lords. Thus, when in 1273 Owain of Ceredigion made a grant of land to his wife Angharad, the grant was made with the explicit confirmation of Llywelyn.[13] Llywelyn was asserting his feudal overlordship of Owain's lands and his control over Owain's power to dispose of them. He reinforced his dominance over the leading native lords by requiring some of them to provide sureties and hostages for their good behaviour and continued loyalty: thus, in May 1275, the good behaviour of a lesser nobleman, Madog ap Cynwrig, lately released from prison, was secured to Llywelyn by the pledge of £32 by Hywel ap Rhys Gryg, one of the major lords in Deheubarth, and by Trahaearn ap Gruffudd.[14] Other Venedotian princes had taken hostages for good behaviour, and intervened in the internal affairs of their neighbours, but Llywelyn sought both to extend and to formalize his powers to interfere and control activities in the rest of native Wales. He also made use of law. Welsh law, while distinct from the law of England, was not uniform throughout Wales, and control over it was not a princely prerogative (it was largely customary). Llywelyn made use of Welsh law to extend his influence.[15] His jurisdiction in theory was restricted to Gwynedd, but he sought to extend it, summoning native lords who crossed his will to his own court, as he had done with Maredudd ap Rhys Gryg in the later 1250s.[16] The maintenance of his hegemony was a complex task, and one in which he received little support from the Crown.

Problems within native Wales became overt in April 1274, when word reached his court of a conspiracy against him involving his brother Dafydd and Gruffudd ap Gwenwynwyn. Dafydd was questioned in front of Llywelyn's court at

Rhuddlan, and Gruffudd was summoned to a hearing at Dolforwyn. No hard proof was immediately forthcoming, but Llywelyn continued to be suspicious. On 24 April, he gave his response to the rumours. He required as a hostage Gruffudd's eldest son Owain, and further demanded that Gruffudd surrender to himself the homage of twenty-five of the leading men of Powys Wenwynwyn, thus increasing Llywelyn's direct power there, and reducing that of Gruffudd. He deprived Gruffudd of Arwystli and part of Cyfeiliog. No punishment was meted out immediately to Dafydd, but he was ordered to present himself shortly for further questioning at Llanfor in Penllyn. This latter never took place, and in November 1274, Dafydd fled over the border into England, where he sought refuge with Edward I. This was tantamount to an admission of guilt, and the hostage, Owain, made a confession of the details of the conspiracy to the bishop of Bangor.

The conspirators, Owain revealed, were himself, his mother Hawise, his father Gruffudd, and Dafydd. They had planned to assassinate Llywelyn, placing Dafydd on the throne of Gwynedd in his stead. Dafydd, once prince, would reward Gruffudd with the lands of Ceri and Cydewain, and would give Owain one of his daughters in marriage. Llywelyn was to have been killed in February 1274, and Owain had in fact set out with a troop of men to do this, but had been prevented from reaching Llywelyn by bad weather and flooding. He had retreated back into Powys and the conspiracy had lapsed. Word of their intentions, had, however, leaked out.

A number of possible motivations for this conspiracy arise. Dafydd had long been excluded from power in Gwynedd, which he seems to have resented throughout his life. All his lands lay in the north-east, vulnerable to English aggression. He may also have felt that Llywelyn did not trust him. The hostility and distrust between Llywelyn and Gruffudd was long-standing: the princes of Powys Wenwynwyn had never been more than reluctant allies and vassals, and there were long-running disputes over rights in Arwystli, Cyfeiliog, Ceri and Cydewain. The financial exactions Llywelyn had had to make on his own lands to fulfil the Treaty of Montgomery may also have played a part – in later years, resentment of his government became explicit within Gwynedd, and it may be that at least some of the nobility there were growing restless under his rule. Dafydd may have expected to capitalize on this.[17]

In the wake of Owain's confession, Llywelyn sent messengers to Gruffudd at Welshpool. Gruffudd received them hospitably, but in the middle of the night fled with his family to Shrewsbury, leaving instructions to his castellan to imprison the messengers and to hold the castle against any attack. Llywelyn marched into Powys Wenwynwyn, attacked and destroyed the castle, and seized all Gruffudd's lands.

All the records relating to the conspiracy emanate from the side of Llywelyn and his court, and there are gaps and uncertainties in them, not least regarding the level of Dafydd's involvement and Llywelyn's knowledge of this.[18] The murder was to have occurred at a grange belonging to Aberconwy abbey, and early rumours of the plot probably came from abbey circles. But the question of complicity of any of the community of Aberconwy is not discussed in the records. Aberconwy was the favoured monastery of the princes of Gwynedd, Llywelyn ap Iorwerth having been buried there. Its monks supported Llywelyn ap Gruffudd in a quarrel with the bishop of St Asaph, and it may have served as an unofficial chancery for princely records.[19] Given the intended location of the assassination, it may be that some of the community knew of the plot before April 1274. The existence of the plot makes plain that Llywelyn's position in the years after Montgomery was not wholly secure.[20] The plot moreover contributed to the break-down of relations between prince and king, as Edward gave refuge to both Dafydd and Gruffudd – a move interpreted by Llywelyn as hostile and damaging to his own jurisdiction. Edward seems to have viewed the refugees as assets and potential tools in his growing effort to impose submission on Llywelyn.

Alongside his difficulties with Dafydd and Gruffudd, Llywelyn faced problems with the church over the rights of the sees of Bangor and St Asaph. Two agreements had been drawn up between Llywelyn and the bishop of Bangor before 1267, to resolve disputes over territory between bishop and prince. But after 1267, Llywelyn faced a heavy fiscal burden, and church lands and revenue may have been a tempting potential source of income. He laid claim to sums of money arising from lawsuits which had previously been paid to the bishops. He also tried to increase the degree of control he could exercise over episcopal lands and property. Disputes between Llywelyn and the bishops on this subject had begun before 1267, but friction became particularly strong in the 1270s. In 1274, the bishops of Bangor and St Asaph made a joint protest to him over his treatment of his brother Dafydd. In 1274-5, Bishop Anian of St Asaph appealed to the pope for aid against Llywelyn. The pope responded by a condemnation of the prince. Anian also enlisted the support of the archbishop of Canterbury, obliging Llywelyn to write a letter to the archbishop in his own defence.[21] In 1276, Anian produced a long list of complaints against Llywelyn, who was forced to try and placate him, granting him a new charter of liberties. By this time, Llywelyn was on the verge of open conflict with the king, and the support of his bishops was of increasing importance to him, as was that of the pope. His attempt came too late, however, and by 1277 both Anian of St Asaph and the bishop of Bangor (also named Anian) were openly leagued with Edward. Llywelyn's dispute with Anian of St Asaph provided his enemies with an excuse to accuse him of ignoring Welsh custom and practice in order to increase his revenues. Although the bishop of Bangor eventually returned to supporting Llywelyn, the breach with Anian of St Asaph was to prove permanent,[22] and by 1277, the bishop of St Asaph was openly siding with Edward I.

After the death of Henry III in 1272, Llywelyn had been summoned on several occasions to the English court to do homage to the new king. Llywelyn, however, had consistently prevaricated. He did not attend the coronation of Edward in 1274. In letters to the English court, he justified his actions: the Marcher lords and others were flouting the terms of the Treaty of Montgomery, the king himself had given refuge to Llywelyn's enemies. Consequently he could not perform his own obligations until his complaints were dealt with, and he felt it unsafe to journey into England. In many respects, his grievances were reasonable. The behaviour of the Marchers threatened his authority, and crown response had been less than satisfactory. To Edward, however, Llywelyn's behaviour verged on the rebellious: his refusal to do homage offended royal dignity and undermined the supremacy over all Wales claimed by the king. Neither side was prepared to compromise. In late 1275, Edward moved to force Llywelyn's hand. Llywelyn had decided to honour his betrothal to Eleanor de Montfort, who had been living on the continent in exile with her mother and brothers. The two were married by proxy in France, then Eleanor took ship for Wales, accompanied by her brother Amaury. The ship was intercepted by a pirate vessel hired by Edward, and Eleanor conveyed into England. Edward had not forgotten his enmity towards the Montforts, and viewed Llywelyn's marriage as an act of hostility.[23] Llywelyn's decision to marry was probably motivated by the need to have an heir: Dafydd, his heir to this time, had once again demonstrated his unreliability, and Llywelyn was no longer young. To Edward, however, the renewal of the tie to the Montforts may have looked like one more act of provocation and resistance to his own authority.

Open conflict between prince and king erupted in 1276. Llywelyn had interpreted the Treaty of Montgomery as a guarantee of his rights and independence. Edward saw Llywelyn as no more than a feudal vassal, and a rather unreliable and untrustworthy one, and the treaty as a grant which he might confirm or withhold at his pleasure. During 1276, as the precariousness of Llywelyn's position became clearer, native Welsh lords began to desert him, and to give their allegiance to Edward. On 12 November 1276, Edward declared Llywelyn a rebel and began preparations for war. He deployed royal forces from bases at Chester, Montgomery and Carmarthen to attack Llywelyn from all sides and to entice away his supporters. In December 1276, Llywelyn ap Gruffudd Maelor ap Madog of Powys Fadog, formerly one of Llywelyn of Gwynedd's main allies, submitted to the king. Dolforwyn castle was seized and mid Wales from Brecon to Cydewain taken into English hands. Gruffudd ap Gwenwynwyn was reinstated in Powys Wenwynwyn. In spring 1277 in the south, Rhys ap Maredudd, lord of Dryslwyn, submitted to the kings representative.[24] Rhys's cousin, Rhys Wyndod, surrendered his castles of Dinefwr and Llandovery, and the Welsh lords of Ceredigion did homage to Edward at Worcester. Ceredigion was refortified for the king. By August, Edward himself, with the army from Chester, had penetrated Gwynedd as far as the Conwy. Llywelyn retreated into Snowdonia. Cut off from most of his lands, and with few allies, he was forced to surrender. On 9 November 1277, a new treaty was agreed between him and the king – the Treaty of Aberconwy.

The new treaty reversed nearly all the gains Llywelyn had made under the Treaty of Montgomery. Edward reclaimed for himself the homage of all but five of the native Welsh lords. The remaining five were to give homage to Llywelyn

Dryslwyn Castle.

only for the remainder of his lifetime, and not to his heirs. Llywelyn was made to surrender all his lands, including the Perfeddwlad, with the exception of Gwynedd uwch Conwy, He was to release from prison his brother Owain Goch, and grant Llŷn to him. He was to indemnify his youngest brother, Rhodri, to the sum of 1,000 marks in return for the latter withdrawing any claim he might have over any part of Gwynedd. Llywelyn was to pay the king a fine of £50,000,[25] plus 1,000 marks a year for Anglesey. Edward made provision for Dafydd, giving him lands in Dyffryn Clwyd and Rhufoniog, plus the lordship of Hope: however, Llywelyn was forced to concede that Dafydd had a claim to part of Gwynedd uwch Conwy, which land Llywelyn might hold only at the king's grace, and which he might not transmit to any heir. Gruffudd ap Gwenwynwyn was restored to his lands in Powys Wenwynwyn. The Treaty of Aberconwy represented a dramatic reversal of fortune for Llywelyn ap Gruffudd, reducing him effectively to the territory and status he had held under the Treaty of Woodstock thirty years before.

The last years of Gwynedd

In the wake of the Treaty of Aberconwy, Eleanor de Montfort was finally allowed to meet her new husband. Eleanor was Edward's cousin – her mother, also Eleanor, was the sister of Henry III, and in other circumstances, the marriage of Eleanor to Llywelyn might have marked a new closeness between the prince of

Gwynedd and the king of England. However, Henry had disliked the first Eleanor's marriage to Simon de Montfort, and the family was subsequently tainted with rebellion. In 1278, Edward released Eleanor and presided himself over a second marriage ceremony between her and Llywelyn at Worcester. It appeared to be a graceful gesture by the king, but it served to reinforce his new control over Llywelyn, and he used the occasion to extract from Llywelyn an agreement not to shelter anyone in his lands against the king's will.[26]

Royal control was being strengthened in Wales, and Llywelyn's authority was not simply diminished, but repackaged in such a way as to remind him regularly of his subordination to Edward. It was not solely Gwynedd which was subjected: in Powys Wenwynwyn, Gruffudd ap Gwenwynwyn was required to accede to terms which ensured his acceptance of English law and authority.[27] Gruffudd was not permitted to retain the strategically important lands of Ceri and Cydewain: in 1279, Edward entrusted these to Roger Mortimer. Powys Fadog had also come under royal control during 1277, when Edward's forces imposed a land settlement. When one of its lords, Madog Fychan ap Gruffudd Maelor, died later in the same year, leaving only underage sons, Edward took his lands into wardship. In the south, he deprived local native lords of key strongholds, including Dinefwr, Llandovery and Carreg Cennen. The only one of the native lords of the south-west who did not suffer was Rhys ap Maredudd, who had held loyal to the king and was rewarded with confirmation of his lands. Finally, Edward cut Llywelyn off from the south by annexing Ceredigion wholesale to the English crown. The new royal holdings were consolidated with a programme of encastellation. Castles were constructed or rebuilt, including Flint, Rhuddlan, Buellt and Aberystwyth, which served both to control neighbouring lands and to secure routes by land and sea into Welsh territories. For much of Wales, 1277 marked the effective beginning of the Edwardian conquest.

The increased power of the king led to inevitable tensions. Problems arose concerning control and operation of law. Native Welsh law represented an important social force outside Edward's control, and a focus for native independence. He took steps to curb its use, arrogating to himself the right to arbitrate disputes (including some which would formerly have been subject to Llywelyn's courts). He appointed Justices to oversee lawsuits on his behalf, requiring Llywelyn and Llywelyn's men to submit to the authority of these new officers. From 1277 onwards, Edward operated as a formal overlord, confirming Llywelyn's charters, interfering in his jurisdiction, and using his enemies and rivals to check his authority. The new circumstances began to have effects on Llywelyn's relations with the nobility of Gwynedd.[28] The release from prison of Owain Goch, and the restoration of Dafydd served further to weaken ties between prince and nobility.

It seems unlikely that either Edward or Llywelyn expected this new situation to last. Edward, after his long dealings with Llywelyn, may have realized that the new pressures would provoke a reaction. Llywelyn hoped to rebuild his former position. As early as May 1278, he reopened communication with some of the

Dolwyddelan Castle.

native lords of the south-west, who visited him at Dolwyddelan.[29] He embarked on a complex legal battle with Gruffudd ap Gwenwynwyn over the control of Arwystli, long debated between Powys and Gwynedd.[30] In 1263, it had been confirmed to Gruffudd by Llywelyn, but in the wake of the conspiracy of 1274, it had been declared forfeit to the prince. In 1278, Llywelyn brought a formal claim for possession of it before Edward's Justices for Wales. Possession of Arwystli would be an important step towards recovery: it would not only weaken Gruffudd ap Gwenwynwyn, but would move Llywelyn's influence back into mid Wales towards the important border lands of Ceri, Cydewain and Maelienydd. Llywelyn's case was built on a combination of Welsh law and on the Treaty of Aberconwy itself. The latter had promised to him justice from the king according to the appropriate laws and customs of the place under dispute. Llywelyn argued that Arwystli was part of Wales and thus rightly subject to Welsh law (which included the provision that any land dispute be heard on the disputed land itself).

He further claimed a right to arbitration on the basis of his earlier dealings with Gruffudd ap Gwenwynwyn, of whom he had formerly been the feudal lord and who had surrendered Arwystli to him in 1274. Llywelyn seems to have identified Gruffudd as both an enemy and as an easier target than the Marchers. Alongside the suit over Arwystli, he entered into communication with some of Gruffudd's nobility, seeking to attract them to himself, and, in 1281, signed an agreement of friendship with Roger Mortimer, whose lands abutted Gruffudd's and who had long been an enemy to Welsh expansion. Gruffudd undoubtedly felt threatened, and looked for a means of defence. He chose – cleverly – to exploit the king's desire to control jurisdiction in Wales. He declared himself to be, in effect, a Marcher lord, and argued therefore that any lawsuit over him or his lands should be subject to the appropriate law of the March and heard in the king's, rather than a Welsh, court. The dispute would continue to the end of Llywelyn's life, and would make plain Edward's resistance to Welsh law and indeed, to Llywelyn. To allow Llywelyn to win the suit would have served to undermine Edward's claims to control the law in Wales, in addition to giving Llywelyn control over a strategically important area. The lawsuit nevertheless placed Edward in a difficult position: simply to overrule Llywelyn's claim might be seen as a breach of the Treaty of Aberconwy, and fuel resentment of the Crown. Edward therefore picked a path of prevarication, introducing into the conduct of the lawsuit the question of the nature of royal jurisdiction. He insisted on treating Llywelyn as a simple litigant, subject to common law, on the grounds that all land-disputes were subject to royal control. He implied that in such cases, the litigants did not have the right to decide what kind of law – Welsh or English – was appropriate. This right was vested in the crown only, and must be decided in the royal court before the case might proceed. The dispute raised serious issues regarding the application of law within native Wales and the extent therein of Crown right: it would become one of Llywelyn's key grievances against the king.

Llywelyn was not alone in suffering dispossession and denial of his claims. In the south-west, Rhys Wyndod was deprived of Dinefwr and Llandovery, Gruffudd and Cynan, sons of Maredudd, lost their lands in Ceredigion. Dafydd ap Gruffudd was denied full jurisdiction over his lands in eastern Gwynedd. In Powys Fadog, Llywelyn ap Gruffudd Maelor discovered his lands subject to the interference of the sheriff of Oswestry, and to claims against himself from within his own family and supported by the king. In the years following after the Treaty of Aberconwy, resentment, friction and discontent grew between Welsh and English throughout Wales and the March.

Rebellion came on the night of 21 March 1281. Dafydd ap Gruffudd launched a sudden attack on the border castle of Hawarden, killing its garrison and imprisoning its castellan, Roger Clifford. Within days, there were further Welsh attacks. On 22 March, Llywelyn ap Gruffudd Maelor of Powys Fadog raided Oswestry, and in the following days native lords in the south seized Carreg Cennen, Llandovery and Aberystwyth. It is not known if Dafydd acted solely on his own initiative, or if Llywelyn knew of or was implicated in the initial rising.[31]

Graves at Strata Florida, probably of the descendants of the Lord Rhys.

The timing was not good: Llywelyn had yet to rebuild the network of alliance and support with other native leaders which was necessary to successful and long-term resistance. It may be that his hand was in some degree forced. However, the uprising looks to a degree planned and coordinated. Perhaps the original plan did not originate with Llywelyn: Dafydd, previously a political weathercock, was to prove himself in this final rising to be willing to fight for his rights as an independent lord to the bitter end. Yet Dafydd's position within the north Welsh polity had never been particularly secure, and his history of changing sides was unlikely to have made him an attractive figurehead or ally, even with the resentments of the early 1280s. Llywelyn had been in contact with the southern lords from 1278: it seems to me likely that the hand behind the uprising was his, although Dafydd may have pre-empted the timing. Exactly when Llywelyn joined the rebellion openly is uncertain, but by the summer at the latest, he was involved. In the midst of this, in June, his new wife Eleanor died giving birth to his sole child, a daughter, Gwenllian.

Edward's response to the uprising was swift, and by August 1282, royal forces regained control over Ceredigion and Ystrad Tywi. The king found himself facing far more determined resistance than he had in 1276-7, however, and northern and mid Wales, with their difficult terrain, proved challenging. A coastal assault on Gwynedd failed. In October 1282, Edward opened negotiations with the north Welsh, offering terms through the archbishop of Canterbury, John Pecham. The king was no longer willing to tolerate Welsh rule within Wales. Llywelyn was offered land up to £1,000 in value plus an English earldom, in place of Gwynedd. Dafydd was offered financial incentives to leave Britain entirely and go on crusade. Edward additionally required that their legal heirs – Dafydd's two young sons, and Llywelyn's newborn daughter – be handed over to him. The terms were refused, and Llywelyn and Dafydd responded with a list of their own grievances against the king. Armed conflict continued. Llywelyn found himself driven into Snowdonia, from whence he sought to move east towards the border. From there, he would be able to redirect the attack on English holdings and forces. There was a power-vacuum in the middle March, caused by the death in October 1282 of Roger Mortimer, which Llywelyn hoped to exploit. He moved into Buellt, perhaps on his own initiative, perhaps lured with promises of aid from one of Mortimer's kinsmen or followers. On 11 December 1282, he was in the vicinity of Llanganten. *Brut y Tywysogyon* records 'And then Roger Mortimer[32] and Gruffudd ap Gwenwynwyn and with them the king's host came upon them without warning, and then Llywelyn and his foremost men were slain...'[33] His head was taken to the king, and subsequently displayed at the Tower of London.

Llywelyn ap Gruffudd had ruled Gwynedd for almost forty years, rebuilding his principality from the small core to which it had been reduced by the Treaty of Woodstock in 1247. It is likely that, after 1277, he expected to be able to repeat this feat in the same careful and effective fashion. At the peak of his career, in the 1260s and earlier 1270s, he possessed unquestioned hegemony over all of native Wales, north and south, and operated at the highest level of political life in the English state. To support his expanded authority, he had built upon the foundations laid by his grandfather, Llywelyn ap Iorwerth, anticipating and revising the system of government within his lands. Other native lords were drawn into a feudal relationship with him. He successfully excluded two brothers (Owain and Rhodri) from power in Gwynedd. He resisted increasingly determined attempts by English kings to undermine his authority, upholding native law and right to independence within native lands. He was perhaps not as a gifted a diplomat as Llywelyn ap Iorwerth, less willing to wait or to compromise in order to head off serious conflicts. In his last years, he faced Edward I, perhaps the English king most set upon destroying Welsh native lordship, where Llywelyn ap Iorwerth had benefited from the social unrest in the last years of John, and the relative caution of the regency of Henry III. Llywelyn ap Gruffudd had a weakness, too, perhaps, for his erratic and sometimes unreliable brother Dafydd, whose position as his heir exposed Llywelyn to manipulation and interference from both Henry III and Edward I. He was charismatic and compelling, a talented war-leader, and a champion of Welsh independence.

His death did not end the rebellion. He had left Dafydd in charge of the defence of what remained of Gwynedd. Edward was in control of the Perfeddwlad; in January 1283, his troops crossed the river Conwy into Gwynedd uwch Conwy, and took Dolwyddelan castle before moving into Anglesey. Dafydd – after nearly thirty years – was prince of Gwynedd, but he had almost no support. The southern lords had mainly surrendered to the king, and English troops had, by spring, entered Snowdonia. The last castle to hold for Dafydd, Castell y Bere, fell on 25 April. In June, Dafydd was betrayed to Edward and

ER COF AM
In Memory Of
GWENLLIAN,
MERCH LLYWELYN EIN LLYW OLAF,
Daughter of the last Prince of Wales,
GANED YN ABERGWYNGREGYN 12.6.1282.
Born at
BU FARW YN SEMPRINGHAM 7.6.1337
Died at
WEDI BOD YN GARCHAROR YMA AM 54 MLYNEDD,
Having been held prisoner here for 54 years.

Memorial to Gwenllian ferch Llywelyn at Sempringham, Lincolnshire.

captured. He was taken for trial to Shrewsbury, and convicted of treason. On 2 October, Dafydd ap Gruffudd, the last native prince of Gwynedd, was hanged, drawn and quartered. His head was sent for display outside the Tower of London, where it was fixed next to that of Llywelyn. Edward was willing to take no chances of a new rebellion. Dafydd's young sons were imprisoned for life at Bristol castle, and his daughters sent to Sixhills convent in Lincolnshire. Llywelyn's daughter, less than a year old, was committed to the nunnery of Sempringham. The long reign in Gwynedd of the Line of Merfyn Frych was over.

Gruffudd ap Gwenwynwyn

In the wake of Dafydd's death, the whole of native Wales was subject to the authority of Edward I. In the south, he dispossessed all the native lords, with the exception of Rhys ap Maredudd. Rhys had supported Edward throughout the conflicts of the later 1270s and 1280s, and initially was rewarded with substantial lands in Cantref Mawr. But Edward did not intend to permit him any delusions of independence. He was required to surrender the key castle of Dinefwr in October 1283, his ambitions for further expansion at the expense of the Giffard family were blocked, and he was forced to accept the judicial authority of the royal Justiciar in west Wales. In June 1287, he rebelled. His rebellion was in no sense national: Rhys was concerned with his own grievances, not with Welsh independence. He found little support even in the south-west, and in less than six months, he had lost all lands, castles and status. He escaped capture, remaining an outlaw until April 1292, when he was finally caught and executed. His dispossession had marked the end of substantial native lordship in the former kingdom of Deheubarth.[34]

In 1282-3, Edward deprived the heirs to Powys Fadog of their lands. But one native lord – arguably the greatest of the time after Llywelyn ap Gruffudd – still survived in possession of his patrimony. This was Gruffudd ap Gwenwynwyn of Powys Wenwynwyn. Gruffudd had remained loyal to Edward throughout the wars of 1277-1283, and emerged with his lands intact. He had faced a long struggle to retain them. He had inherited Powys Wenwynwyn as a minor in 1216, in the wake of the expulsion of his family from their lands by Llywelyn ap Iorwerth. Llywelyn had been granted the lands in wardship until Gruffudd was of age, but Gruffudd in the end had to wait far longer. Llywelyn retained Powys Wenwynwyn in his own hands until his death in 1240. Henry III's government provided the exiled Gruffudd with lands in Derbyshire to support him, and lent half-hearted aid to his attempts at restoring himself in the late 1220s and 1230s. After 1240, Gruffudd found himself caught between the Marcher lords, the ambitions of the princes of Gwynedd, and the king. He faced demands and aggression from all three, and adapted his policy to suit the conditions of the time. His allegiance changed between England and Gwynedd as the fortunes and actions of both dictated,[35] although he was perhaps always a more willing ally of the Crown than of the prince. This was unsurprising: to Gruffudd, growing up in exile, the princes of Gwynedd were the usurpers of his inheritance, dangerous, ambitious and sometimes unscrupulous neighbours seeking to undermine and trammel his authority. The kings also checked his powers, but at a greater distance, and without showing a desire to possess his lands. Gruffudd's main aim, throughout his life, seems to have been to retain his inheritance as intact as possible, and as free as was practical from outside control. As a result of this, his reputation has suffered. He is remembered for his desertion of Llywelyn in 1274, and for his way of changing sides in warfare, but such a judgement is retrospective. Gruffudd was the heir to lands which, as recently as the late eleventh century, had been free from all outside dominion and control. There was a long history of usurpation, conflict and hostility between Gwynedd and Powys, and to Gruffudd, Llywelyn's activities looked less like protection of Welsh independence than like attempts to deprive him of his own freedom.

Accordingly, Gruffudd adapted to his times. He made his lands over into the shape of a Marcher lordship, employing English law in the dispute over Arwystli, and in his provisions for his sons. In 1278, he laid out the conditions for the succession. He ignored the tradition of partible inheritance, instead securing his lordship to his eldest son, Owain, and gaining royal approval for this. He lacked the charisma and perhaps the wide vision of Llywelyn, but he possessed qualities of his own. Adept at reading the times, he retained his lands more or less intact through one of the most turbulent periods in the history of Wales. He was never permanently dispossessed by his rivals; he transmitted his lands to his son under terms which English law would recognize and accept. And, alone of the major native leaders of the late thirteenth century, when he died in 1286 it was in his bed, not in war or by execution, in full possession of his lands. His heir inherited without difficulty.

The Wales in which Gruffudd died was very different from the Wales into which he was born. Gwynedd was in English hands; native lordship was dismantled or transformed into something closer to the lordships of the March. The old dynasties which had ruled Wales had been dispossessed. At the end of the fourteenth century, Owain Glyndŵr, a descendant in the male line of the kings of Powys and in the female line of the kings of Deheubarth, would declare himself prince of Wales, and seek to rebuild native independence. But with the fall of Gwynedd in 1283, the last of the old kingdoms of Wales had passed away.

Notes

Introduction

1 R.R. Davies, *Conquest, Coexistence and Change: Wales 1063-1415* (Oxford 1987), p. 19.

1 From Vortigern to Merfyn Frych:

1 P.V. Webster, 'The Roman Period', in H.N. Savory, ed., *Glamorgan County History Volume II: Early Glamorgan* (Cardiff 1984), 277-313, pp. 292-8.

2 For example, *llyfr*, book, from Latin *liber*, *ysgrif*, script, from *scribo*, *ffenestr*, window, from *fenestra*, although not all of these words may have entered the Welsh language during the Roman period.

3 For example at Moel Fenlli, near Llanbedr Dyffryn, Clwyd.

4 P.J. Casey, 'Magnus Maximus in Britain: a reappraisal', in P.J. Casey, ed., *The End of Roman Britain* (BAR series 71, 1979), 66-79.

5 P. Bartholomew, 'Fifth Century Facts', *Britannia* 13 (1982), 261-70; P.J. Casey & M.G. Jones, 'The Date of the Letter of the Britons to Aetius', *BBCS* 37 (1990), 281-90; E.A. Thompson, 'Britain AD 406-410', *Britannia* 8 (1977), 303-18; E.A. Thompson, 'Procopius on Brittia and Britannia', *Classical Quarterly* New Series 30 (1980), 498-507; E.A. Thompson, *Saint Germanus of Auxerre and the End of Roman Britain* (Woodbridge 1984); E.A. Thompson, 'Zosimus 6.10.2 and the letters of Honorius', *Classical Quarterly* New Series 32 (1982), 445-62.

6 See note 5. There is some supporting evidence for this: the *Gallic Chronicle of 452* records a barbarian invasions of Britain and Gaul (by Saxons and Vandals respectively)

7 For discussion of Gildas see M. Lapidge and D.N. Dumville, eds., *Gildas: New Approaches* (Woodbridge 1984).

8 Gildas, *Ruin*, ch. 23-4.

9 Gildas, *Ruin*, ch. 25-6.

10 See note 8. See also N.J. Higham, *The English Conquest: Gildas and Britain in the fifth century* (Manchester 1994).

11 Bede, *HE*, Bk I, ch. 15.

12 D.P. Kirby, 'Vortigern', *BBCS* 23 (1970), 37-59, pp. 40-1.

13 Bede, *HE*, Bk I, ch. 15 gives these names as the early Saxon leaders, but does not explicitly connect them with Vortigern. The Anglo-Saxon Chronicle (first compiled in its extant form in the later ninth century, but drawing upon earlier materials) does make the association, and gives short notices of Hengist's campaigns against Vortigern and other Welsh. The early ninth century Welsh text, *HB*, contains the most elaborate account of Vortigern and his career: *HB* ch. 31, 37, 38, 39-49, 62, 66.

14 *HB* ch. 31, 36, 37, 38, 43, 44, 45, 46.

15 *HB* ch. 39.

16 *HB* ch. 40-42.

17 *HB* ch.47.

18 *HB* ch. 48

19 D.P. Kirby, 'Vortigern'. For problems with this, and other material relating to the sub-Roman period, see D.N. Dumville, 'Sub-Roman Britain: History and Legend', *History* 62 (1977), 173-92, especially pp. 184-7.

20 J Rhys, 'All Around the Wrekin', *Y Cymmrodor* (1908), 1-62, pp. 39-47; A.H. Sayce, 'The Inscription on Pillar of Eliseg', *Arch. Camb.* 6th ser., 9 (1909), 43-8; R.A.S. Macalister, 'Notes on Some of the Early Welsh Inscriptions', *Arch. Camb.* 7th ser., 2 (1922),198-219, pp. 217-8; V.E. Nash-Williams, *The Early Christian Monuments of Wales* (Cardiff 1950), 123-5. Part of this monument, known as the Pillar of Elise, is still extant, close to the ruins of the monastery of Valle Crucis, near Llangollen, although the inscription is now lost.

21 D.P. Kirby, 'Vortigern'; D.P. Kirby, 'British Dynastic History in the Pre-Viking Period', *BBCS* 27 (1978), 81-114, pp. 101-2.

22 *HB* ch. 32, 33, 34, 35.

23 See note 21.

24 Gildas, *Ruin*, ch. 24.

25 *HB* ch. 31, 40, 42, 48, 66. This text has a far more ambivalent attitude to the Romans, and a far more positive one to the Britons, than that of Gildas: fear of Roman invasion is cited as a further reason for Vortigern's invitation to Hengist.

26 *HB* ch. 48.

27 John Morris, *The Age of Arthur A History of the British Isles from 350 to 650* (London 1973).

28 *HB*, ch. 56.

29 See his appearances in the Lives of Saints Padarn, Carannog, Illtud, Gildas and Cadog. Jon B. Coe and Simon Young, eds. and trans., *The Celtic Sources for the Arthurian Legend* (Llanerch 1995), pp. 14-37.

30 Dark, *Civitas*, p. 80.

31 Gildas, *Ruin*, ch.27-36.

32 For detailed discussion of this problem, see D.N. Dumville, 'Gildas and Maelgwn: Problems of Dating', in Lapidge and Dumville, eds., *Gildas*, pp. 51-9.

33 The earliest version of the pedigree of the First Dynasty of Dyfed is that in the Irish text the *Expulsion of the Deisi*, composed before the ninth century. See Bartrum, *Tracts*, p. 4. It should be borne in mind that the presence of the name Vortepor in the genealogies may simply be a product of influence upon whoever composed them of either the writing of Gildas or of the inscription on the Vortepor stone.

34 *History of the Britons*, ch. 62.

35 Gildas, *Ruin*, ch. 33-6.

36 Lloyd, *A History*, I, 132, n.31.

37 Bartrum, *Tracts*, (HG2), p. 12. Another suggestion is that he was associated with the area around Carmarthen: K.H. Jackson, 'Varia: II. Gildas and the Names of the British Princes', *CMCS* 3 (1982), 30-40, p. 31.

38 Lloyd, *A History*, I, 132.

39 Lloyd, *A History*, I, 133; Wendy Davies, *Wales*, p. 99; Jackson, *Varia*, pp. 32-4; Higham, *English Empire*, pp. 179-80; Kirby, 'British Dynastic History', p. 94.

40 Dumville, 'Gildas', pp. 56-9; and see note 39.

41 Gildas, *Ruin*, ch. 14-17, 19, 21, 23.

42 This is extant now in manuscripts of the twelfth century and later, but on linguistic grounds probably composed at a much earlier date (before the ninth century). Kuno Meyer, ed., 'The Expulsion of the Dessi', *Eriu* 3 (1907), 135-42; Bartrum, *Tracts*, p.4.

43 *HB* ch. 62.

44 Dillon 'The Irish Settlements in Wales', *Studia Celtica* 12 (1977), 1-11; Molly Miller, 'Date-guessing and Dyfed', *Studia Celtica* 12-13 (1977-8), 33-61; T.O. Cathasaigh, 'The Deisi and Dyfed', *Eigse* 20 (1981) 1-33; K. D. Pringle, 'The Kings of Demetia I & II', *THSC* (1970), 70-6 & (1971), 140-4; M. Richards, 'The Irish Settlements in South-West Wales', *Journal of the Royal Society of Antiquaries of Ireland* 89-90 (1959-60), 135-52; C. Thomas, 'The Irish Settlements in Post-Roman Western Britain: A Survey of the Evidence', *Journal of the Royal Institution of Cornwall* New Series 6 pt. 4 (1969-72), pp. 251-274.

45 Whitley Stokes, ed., *Three Irish Glossaries* (London and Edinburgh 1862), p. 29; J. O'Donovan and Whitley Stokes, ed. and trans., *Sanas Chormaic Cormac's Glossary* (Calcutta 1868), p. 111.

46 *HB* ch. 14 locates the Uí Liatháin largely in south-west Wales.

47 *ECMW*, p.55, no. 9.

48 *ECMW*, p. 67, no. 39.

49 *ECMW*, p. 93, no. 106.

50 *ECMW*, p. 86, no. 84.

51 *ECMW*, p. 121, no. 176.

52 *ECMW*, p. 125, no. 183

53 *HB* ch. 62.

54 Bartrum, ed. *Tracts*, p.13 (my translation).

55 Lloyd, *A History*, I, 117-8; Wendy Davies, *Wales*, pp. 98-9; Molly Miller, 'Forms and uses of Pedigrees', *THSC* (1978), pp. 195-206; Molly Miller, 'The foundation legend of Gwynedd in the Latin Texts', *BBCS* 27 (1976-8), pp. 515-32, pp. 523-8.

56 Miller, 'Foundation Legend', pp. 523-8. For further discussion of Venedotian pedigrees, see Molly Miller, 'Date Guessing and Pedigrees', *Studia Celtica* 10/11 (1975/6), 96-109, pp. 101-9; Kirby, 'British Dynastic History', pp. 92-3.

57 Dark, *Civitas*, 77-8.

58 Lloyd, *A History*, I, 100, 116-20, seems largely to have accepted the tradition, as more recently, have Leslie Alcock, *Arthur's Britain* (Harmondsworth 1971), pp. 37-8, 125-9; Morris, *The Age of Arthur* pp. 66-8. A more sceptical approach is found in Wendy Davies, *Wales*, p. 89; Dumville, 'Sub-Roman Britain', pp. 181-3; N.K. Chadwick, *Studies in the Early British Church* (Cambridge 1958), pp. 32-4.

59 J. Rhys, *Celtic Britain*, (3rd ed., London 1904) p. 118; Morris, *Age of Arthur*, p. 65.

60 R.G. Collingwood and J.N.L. Myres, *Roman Britain and the English Settlement*, (2nd ed., Oxford 1937), pp. 289-90 suggest Stilicho was the organizer of the migration; A.H.A Hogg, 'The Date of Cunedda', *Antiquity* 22 (1948), 201-5, p. 205, suggested Maximus; H.M. Chadwick, *Early Scotland*, (1945), pp. 148-9, proposed Vortigern, or Coel Hen, or both. S.S. Frere, *Britannia* (London 1967), p. 426, suggested Vortigern. Morris, *Age of Arthur*, p. 68, seems to view the migration as subject to the agreement, if not the planning, of Vortigern.

61 Dark, *Civitas*, p. 74; Dumville, 'Sub-Roman Britain', 173-92;. Miller, 'Foundation Legend', pp. 523-8; Miller, 'Date Guessing and Pedigrees, pp. 101-9; Kirby, British Dynastic History', pp. 89-94.

62 K.S. Brassil, W.G. Owen, and W.G. Britnell, 'Prehistoric and early medieval cemeteries at Tandderwen, near Denbigh, Clwyd', *Archaeological Journal* 148 (1991), 46-97.

63 K.R. Dark, *Discovery by Design*, (B.A.R. British Series 237, 1994) pp. 134-8.

64 Dark, *Civitas*, pp. 75-6.

65 See note 61.

66 Bede, *HE*, Bk II, ch. 2.

67 For example, Oswy, king of Northumbria, married Rieinmellt, a princess of the north British kingdom of Rheged. *HB*, ch. 57.

68 Kate Pretty, 'Defining the Magonsaete', in Steven Bassett, ed., *The Origins of Anglo-Saxon Kingdoms*, (Leicester 1989), 171-83, pp. 125-7.

69 *HB* ch. 63.

70 Lloyd, *A History*, I, 181. Lloyd doubted that Iago was involved the battle.

71 Bede, *HE* Bk II, ch. 2.

72 Lloyd, *A History*, I, 181.

73 *ECMW*, pp. 55-7, no. 13.

74 D.P. Kirby, *The earliest English kings*, (London 1991), pp. 77-88.

75 Bede, *HE*, Bk II, ch. 5.

76 Rachel Bromwich, ed, and trans., *Trioedd Ynys Prydein The Welsh Triads* (Cardiff 1961), p. 167.

77 Bromwich, *Trioedd*, p. 57

78 Bromwich, *Trioedd*, pp. 47-8, 167.

79 Bede, *HE*, Bk II, ch. 20.

80 Bede, *HE*, Bk III, ch. 1. Deira and Bernicia were the two constituent kingdoms from which the over-kingdom of Northumbria was formed.

81 Bede, *HE*, Bk III, ch. 1.

82 Bede, *HE*, Bk III, ch. 2.

83 *HB* ch. 65.

84 *HB*, ch. 65.

85 Bede, *HE*, Bk III, 9.

86 *HB*, ch. 65.

87 Bede, *HE*, Bk III, ch. 24.

88 *HB*, ch. 65.

89 Such names, however, are not easy to date. Graham Jones, 'Penda's Footprint? Place-Names Containing Personal Names Associated with those of Early Mercian Kings', *Nomina* 21 (1998), 29-62, pp. 42-3.

90 Dark, *Civitas,* p. 79; Charles Thomas, *Celtic Britain* (London 1986), p. 116.

91 Dark, *Civitas*, p. 79.

92 Margaret Gelling, *The West Midlands in the Early Middle Ages*, (Leicester 1992) p. 27.

93 Bede, *HE*, Bk II, ch. 2.

94 C. Fox, *Offa's Dyke* (1955); F. Noble, *Offa's Dyke Reviewed* (1983); D. Hill, 'Offa's and Wat's Dykes – some exploratory work on the frontier between Celt and Saxon', in T. Rowley, ed., *Anglo-Saxon Settlement and Landscape* (B.A.R. vol. 6), pp. 102-7; D. Hill, 'Offa's and Wat's Dykes', *Transactions of the Lancashire and Cheshire Antiquarian Society* 79 (1977), pp. 21-33; D. Hill, 'The construction of Offa's Dyke', *Antiquaries Journal* 65 (1985), pp. 140-2; D. Hill, 'Offa's, Wat's and shorter dykes', *Medieval Archaeology* 25 (1981), pp. 184-6 & 30 (1986), pp. 150-3; Dark, *Civitas*, pp. 23-4; Gelling, *West Midlands*, pp. 1,2-4. The dyke as extant is a composite work, built in sections over time, and perhaps connected up into a semi-unified artefact in the reign of Offa.

95 See note 94.

96 See p. 18 above.

97 The inscription no longer survives but was transcribed in the late seventeenth century by Edward Lhuyd, Bartrum, *Tracts*, p. 1, and see note 21 above.

98 Gelling, *West Midlands*, pp. 72-6.

99 For the continuing debate, see Wendy Davies, *The Llandaff Charters* (Aberystwyth 1979); Wendy. Davies, *An Early Welsh Microcosm* (1978); Wendy Davies, '*Liber Landauensis*: its construction and credibility', *English Historical Review* 88 (1973), pp. 335-51; Dark, *Civitas*, 137-48; C.N.L. Brooke, *The Church and the Welsh Border in the Central Middle Ages* (Woodbridge 1986), pp. 16-94; K.L Maund, 'Fact and Narrative Fiction in the Llandaff Charters', *Studia Celtica* 31 (1997), 173-93; John Reuben Davies, 'Church, Property and Conflict in Wales, AD 600-1100', *WHR* 18 (1997), pp. 387-406.

100 See note 45.

101 This will be discussed in chapter two.

2 From Rhodri Mawr to Hywel Dda:

1 This dynasty is often referred to as the dynasty of Rhodri Mawr, or the Second Dynasty of Gwynedd, but as it was effectively founded by Merfyn, and as its sphere of power would come to encompass more than just Gwynedd, in this book it will be called the Line of Merfyn.

2 Wendy Davies, *Patterns of Power in Early Wales*, (Oxford 1990), 48-60; Nancy Edwards, 'A possible viking grave from Benllech, Anglese'y, *Transactions of the Anglesey Antiquarian Society and Field Club* (1985), 19-24; H.R. Loyn, *The Vikings in Wales* (London 1976); Mark Redknapp. 'Glyn, Llanbedrgoch, Anglesey', *Archaeology in Wales* 34 (1994), 58-60; 35 (1995), 58-9; 36 (1996), 81-2; M. Richards, 'The Norse Place Names in Wales', in B. O'Cuiv, ed., *The Impact of the Scandinavian Invasions on the Celtic-Speaking Peoples* (Dublin 1975), pp. 51-60; F.T. Wainwright, 'Ingimund's Invasion', in his *Scandinavian England* (Chichester 1975), pp. 131-61.

3 Place-names showing Scandinavian interest are scattered along the Welsh coast-line, and tend to be attached to noticeable features, such as natural harbours, rocks, islands and shoals, such as Anglesey, Bardsey, Skomer, Grassholm and Ramsay. There are also settlements sites in south-west Wales which may show Scandinavian influence, such as Fishguard and Hasguard. However, place-names are notoriously hard to date, and it can be difficult in some cases to tell the difference between names influenced by Scandinavians and names influenced by later Flemish settlers. See Loyn, *The Vikings in Wales*, pp. 8-11, and see note 2.

4 *HB* ch. 16.

5 Bartrum, *Tracts*, p. 9 (HG 1).

6 Bartrum, *Tracts*, p. 36 (*HGK*, no. 1); p. 91(*Bonedd yr Arwyr*, 27c); p. 95 (*ABT* no. 1).

7 D.S. Evans, ed. and trans., *A Medieval Prince of Wales: the Life of Gruffudd ap Cynan* (Llanerch 1990), pp. 23, 53.

8 Merfyn Frych from the land of *Manaw*. W.F. Skene, *The Four Ancient Books of Wales,* 2 vols, Edinburgh 1868), II, p.222.

9 Bartrum, *Tracts*, p. 36 (*HGK*, no. 2).

10 Lloyd, *A History*, I, 324 and n. 14.

11 Davies, *Wales*, p.104.

12 Lloyd, *A History*, I, 324.

13 Bartrum, *Tracts,* p.46 (JC 20, no. 18), p. 99 (*ABT*, no. 6k).

14 These are now recorded in manuscripts no earlier than the later fourteenth century, but the spelling in the texts may indicate that they were copied from a source composed before 1200.

15 Bartrum, *Tracts*, p. 46 (JC 20, no. 18).

16 Bartrum, *Tracts*, p. 38 (MG no. 1).

17 Bartrum, *Tracts*, p. 95 (*ABT* no. 1).

18 That is to say, by the twelfth century at the latest, and probably earlier.

19 Dafydd Jenkins and Morfydd E. Owen, eds., *The Welsh law of Women: Studies Presented to Professor Daniel A. Binchy on his Eightieth Birthday, 3 June 1980* (Cardiff 1980), pp. 29, 85, 98.

20 See also above, pp. 18, 34.

21 Dark, *Civitas*, p. 226.

22 Bartrum, *Tracts*, pp. 46-7, (JC 20, nos. 20, 21, 42).

23 Bartrum, *Tracts*, p. 100, (*ABT* no. 6j).

24 S. Keynes and M. Lapidge, *Alfred the Great: Asser's Life of King Alfred and other Contemporary Sources* (Harmondsworth 1983), ch. 80.

25 Bartrum, *Tracts*, pp. 46-7 (JC 20 no. 20)

26 Bartrum, *Tracts*, p. 101 (*ABT* no. 7a).

27 Keynes and Lapidge, trans, *Asser*, ch. 80.

28 D.N. Dumville, 'The "Six" Sons of Rhodri Mawr', *CMCS*, 4 (Winter 1984), 5-18.

29 Gerald of Wales, *The Description of Wales*, Book I, ch. 2 in J.S. Brewer *et al, Giraldi Cambrensi Opera*, 8 vols (Rolls Series, London 1861-1891) vol. VI (London 1868). For an English translation, see Gerald of Wales, *The Journey through Wales and the Description of Wales* trans. Lewis Thorpe (Harmondsworth 1978), p. 221.

30 Shared rule between brothers is not unknown in early Wales: this arrangement occurred in Gwynedd in the second part of the tenth century, for example.

31 Keynes and Lapidge, trans, *Asser*, ch. 80.

32 Keynes and Lapidge, trans, *Asser*, ch. 80.

33 J.N. Radner, ed. and trans., *The Fragmentary Annals of Ireland* (Dublin 1978), [?907], pp. 166-73.

34 It is tempting to wonder if Merfyn's death might have been a contributory factor, also: he may perhaps have been less expansionist than his brothers. However, this can be no more than speculation, given the scantiness of our sources for these years.

35 T.M. Charles Edward, *Early Irish and Welsh Kinship*, (Oxford 1993) pp. 217-8.

36 D.P. Kirby, 'Hywel Dda: Anglophil?', *WHR* 8 (1978-9), 1-13, pp. 910.

37 J. Manley, '*Cledemutha*: A Late Saxon Burh in north Wales', *Medieval Archaeology* 31 (1987), 13-46.

38 ASC D *s.a.* 915; ASC A *s.a.* 918 [917].

39 ASC A *s.a.* 922 [921]; ASC D *s.a.* 926.

40 Bartrum, *Tracts*, p. 9 (HG no. 2)

41 *AC* (C) [928]; *ByT* (Pen. 20) [920-929]; *ByT* (RB) [920-929]; *BS* [926-929].

42 D.N. Dumville, 'Brittany and *Armes Prydein Fawr*', *Etudes Celtiques*, 20 (1983), 145-59, pp. 149-50.

43 See note 42.

44 W. Stubbs, ed. and trans., *Willelmi Malmesbiriensis Monachi De Gestis Regum Anglorum*, (2 vols, Rolls Series, London 1887/9), I, 165; Lloyd, *A History*, I p. 335 accepts 926 or 927 as the date of Idwal's rebellion (if it occurred at all), but D.P. Kirby, 'Hywel', pp. 4-5, suggests a date of around 934, on the ground that it is said that Constantine, king of Scotland, was deprived of his lands by Athelstan at the same time as Idwal, and Constantine is known to have rebelled against Athelstan in 934, but not in 926-7.

45 H.R. Loyn, 'Welsh and English in the tenth century: the context of the Athelstan charters', *WHR* 10 (1980-1), 283-301.

46 In the case of Idwal it may have been not that Hywel had any seniority over him, but that Hywel was better regarded than Idwal by the English court.

47 Lloyd, *A History*, I, 336-8.

48 Kirby, 'Hywel', pp. 6-8.

49 Dumville, 'Brittany', pp. 148, 150-1.

50 Ifor Williams and Rachel Bromwich, eds. and trans., *Armes Prydein, The Prophecy of Britain, from the Book of Taliesin* (Dublin 1972), pp. xii-xxvi.

51 See note 42.

52 Lloyd, *A History*, I, 338-43.

53 Huw Pryce, 'The Prologues to the Welsh Law Books', *BBCS* 33 (1986), 151-87.

54 Pryce, 'The Prologues'; J. Goronwy Edwards, 'Hywel Dda and the Welsh Lawbooks', in Dafydd Jenkins, ed., *Celtic Law Papers* (Brussells 1973), 135-60.

3 From Owain ap Hywel to Gruffudd ap Llywelyn:

1 K.L. Maund, 'Dynastic Segmentation and Gwynedd', *Studia Celtica* 32 (1998), 155-167, pp. 157-8.

2 Rhodri had died in 953.

3 Evans & Rhys, edd., *The Text of the Book of Llan Dâv* . The *Book of Llandaff* was compiled in the early twelfth century under the auspices of Urban, bishop of Llandaff, against a background of Norman aggression and expansionism against Welsh territories.

4 See chapter one, note 99.

5 See Lloyd, *A History*, I, 347-8.

6 K. Hughes, 'The Welsh Latin Annals', in her *Celtic Britain in the Early Middle Ages: Studies in Scottish and Welsh Sources* (Woodbridge 1980), no. V, pp. 68-73.

7 *AC* (B) [982]; *ByT* (Pen.20) [982-983]; *ByT* (RB) [983]; *ByS* [982-983].

8 Lloyd, *A History*, I, 345.

9 We do not know how they divided the kingdom between them: they may perhaps have followed the pattern set by Anarawd ap Rhodri and his brothers, with one of them — perhaps Iago — operating as senior king and the others as his junior associates. They may have divided Gwynedd and Powys between them along geographical lines (there is a faint hint of this in the written sources). K. L. Maund, 'Dynastic Segmentation', p. 159.

10 Davies, *Patterns*, pp. 57-60; for a more reductionist approach, see, Maund, 'Dynastic Segmentation', pp. 159, 162-67.

11 Pauline Stafford, *Unification and Conquest: A Political and Social History of the Tenth and Eleventh Centuries* (London 1989), p.56.

12 See Maund, 'Dynastic Segmentation', p. 160 & n. 23.

13 Edgar had died in 975, and been succeeded briefly by his son Edward, but the murder of the latter in 978 had resulted in a regency in the name of Aethelred. Hywel's ally, Earl Aelfhere, had belonged to the faction of Edward: he was dead by 985. By striking at Hywel, the new king and his council removed a potential source of controversy on their borders.

14 David E. Thornton, 'Maredudd ab Owain: most famous king of the Welsh', *WHR* 18 (1997), pp. 567-91; but compare Davies, *Patterns*, p. 57.

15 Davies, *Patterns*, p. 57.

16 Thornton, 'Maredudd', p. 582.

17 In 1991, I considered that after *c.*989, Maredudd's power was restricted to south Wales (Maund, *Ireland*, p. 18), but in the light of arguments advanced by Thornton, and my own further research into Venedotian dynastic politics in the later tenth century (Maund, 'Dynastic Segmentation', p. 163), I have revised my views.

18 Thornton, 'Maredudd', pp. 582-5

19 See note 18.

20 Thornton, 'Maredudd', p. 589, argued that the victory of the sons of Meurig was short-lived, ending with the death of one of them, Idwal, in 996. However, I fail to see why the death of Idwal should mean that his brothers also lost power: indeed, it is more likely that he died as a result of yet another internal feud within the northern house. There is nothing to suggest Maredudd was active in the north at all after 994.

21 *ByT* (Pen.20) [998-999].

22 Bartrum, *Tracts* p. 47 (JC 20, no. 27), p. 48 (JC 20, no. 31), p. 96 (*ABT*, no. 1e), p. 97 (*ABT*, no. 2f), p. 101 (*ABT*, no.s 7j, k).

23 None of these men are explicitly said in the Welsh Chronicles to have reigned as kings, but later kings of Deheubarth traced their ancestry through Cadell ab Einion ab Owain.

24 The model was developed by Sir John Lloyd. See Lloyd, *A History*, I, 346-7.

25 Annals of Tigernach [1023]; Annals of Loch Cé [1023]; Annals of Clonmacnoise [1023]; Annals of Ulster [1023]; *Chronicon Scottorum* [1021].

26 Lloyd, *A History,* I, 346-7.

27 *ByT* (Pen. 20) [1113-1116]; *ByT* (RB) [1113-1116]; *BS* [1113-1116].

28 Bartrum, *Tracts,* p. 101 (*ABT,* no. 7f).

29 Furthermore, if Llywelyn was a grandson of a son of Anarawd, this would place him in the same generation as Hywel ab Ieuaf and Maredudd ab Owain. Both the latter were dead before 1000 (Hywel by violence) and Hywel's son was adult in 1000; moreover, Llywelyn is known to have married Maredudd's daughter. It is possible that a person of Maredudd's generation might have been active in the first two decades of the eleventh century, given that Welsh kings often had children by more than one woman and spread out over most of their adult lives. Prawst and Elise if they lived at all could both have been young in their respective generations. However, this connexion of Llywelyn to the northern branch through the female line is reminiscent of the fictional links claimed for Merfyn Frych and Rhodri Mawr, and is unlikely to be genuine.

30 *AC* (B) [1021]; *AC* (C) [1023]; *ByT* (Pen. 20) [1020-1022]; *ByT* (RB) [-1022]; *BS* [1020-1022]. The name Rhain occurs in the pedigree of the first royal line of Dyfed: *Regin map Catgocaun,* (Rhain ap Cadwgan), Bartrum, *Tracts,* pp. 9-10 (HG no. 2).

31 It is worth noting that Rhain alone among those who claimed kingship anywhere in Wales during the eleventh century attracts the censure of the annalist as an usurper and an intruder. This is further reason to suspect the validity of the doctrine of the legitimacy of the Line of Merfyn to be the only legitimate kings in Deheubarth and Gwynedd during this century.

32 *ByT* (Pen.20) [1020-1022]; *ByT* (RB) [-1022], supreme king of Gwynedd and foremost and most praiseworthy king of all the Britons; *BS* [1020-1022], the most renowned king that was known from the one sea to the other.

33 His son Gruffudd did not become politically active until 1039, and was killed in 1063 or 1064, still an active and effective ruler.

34 Bartrum, *Tracts,* p. 47 (*ABT* no. 17, note I). This is the sole pedigree to mention Rhydderch, probably because although his family enjoyed considerable success in the mid-eleventh century, they had disappeared from the highest political sphere before 1090.

35 R. R. Davies, *Conquest,* p. 61, has accepted this tradition, but given the lack of any early evidence to support it, and the evidence for confusion about the antecedents of Rhydderch in *ABT,* I am unable to follow him here.

36 Evans and Rhys, edd, *The Text,* p. 253.

37 Maund, *Ireland,* pp. 188-9.

38 *ByT*(RB) [-1039].

39 *AC* (C) [1046]; *ByT* (Pen. 20) [1043-1045]; *ByT* (RB) [-1045]. *BS* [1043-1045] reads *lladua vaur,* great massacre.

40 I have argued elsewhere for identifying the leader of this raid as Gruffudd ap Llywelyn. Maund, *Ireland,* pp. 27, 132-3.

41 For the reign of Edward the Confessor, see Frank Barlow, *Edward the Confessor,* (London 1970, new ed. 1997).

42 ASC C [1053]; ASC D *s.a.* 1055; ASC E *s.a.* 1055.

43 Magnus was in the Irish Sea with a fleet, trying to impose his authority over Man and the Isles.

44 Maund, *Ireland,* pp. 131-36; K. L. Maund, 'The Welsh Alliances of Earl Aelfgar of Mercia and his family in the eleventh century', *Anglo-Norman Studies* 11 (1988), 181-90.

45 That Gruffudd had killed his uncle may not have had any bearing. Aelfgar in 1039 may have been too young to remember or be moved by this event; also changes in the political landscape would tend to dictate a pragmatic approach.

46 See note 42.

47 ASC (C) *s.a.* 1056; ASC (D) *s.a.* 1056; John of Worcester, *Chronicle, s.a.* 1056.

48 Marjorie Chibnall, ed. and trans., *The Ecclesiastical History of Orderic Vitalis* (6 vols Oxford 1969-1980) II, 138, Book III.

49 Gerald, *Itin.,* Bk I, ch. 2.

50 Edward had been raised at the Norman court, having been driven into exile in late 1013 or early 1014.

51 Domesday Book, Warwickshire, fo. 238d.

52 M. R. James, C. N. L. Brooke and R. A. B. Mynors, edd. and trans., *Walter Map: De Nugis Curialium, Courtiers Trifles* (Oxford 1983), pp. 186-96.

53 Thus the author of *HGK* depicted his hero, Gruffudd ap Cynan , as being invested with the mantle of Gruffudd ap Llywelyn. (Evans, *A Medieval Prince,* pp. 29, 60.)

4 From Bleddyn ap Cynfyn to Owain ap Cadwgan:

1 *Domesday Book,* Gloucestershire, fo. 162a. This reference assigns no date to the raids, however, so they may have occurred rather later.

2 C. P. Lewis, English and Norman Government in the Welsh Borders 1039-1087, (Unpublished D.Phil. dissertation, University of Oxford 1985).

3 I have argued elsewhere for the involvement of the new earl of Hereford, Roger of Breteuil; Maund, *Ireland,* pp. 146-7.

4 *ByT* (Pen. 20) [1073-1075]

5 *ByT* (Pen. 20) [1076-1078].

6 D. Simon Evans, ed. and trans., *A Medieval Prince of Wales: The Life of Gruffudd ap Cynan* (Llannerch 1990). For recent discussion of the text and its problems, see K. L. Maund, ed., *Gruffudd ap Cynan: A Collaborative Biography* (Woodbridge 1996).

7 Evans, *A Medieval Prince,* p. 59.

8 Evans, *A Medieval Prince,* pp. 31-2, 62-3.

9 For further discussion of Cynwrig, see Maund, *Ireland,* pp. 93-4.

10 Maund, *Ireland,* pp. 94-5.

11 J. E. Caerwyn Williams, ed. and trans., 'Meilyr Brydydd and Gruffudd ap Cynan', in Maund, ed., *Gruffudd,* pp. 165-186.

12 See Maund, 'Trahaearn ap Caradog: Legitimate Usurper?', *WHR* 13 (1986/7), pp. 468-76.

13 It should be noted that apart from *HGK,* there is only very scanty evidence for warfare between Trahaearn and the Normans. The Anglo-Norman writer Orderic Vitalis notes an encounter between Robert of Rhuddlan and one *Trehellum* who probably should be taken to be Trahaearn, which Robert is said to have won. (Orderic Vitalis, *Ecclesiastical History,* ed. and trans. Chibnall, IV, 144.) However, the encounter is not documented elsewhere (in particular, it is not recorded by the Welsh Chronicles or by the contemporary *Chronicle* of John of Worcester). By the time of Domesday Book, Robert was at least claiming to hold part of north Wales, but the nature and extent of his claim is not known (*Domesday Book,* Cheshire, fo. 269ra-rb). It seems likely that some erosion of north-eastern parts of Wales had occurred, but most of this is likely to have occurred after Trahaearn's death in 1081.

14 Bartrum, *Tracts,* p.48, (JC 20 no. 31).

15 For a discussion of this relationship, see Maund, *Ireland,* pp. 45-50, 80-82. If Iorwerth was a genuine historical figure, he probably lived in the later ninth century.

16 *ByT* (Pen.20), [1076-1078]; *ByT* (RB),. [-1078]; *BS.*[1076-1078].

17 Meilyr does not seem to have resented Trahaearn's hegemony in the north, even though he — as a son and a nephew of former kings — had a considerable claim to that kingdom. It is possible that he may have been Trahaearn's recognised heir.

18 *Domesday Book,* Herefordshire, fo. 179rb.

19 There is considerable literature on the Normans in Wales. The following provide an overview. Janet Meisel, *Barons of the Welsh Frontier: the Corbet, Pantulf and Fitzwarin Families 1066-1272* (Lincoln, Nebraska 1980); L. H. Nelson, *The Normans in south Wales 1070-1171* (Austin, Texas 1966); J. G. Edwards, 'The Normans and the Welsh March', *PBA* 42 (1956), 155-77; J. E. Lloyd, 'Wales and the coming of the Normans', *THSC* (1899-1900), 122-79; I. C. Rowlands, 'The making of the March: aspects of the Norman settlement of Dyfed', *ANS* 3 (1981), 142-57; D. G. Walker, 'The Norman settlement in Wales', *Proceedings of the Battle Conference on Anglo-Norman Studies* 1 (1978), 131-43.

20 *ByT* (RB) [1090-1093].

21 See Robert S. Babcock, 'Rhys ap Tewdwr, king of Deheubarth', *Anglo-Norman Studies* 16 (1993), 21-35.

22 Babcock, 'Rhys', pp. 26, 28, 31-5.

23 See Maund, *Ireland*, pp. 148-53.

24 Evans, *A Medieval Prince*, pp. 38, 39, 69, 70.

25 Lloyd, *A History*, II, 404.

26 ASC E [1097].

27 Roger of Montgomery had died in July 1094. and been succeeded by his middle son Hugh.

28 The date of this is unknown, but Cadwgan died in 1111, and Uchdryd still held these lands in 1116. He may have received from Cadwgan between 1088 and 1098, when the power vacuum in Gwynedd, combined with the deaths in battle of Cadwgan's two elder brothers meant that Cadwgan was effectively the leading native ruler throughout north Wales. He may alternatively have been granted them after 1099, when Cadwgan came to terms with the Normans.

29 Gruffudd, despite his partly Norse blood, may have already experienced some difficulties with such a fleet. According to the *History*, at some point before his first expedition to Wales (1075) and Mynydd Carn (1081), Gruffudd made a raid on Anglesey, Llyn and Arfon: he obtained a victory, but rather than letting him establish his power, his Hiberno-Norse allies plundered, took him captive, and bore him with them back to Ireland. It should be noted that this incident is not related anywhere other than in the *History*, and may thus not be reliable as evidence (in particular, that this was a separate raid to that of 1075 is debatable). The incident may even have been provided by the *History* to prepare the reader for the treachery of the Hiberno-Norse in 1098, which is known from the Chronicles. However, it seems that Viking mercenaries were considered to be potentially treacherous, and the chronicler who recorded the incident in 1098 in the *Brutiau* seems unsurprised by their behaviour.

30 Owain cannot have known that the earls would be defeated, but his rebellion seems to me to suggest not only that he had aided them from fear or coercion, rather than friendship, but that he did indeed have ambition to kingship in Gwynedd for himself.

31 *ByT* (Pen.20) [1100-1102].

32 See Maund, 'Owain ap Cadwgan: a rebel reviewed', *Haskins Society Journal*, (forthcoming).

33 It should be borne in mind that some of these lands were probably held by Cadwgan of Earl Robert: we know nothing of the terms on which they were held.

34 There is an implication of this in the *Brutiau*, but the retrospective nature of their account should be remembered.

35 *ByT* (Pen. 20) [1100-1102]; *ByT* (RB) [1100-1102]; *BS* [1100-1102].

36 See note 35.

37 It is difficult to ascertain when this marriage or liaison occurred, although 1098-99 is attractive, as the period in which Cadwgan and Gruffudd were certain allies. We know from the *Brutiau* that it resulted in a son, Madog, who was old enough to hold a lordship by 1118 (meaning he must have been born no later than 1104, Gruffudd ap Cynan had at some point married Angharad, daughter of Owain ab Edwin (she died in 1162, twenty five years after her husband). Gwenllian however can hardly have been a daughter of this marriage, as it is unlikely to have occurred before 1098, and Cadwgan died in 1111. It is likely that Gwenllian resulted from an earlier relationship of Gruffudd's before 1081. Lloyd, *A History*, II, 417 n. 57, also came to this view.

38 In this Cadwgan may have been following the example of his father Bleddyn, and half-uncle, Gruffudd ap Llywelyn, involving himself in high-level English politics.

39 Lloyd, *A History*, II, 417-20; R. R. Davies, 'Henry I and Wales' in H. Mayr-Harting and R. I. Moore, edd., *Studies in Medieval History Presented to R. H. C. Davis* (London 1985), 132-47, pp. 137-42.

40 Lloyd, *A History*, II, 417-22, R. R. Davies, *Conquest*, 43, 71. For a revisionist view, see Maund, 'Owain'.

41 Maund, 'Owain'.

42 Lloyd, *A History*, II, 418 & n.59.

43 Uchdryd seems to have been playing a waiting game, anxious to avoid potentially damaging reprisals from England while simultaneously trying to minimise problems with Cadwgan.

44 Lloyd, *A History*, I, 417.

45 Rhys ap Gruffudd of Deheubarth in the late twelfth century, and Llywelyn the Great in the mid-thirteenth were far less successful in securing the succession upon a chosen son.

46 Maund, 'Owain'.

5 From Owain Gwynedd to Rhys ap Gruffudd:

1 Evans, *A Medieval Prince*, pp. 49, 81.

2 *ByT* (Pen. 20) [1113-1116].

3 Robert S. Babcock, 'Imbeciles and Normans: The *Ynfydion* of Gruffudd ap Rhys Reconsidered', *Haskins Society Journal* 4 (1992), 1-9.

4 That Gruffudd fled to Gwynedd and not Powys may be some small evidence to support the claim of the *Brutiau* that Owain ap Cadwgan was absent from Wales in Normandy in 1115. Owain was at the time more powerful than Gruffudd ap Cynan, and had a history of successful resistance to Norman rule. However, Owain was known to have ambitions in Deheubarth himself: Gruffudd ap Rhys may have considered him more a rival than a potential ally.

5 Owain ap Cadwgan had killed two of Llywarch's brothers in 1108, and Llywarch had been amongst those opposed to Owain in his years of rebellion.

6 *ByT* (Pen.20), [1129-1132].

7 For a detailed account, see A. D. Carr, 'A Debatable land: Arwystli in the Middle Ages', *Montgomeryshire Collections*, 80 (1992), pp. 39-54

8 Gerald, *Itin*, Bk. 1, ch. 9.

9 Earl Ranulf was a partisan of Matilda, and was captured by the supporters of Stephen in 1146.

10 The death in 1153 of Earl Ranulf helped secure Owain's position, as the earl's heir, a minor, offered little resistance to Owain's expansion into Iâl and Tegeingl.

11 Son of Owain's brother Cadwallon, who had been killed in Nanheudwy in 1132.

12 He had married Alice de Clare.

13 Cadwaladr and Iorwerth Goch probably were amongst his allies: from the testimony of the *Brutiau*, Madog may have played a waiting game, standing aloof from both sides at least initially.

14 Two version of the *Brutiau* speak of large forces brought by the three: *ByT* (RB) [1157-1159]; *BS* [1158-1159], which suggests that Owain must have at the least been aware of their actions and probably willing to lend his warriors.

15 'The Dream of Rhonabwy', in Jeffrey Ganz, trans., *The Mabinogion* (Harmondsworth 1976), p. 178.

16 The latter Owain owed his by-name to his place of birth, Porkington in Shropshire, which testifies to the wide scope of Madog's power in the 1140s and 1150s.

17 Lloyd, *A History*, II, 505-22; J. Beverley Smith, 'Owain Gwynedd', *Transactions of the Caernarvonshire Historical Society*, 32 (1971), 8-17. .

18 Davies, *Conquest*, p. 52.

19 *ByT* (RB) [1163-1165].

20 For the texts of the letters, and an important discussion of their significance, see Huw Pryce, 'Owain Gwynedd and Louis VII: the Franco-Welsh diplomacy of the first prince of Wales', *WHR* 19 (1998), pp. 1-28.

21 *ByT* (Pen.20) [1169-1170].

22 For recent scholarship on Rhys, see Roger Turvey, *The Lord Rhys* (Llandysul 1997); N. A. Jones & A. H. Pryce, edd., *Yr Arglwydd Rhys* (Caerdydd 1996) (in Welsh).

23 Michael Dolley, *Anglo-Norman Ireland* (1974); Marie Therese Flanagan, 'Strongbow, Henry II and Anglo-Norman Intervention in Ireland', in J. B. Gillingham and J. C. Holt, edd., *War and Government in the Middle Ages* (Woodbridge 1984), 62-78; Marie Therese Flanagan, *Irish Society, Anglo-Norman Settlers, Angevin Kingship: interactions in Ireland in the late twelfth century* (Oxford 1989); Robin Frame, *Ireland and Britain 1170-1450* (London 1998); J. F. O'Doherty, 'The Anglo-Norman invasion of 1167-1171', *Irish Historical Studies* 1 (1938-9), 154-7.

24 See T. Jones Pierce, 'Medieval Cardiganshire a study in Social origins', in J. B. Smith, ed., *Medieval Welsh Society* (Cardiff 1972), pp. 309-27

25 Turvey, *The Lord Rhys*, pp. 94-5,

26 The exact form varies, although this variation may owe as much to later copyists as to Rhys's own practice. He is found in charters as *princeps Wallie*, prince of Wales, *Walliarum princeps*, prince of the Welsh, and *proprietarius princeps Sudwallie*, proprietary prince of south Wales.

27 Turvey, *The Lord Rhys*, pp. 87-94; Pryce, 'Owain Gwynedd and Louis VII', pp. 2, 21-4. Owain himself used both 'prince of the Welsh' and 'king of Wales'.

28 Although it is not clear that this was uniformly accepted across Wales even in the very last years of independence, it would become a powerful doctrine which is, to some degree, still accepted by some scholars today.

29 Turvey, *The Lord Rhys*, pp. 98-108, Lloyd, *A History*, II, pp. 574-6; Davies, *Conquest*, pp. 223-4.

30 Gerald, *Itin,* Bk. I, ch. 1.

31 *ByT* (Pen. 20) [1197].

6 Llywelyn ap Iorwerth:

1 He was additionally an accomplished poet, as talent which may well also have served to enhance his standing in his community, and to increase his renown.

2 The *Brutiau* note that he gained possession of all Gwynedd in this year, but the struggle for control continued into 1175, suggesting the initial seizure was only temporary. *ByT* (Pen. 20) [1174]; *ByT* (RB) [1174].

3 Gerald, *Itin.*, Bk II, ch. 12.

4 That is was a marriage and not some other form of liaison is perhaps suggested by the assertion of Gerald, *Itin.*, Bk II, ch. 8, who claimed that Llywelyn alone amongst the sons of Owain was legitimate. On the other hand, when Gerald wrote, Llywelyn ap Iorwerth was in the ascendant against his uncles, the sons of Owain by Cristin, and such an assertion might well have been politic, or in line with current Venedotian propaganda.

5 Lloyd, *History*, II, 550 and n. 69.

6 W. Dugdale, *Monasticon Anglicanum*, edd. J. Caley, H. Ellis and B. Bandinel, 6 vols in 8 (London 1817-30), VI, 497; Lloyd, *History*, II, 587 n. 62.

7 I have argued elsewhere that *HGK* may have been written as a paradigm and justification of the early career of Llywelyn: its focus on Gruffudd as the legitimate outsider also may be evidence that Llywelyn was not raised in Gwynedd, or indeed in Wales. Maund, *Ireland*, p. 173.

8 Davies, *Conquest*, pp. 294-5.

9 *ByT* (Pen. 20), [1202]; *ByT* (RB) [1202].

10 Lloyd, *A History*, II, 582-7; Davies, *Conquest*, pp. 227-30.

11 Davies, *Conquest*, p. 229.

12 During the course of the thirteenth century, hostility by Gwynedd and intransigence from the princes of Powys would become the norm for their relations.

13 As the Lord Rhys did in 1173-4.

14 As Gruffudd ap Llywelyn did in 1054-5 and 1057, and Bleddyn ap Cynfyn did 1069-71.

15 According to the *Brutiau*, Owain accompanied Henry I to Normandy in 1114-15. Hywel Sais was sent with troops to aid Henry II in France in 1173.

16 *ByT* (Pen.20) [1210-1211].

17 John and Philip were in dispute over Normandy and Anjou, which Philip had seized from the English crown in 1204.

18 For the history of the many native lords in Deheubarth in the thirteenth century, see J. Beverley Smith, 'The Cronica de Wallia and the Dynasty of Dinefwr', *BBCS* 20 (1962-4), 261-82.

19 Davies, *Conquest*, p. 246.

20 Davies, *Conquest*, pp. 298-9, Lloyd, *A History*, II, 661-2.

21 He also asked for and received a substantial ransom.

22 Lloyd, *A History*, II, 669-70.

23 For discussion of the death of Gruffudd, see J. B. Smyth, *Llywelyn ap Gruffudd Prince of Wales*, (Cardiff 1998), pp. 47-8.

24 Davies, *Conquest*, p. 302.

25 For a detailed discussion of Dafydd, see Michael Richter, 'David ap Llywelyn, the first prince of Wales', *WHR*, 5 (1970-1), pp. 205-19.

7 Llywelyn ap Gruffudd:

1 Llywelyn is much discussed in modern historiography: for detailed accounts of his reign, see particularly Smith, *Llywelyn*; A. D. Carr, *Llywelyn ap Gruffudd* (Cardiff 1982).

2 As occurred over rights in Deheubarth and in Powys Fadog 1247-8.

3 Rhys Fychan, and Maredudd ap Rhys Gryg. Davies, *Conquest*, p 309; Smith, *Llywelyn*, pp. 67-8.

4 But see Smith, *Llywelyn*, pp. 172-3.

5 For the importance of these alliances to Llywelyn, see Smith, *Llywelyn*, pp. 90-5.

6 See Smith, *Llywelyn*, pp. 99-100,J. Beverley Smith, 'The Origins of the Revolt of Rhys ap Maredudd', *BBCS* 21 (1964-6), 151-63, pp. 152-3.

7 For a full discussion of these negotiations, see Smith, *Llywelyn*, pp. 116-38.

8 For Simon de Montfort and Wales, see T.F. Tout, 'Wales and the March during the Barons War', in his *Collected Papers*, vol. 2 (Manchester 1933), 47-100; Smith, *Llywelyn*, pp. 166-72; J. R. Maddicott, *Simon de Montfort* (Cambridge 1994), pp. 336-8.

9 On this, see Smith, *Llywelyn*, pp. 165-6.

10 Walker, *Medieval Wales*, pp. 120-1.

11 For detailed discussion of Llywelyn's relations with the Marchers in this period see Smith, *Llywelyn*, pp. 338-63.

12 K. L. Maund, *Handlist of the Acts of Native Welsh Rulers 1132-1282* (Cardiff 1996), no. 288, p. 87.

13 Maund, *Handlist*, no. 15, p. 6.

14 Maund, *Handlist*, no. 302, p. 92.

15 Llywelyn ap Iorwerth and the Lord Rhys may also have taken similar steps.

16 For extended discussion of Llywelyn's government and jurisdiction, see David Stephenson, *The Governance of Gwynedd* (Cardiff 1984); Smith, *Llywelyn*, chapter 6.

17 Ralph Maud has argued for Dafydd as the champion of traditional Welsh custom, against the perceived modernizing of Llywelyn. Ralph Maud, 'David, the Last Prince of Wales: the Ten Lost Months of Welsh History', *Transactions of the Honourable Society of Cymmrodorion*m (1968), 43-62.

18 Smith, *Llywelyn*, pp. 374-7.

19 Stephenson, *Governance*, pp. 34, 181-2.

20 Davies, *Conquest*, pp. 323-4.

21 Maund, *Handlist*, no. 414, p. 124.

22 For a detailed discussion of Llywelyn's relations with the church, see A. H. Pryce, *Native Law and the Church in Medieval Wales*, (Oxford 1993), chapters 8 and 9; Smith, *Llywelyn*, pp. 377-382.

23 The murder in 1271 at Viterbo of Edward's first cousin Henry by two of Eleanor's brothers can only have encouraged Edward in his dislike of the family.

24 This Rhys was the son of the troublesome Maredudd ap Rhys, who had died in 1271

25 This was rescinded on 11th November 1277

26 Smith, *Llywelyn*, p. 449.

27 David Stephenson, 'The Politics of Powys Wenwynwyn', *CMCS* 7 (1984), 39-61, pp. 60-1.

28 R. R. Davies, *Conquest,* pp. 342-3.

29 Davies, *Conquest*, p. 343.

30 For full discussion of this suit, see Smith, *Llywelyn*, pp. 470-89.

31 Indeed, contemporary chroniclers were uncertain on this point. Smith, *Llywelyn*, pp. 465-7.

32 This was the son of the Roger Mortimer who had died in October 1282.

33 *ByT* (Pen. 20) [1282].

34 For detailed discussion, see Smith, 'The Origins'.

35 For a detailed discussion, see Stephenson, 'The politics'; Davies, *Conquest*, pp. 233-5.

Bibliography

BARTRUM, P.C., ed., *Early Welsh Genealogical Tracts,* (Cardiff 1966)

BROMWICH, Rachel, ed, and trans., *Trioedd Ynys Prydein The Welsh Triads* (Cardiff 1961)

BROOKE, C.N.L., *The Church and the Welsh Border in the Central Middle Ages* (Woodbridge 1986)

CARR, A.D., *Llywelyn ap Gruffudd* (Cardiff 1982)

CARR, A.D., *Medieval Wales 1064-1521* (London 1995), chapters 1 & 2

COE, Jon B. and YOUNG, Simon, eds. and trans., *The Celtic Sources for the Arthurian Legend* (Llanerch 1995)

CROUCH, D.A. 'The March and the Welsh Kings', in E. King, ed., *The Anarchy of King Stephen's Reign* (Oxford 1994), pp. 255-89

DARK, K.R., *Civitas to Kingdom: British Political Continuity 300-800* (Leicester 1994)

DARK, K.R., *Discovery by Design*, (B.A.R. British Series 237, 1994)

DAVIES, R.R., *Conquest, Coexistence and Change: Wales 1066-1415* (Oxford 1987) [paperback edition retitled *Age of Conquest: Wales 1066-1415* (Oxford 1990)]

DAVIES, R.R., *Domination and Conquest: the experience of Ireland, Scotland and Wales 1100-1300* (Cambridge 1990)

DAVIES, R.R., 'Henry I and Wales', in H. Mayr-Harting & R.I. Moore, eds., *Studies in Medieval History Presented to R.H C. Davis* (London 1985), 132-47

DAVIES, R.R., 'Kings. Lords and Liberties in the March of Wales 1066-1272', *Transactions of the Royal Historical Society* 5th ser. 29 (1974), 41-61

DAVIES, Wendy, *Patterns of Power in Early Wales* (Oxford 1990)

DAVIES, Wendy, *Wales in the Early Middle Ages* (Leicester 1982)

DUMVILLE, D.N., 'Sub-Roman Britain: History and Legend', *History* 62 (1977), 173-92

EDWARDS, J.G., 'The Normans and the Welsh March', *PBA* 42 (1956) 155-77

EDWARDS, N. & LANE, A., *Early Medieval Settlements in Wales* (Oxford 1988)

EVANS, D S., ed. and trans., *A Medieval Prince of Wales The Life of Gruffudd ap Cynan* (Llanerch 1990)

EVANS, J.G. & RHYS, J., eds., *The Text of the Book of Llan Dâv* (Oxford 1893)

GANZ, Jeffrey, trans., *The Mabinogion* (Harmondsworth 1976)

GELLING, M., *The West Midlands in the Early Middle Ages* (Leicester 1992)

GERALD OF WALES, *The Journey through Wales and the Description of Wales* trans. Lewis Thorpe (Harmondsworth 1978)

HIGHAM, N.J., 'Medieval overkingship in Wales', *WHR* 16 (1992-3), 145-59

HUGHES, K., *Celtic Britain in the Early Middle Ages: Studies in Scottish and Welsh Sources* (Woodbridge 1980)

JENKINS, Dafydd, transl., *The Law of Hywel Dda: Law Texts from Medieval Wales* (Llandysul 1986)

JONES, N.A. & PRYCE, A.H. eds., *Yr Arglwydd Rhys* (Caerdydd 1996) [In Welsh]

JONES, Thomas, ed. & trans., *Brenhinedd y Saesson, or The Kings of the Saxons,* (Cardiff 1971)

JONES, Thomas, trans., *Brut y Tywysogyon or the Chronicle of the Princes, Peniarth MS 20 Version,* (Cardiff 1952)

JONES, Thomas, ed. & trans., *Brut y Tywysogyon or the Chronicle of the Princes, Red Book of Hergest Version,* (2nd edition Cardiff 1973)

KEYNES, S.D. & LAPIDGE, M., trans., *Alfred the Great: Asser's 'Life of King Alfred' and other contemporary sources,* (Harmondsworth 1983)

KIRBY, D.P., 'British Dynastic History in the Pre-Viking Period', *BBCS* 27 (1976-78), 81-114

KIRBY, D.P., 'Hywel Dda: Anglophil?', *WHR* 8 (19776-7), 1-13

KIRBY, D.P., 'Vortigern', *BBCS* 23 (1968-70), 37-59

LAPIDGE, M. and DUMVILLE, D.N., eds., *Gildas: New Approaches* (Woodbridge 1982)

LLOYD, J.E., *A History of Wales from the earliest times to the Edwardian conquest*, 2 vols., (3rd edition, London 1939)

LOYN, H.R., 'Welsh and English in the tenth century: the context of the Athelstan charters', *WHR* 10 (1980-1), 283-301

MAUD, Ralph, 'David, the Last Prince of Wales', *THSC* (1968), pp. 43-62

MAUND, K.L., ed., *Gruffudd ap Cynan: a collaborative biography* (Woodbridge 1996)

MAUND, K.L., ed., *Handlist of the Acts of Native Welsh Rulers 1132-1283* (Cardiff 1996)

MAUND, K.L., *Ireland, Wales and England in the Eleventh Century* (Woodbridge 1991)

MCCLURE, J. & COLLINS, R., trans., *Bede, The Ecclesiastical History of the English People,* (Oxford 1994)

MILLER, Molly, 'Date-guessing and Dyfed', *Studia Celtica* 12-13 (1977-8), 33-61

MILLER, Molly, 'The foundation legend of Gwynedd', *BBCS* 27 (1976-8), 515-32

MORRIS, John, *Domesday Book,* gen. ed. (35 vols. in 40, Chichester 1975-86)

MORRIS, John ed. & trans., *Gildas The Ruin of Britain and Other Works,* (Chichester 1978)

NASH-WILLIAMS, V.E., *The Early Christian Monuments of Wales* (Cardiff 1950)

PRYCE, Huw, 'Owain Gwynedd and Louis VII: the Franco-Welsh diplomacy of the first prince of Wales', *WHR* 19 (1998), 1-28

RICHTER, Michael, 'David ap Llywelyn, the First Prince of Wales', *WHR*, 5 (1970-1),. 205-9

RODERICK, A.J., 'The feudal relations between the English crown and the Welsh princes', *History* 37 (1952), 201-12.

SIMS-WILLIAMS, P. 'Historical Need and Literary Narratives: A caveat from ninth century Wales' *WHR* 17 (1994), 1-40

SMITH, J.B., 'Llywelyn ap Gruffudd and the March of Wales', *Brycheiniog*, 20 (1982-3), pp. 9-22

SMITH, J.B., *Llywelyn ap Gruffudd: Prince of Wales* (Cardiff 1998) English edition

SMITH, J.B., 'Llywelyn ap Gruffudd, Prince of Wales and Lord of Snowdon', *Transactions of the Caernarvonshire Historical Society*, 45 (1984), pp. 7-36

SMITH, J.B., *Llywelyn ap Gruffudd: Tywysog Cymru* (Caerdydd 1986) Welsh edition

SMITH, J.B. 'Magna Carta and the charters of the Welsh princes', *English History Review* 99 (1984), 344-62.

SMITH, J.B. 'The Origins of the revolt of Rhys ap Maredudd', *BBCS*, 21 (1964-6), 151-63

SMITH, J.B. 'Owain Gwynedd', *Transactions of the Caernarvonshire Historical Society*, 32 (1971), 8-17

SMITH, Llinos B., The gravamina of the community of Gwynedd against Llywelyn ap Gruffudd, *THSC* (1983), 158-76

SMITH, Llinos B., 'Llywelyn ap Gruffudd and the Welsh Historical Consciousness', *WHR* 12 (1984-5), 1-28

STEPHENSON, David, *The Governance of Gwynedd* (Cardiff 1984)

STEPHENSON, David, 'Llywelyn ap Gruffydd and the Struggle for the Principality of Wales', 1258-1282, *THSC* (1983), 36-47

STEPHENSON, David, 'The Politics of Powys Wenwynwyn in the thirteenth century', *CMCS*, 7 (1984), 39-61

SWANTON, Michael, trans. and ed., *The Anglo-Saxon Chronicle* (London 1996)

THORNTON, David E., 'Maredudd ab Owain: most famous king of the Welsh', *WHR* (1997)

TURVEY, R., *The Lord Rhys* (Llandysul 1997)

WALKER, David, *Medieval Wales* (Oxford 1990)

WILLIAMS, G.A., 'The succession to Gwynedd 1238-47', *BBCS* 20 (1962-4), 393-413

WILLIAMS (ab Ithel). J., ed, *Annales Cambriae* (London 1860)

WINTERBOTTOM, M., ed. & trans., *Nennius British History and the Welsh Annals,* (Chichester 1980)

WOOD, Michael, *In Search of the Dark Ages* (London 1981).

Index

Numbering in bold refers to illustrations, 'c' denoting a colour plate